A WARRING NATION

✢ A WARRING NATION

HONOR, RACE, AND HUMILIATION IN AMERICA AND ABROAD

Bertram Wyatt-Brown

UNIVERSITY OF VIRGINIA PRESS
CHARLOTTESVILLE AND LONDON

University of Virginia Press
© 2014 by the Rector and Visitors of the University of Virginia
All rights reserved
Printed in the United States of America on acid-free paper
First published 2014

9 8 7 6 5 4 3 2 1

LIBRARY OF CONGRESS CATALOGING-IN-PUBLICATION DATA

Wyatt-Brown, Bertram, 1932–2012.
  A warring nation : honor, race, and humiliation in America and abroad / Bertram
Wyatt-Brown.
      pages   cm
  Includes bibliographical references and index.
  ISBN 978-0-8139-3474-7 (cloth : alk. paper) — ISBN 978-0-8139-3475-4 (e-book)
  1. War and society—United States—History. 2. United States—History, Military.
3. Race—Social aspects—United States. 4. Honor—Social aspects—United States.
5. Humiliation—Social aspects—United States. I. Title.
  E181.W98 2013
  355.00973—dc23

2013023886

CONTENTS

ACKNOWLEDGMENTS

One of the most gratifying aspects of being a historian is the helpfulness and conscientiousness of a host of commentators and contributors to the final product. My debt of gratitude is especially appropriate for the grand assistance of Susan Marbury, my sister-in-law. She helped with the copyediting, which prevented some serious failings on my part. Margaret Hogan, the copyeditor, was meticulous about tightening the prose, insisting on greater precision in elaboration of materials, and making me rewrite vague and unclear passages to improve the text. Beatrice Burton worked assiduously to check the accuracy of all the endnotes and to amplify any that needed improvement. The outstanding staff at the University of Virginia Press has been remarkably helpful throughout the process. My editor, Richard Holway, himself the author of a very significant work on honor in the ancient Greek tradition, has been a source of inspiration and encouragement. Mark Mones, project editor at the press, has been the soul of efficiency and enlightenment.

This book might never have been written without the intellectual stimulation that David Hackett Fischer provided me. His own many works, especially *Albion's Seed* and *Washington's Crossing*, offered indispensable insights into a variety of actions and thoughts. Dave Fischer's report to the press as an in-house reader lifted my spirits and no doubt had a salutary effect on the Board of Editors.

A very special debt of gratitude belongs to Anne Wyatt-Brown. Not only has my wife supported this project in every way imaginable, but she has been a lively and most constructive critic, being a fine editor in her own right, and, most of all, throughout many trials, a caring and solicitous helpmeet. I could never have managed this publication without her able and always welcome assistance.

Others who read the work in whole or part and offered suggestions include Larry Friedman, John Pocock, Charles Joyner, Vernon Burton, Ruth Zollinger, Randall Stephens, John Mayfield, and Jean Baker. It has been a great joy to have all those named above as friends, supporters, and critics of this complicated project.

ADDENDUM BY ANNE M. WYATT-BROWN

After Bert died, many people made it possible for us to complete the work that he was unable to oversee. Margaret Hogan and Beatrice Burton showed great ingenuity and patience in the task of checking all of Bert's statements and citations for accuracy. Occasionally, Bea was stymied in her efforts to track down all of Bert's sources. Friends from Johns Hopkins University and its Sheridan Libraries helped us when we were desperate. For example, Philip Morgan found an article for us that was the source of an important paragraph in Bert's text. Later, when Bea Burton couldn't get her hands on a master's thesis from Hopkins, I asked Betsy Merrill at the Sheridan Libraries for help. She enlisted archivist Jim Stimpert, who read Benjamin T. Swartz's master's thesis several times to verify citations. Georganne Burton, Bea's mother, hunted up the *Yorkville Enquirer,* the source of Swartz's citations, in the Clemson Library. Bea consulted Benjamin Swartz himself, who also answered her questions. Without the help of all these people, Bert's book would have lacked some important points that enriched his text.

INTRODUCTION

Whenever men and women straighten their backs up, they are going somewhere, because a man can't ride your back unless it is bent.

—MARTIN LUTHER KING JR.

There are two sets of laws, the law of honour and the law of justice, which are strongly opposed in many matters.

—MICHEL DE MONTAIGNE

Hadellca xun ayaa xanuum kulul.
Humiliation is worse than death; in times of war,
words of humiliation hurt more than bullets.

—SOMALI PROVERB

Honor, race, and humiliation, though never previously analyzed together, interact throughout America's history. By filtering the interactions among honor, race, and humiliation through the lens of American wars, this study illuminates their interdependence. Other writers have dealt with honor and race. Since the 1960s, racial inquiries, in particular, have multiplied, adding much to our knowledge of American culture. Humiliation, however, never has caught the historical imagination. Yet, it is an emotional state that so often generates the impulse to seek revenge for insult, be it against an individual, a family, or a nation. For instance, in response to the Creeks' massacre of white families in 1812, General Andrew Jackson wrote, "When we figure to ourselves our beloved wives and little prattling infants, butchered, mangled, murdered, and torn to pieces, by savage bloodhounds," feelings reach the highest pitch imaginable. But, the warrior continued, "We are ready and pant for vengeance."[1]

Honor is an elusive, ancient, and often misunderstood ethic. Its principles used to dominate public discourse in America, but people now seldom speak of it except in military circles. The decline in general discourse of the use of the term "honorable" is evident in a Google n-gram chart, a type of visual representation of word usage over time. It shows that the high point was the era of the Civil War, after which a steady declension materialized with only a slight resurgence that began in 2000.[2] Nonetheless, honor and its ethics inform much of our understanding of race and humiliation. Race and racism, the most prominent of the three ingredients in this study, have haunted the American past and even present like an avenging force of nature. And one of the features of racism is humiliation. Scholars and journalists have generally used this idea in individual contexts, but not considered it as an elemental emotion. Like racism and honor, humiliation has a history, one that often concerns the way victors treat the vanquished, those placed at a lower status.

In the American past, honor was used in all sorts of contexts; it even helped to define the very character of the slave South. In offering this appraisal, I use examples both from that past and from more recent illustrative events. Over time, Northern honor resided in large-scale institutions rather than in the more intimate, face-to-face style found in the South in which individuals, family, and community established its basis. Moreover, the psychology of honor varies from one region or nation to another, a subject this volume treats with regard to Hitler's Germany, Tojo's Japan, South Asia, and the Middle East, among others. The United States has lately, for instance, discovered a whole social construction in Afghanistan that it did not fully understand. To train American troops there to avoid harmful but unintended insults has proved necessary.

The Afghan troops are now being instructed by their leaders in American ways, so that they will not be offended if Americans blow their noses in front of an Afghan or pat an Afghan on the back. Likewise, in Iraq, an American, feeling comfortable, might put his feet up on his desk in the presence of an Iraqi. But pointing shoes toward an Arab is considered a serious affront. Throwing footwear is one way for an Islamist to insult an unwelcome foreigner. President George W. Bush in 2008 received this treatment when a journalist hurled two shoes at him, shouting, "You dog!"[3] These examples may seem trivial, but such actions and many others cut deeply among honor-conscious Islamic people.

This study dwells chiefly on race, honor, and humiliation as they affect men. Important though women were in the larger cultural scene, they were not initiators or major actors in the drama that unfolds in these pages. They did faithfully urge husbands, brothers, and male children to be as courageous and manly as possible. And women sometimes had to do more:

take over failing businesses or plantations if their mates were incapable or incapacitated. Women were not the prim, obedient helpmeets that men liked to imagine, and were often quite tough and brave in defending their own ideas and conduct. Many raised their boys thoroughly steeped in the mystique of manliness. Sam Houston, founder of the Republic of Texas, never forgot his mother's words as she placed a musket in his arms: "Never disgrace it; for remember, I had rather all my sons should fill one honorable grave, than that one of them should turn his back to save his life." She then gave Sam a ring engraved with the word "Honor."[4]

An example of female cleverness and ability to twist the honor mode to personal purposes comes from my own family's lore. The story, myth or not, would have it that an ancestor, a formidable widow named Eliza Mathews, arrived at a son-in-law's Alabama plantation. She expected her host to dispense a welcoming and generous example of his hospitality, whether he liked the duty or not, as was the custom in the Old South. A retinue of house slaves followed her carriage. They, like herself and the horses, had to be housed and fed. Mathews announced her plans to stay six weeks or more. Her intent was actually to retrieve funds she had previously lent. The full amount was soon in her hands, and she and her entourage triumphantly left forthwith. Her effort was vindicated.

The literature on Southern females has grown substantially in depth and range in the recent years. Some notable works, though by no means all, include Kristin L. Hoganson, *Fighting for American Manhood*; Margaret S. Creighton, *The Colors of Courage*; Nina Silber, *Gender and the Sectional Conflict*; Amy S. Greenberg, *Manifest Manhood*; and Stephen W. Berry II, *All That Makes a Man*.[5]

Much can be learned from women's diaries, especially those written in the nineteenth-century South. For example, Mary Chesnut, the wife of General James Chesnut of Camden, South Carolina, shrewdly observed the behavior of the men around her. Some she admired for their uprightness and valor, others she found wanting. A few were flagrant womanizers, busy in the slave quarters. Their wives had either to pretend they did not know or return to their parents or brothers.[6]

Needless to say, such beleaguered women could do little about the problem in the early nineteenth-century South. Divorce was out of the question, and most wives had no independent livelihoods. By and large, both rich and poor Southern women stood by their men in the Civil War, bitter in their hostility toward the Yankee invaders. One widow in Union-occupied Chattanooga, Tennessee, managed to hang herself before the very eyes of the soldiers awaiting her appearance.[7]

Confederate women's honor was as much at risk as that of their husbands. Women's reputations depended on the opinion of the community about their men, as well as their own personal behavior. Their belligerence toward the Northern enemy, one suspects, arose out of the rage and vexation they felt about their constricted place in the world. That admission, of course, would never be stated boldly in the face of husbands, brothers, and male offspring.

The decision to exclude female honor reflects the fact that I have written in other studies on this topic; it would be redundant to repeat that wider approach. Military honor actually excluded females throughout much of American military history. In the Second World War, women appeared in uniform in the various armed services, but they served as adjuncts, not warriors. Of course, nursing was indispensable. It was a branch of military operations in which women took a major part, but very rarely did they carry weapons rather than slop pots and bandages. That state of affairs was only recently corrected, most particularly in the twenty-first century's wars in Iraq and Afghanistan. The past, though, was another matter.[8]

✛✛✛

In America, whether considering male or female honor, the concept has largely been seen as an exclusively white ethic. But African Americans also had their own understandings of the role honor plays. For them, honor has meant liberty and equality; for whites, liberty and social and racial hierarchy. In this social order, any white was deemed worthier, more trustworthy, and more courageous than anyone with darker skin. For that reason the emphasis here will be on the racial context of honor.

Many scholars and journalists have provided valuable and incisive explorations of race and racism in recent times. Indeed, race has dominated historical scholarship since the middle of the twentieth century. Only lately, though, have Americans become aware of how deep-seated and how difficult it has been to overcome racial prejudice and reprisals in the current age. To review the literature in this field would be a book-length undertaking. Instead, this study employs an angle of vision that demonstrates how honor, racism, and humiliation have formed a distinctive structure that has existed since whites and blacks first began to settle the continent.

Even today, some whites find that the economic and political advances of African Americans threaten their own sense of self. Black people's success can humiliate whites, whose revenge may range from simply registering discontent in the ballot box with a vote for some congenial politician to outright brutality. The upturning of traditional values and the assertions of self-confidence and self-respect that African Americans have always sought become disturbing to whites. After all, gradations in ranks have prevailed throughout history, and attempts to eliminate them by legal, social, and religious means have had only partial success. Joining racism with the concepts of honor and humiliation provides a fresh approach to each of them.

A major element in this discussion concerns the principles of honor and the counterweight of dishonor. Honor was originally primitive in most of its characteristics. Until modern times, the highest ideal has been to acquire and retain a reputation for honor. To hold honor was to be held in high esteem by others: an individual, a tribe, a nation. To be denied by the public or to lose respect was ignoble, a disgrace. For many past and present cultures that lacked enforceable law, an array of civil institutions, and centralized authority, a convention of honor was the only means to achieve social stability and control. Its original stress on manliness and warrior prowess has gradually eroded over the ages under the tides of commercial and industrial advance, state solidification, and religious pressures. Nonetheless, honor has retained something of its initial character.

A figure in Lope de Vega's honor play *Los Comendadores de Córdoba* declares, "Honor is that which is contained in another: no man grants honor to himself; rather, he receives it from others."[9] Upon retirement in 1828, Senator John Randolph of Virginia voiced this concept when he exclaimed, "I shall receive from [my loyal constituents] the only reward I ever looked for, but the highest men can receive—the universal expression of their approbation." And, as Randolph stated, the man of honor must acknowledge that favorable judgment without losing dignity. To sacrifice honor was the greatest disgrace imaginable. This concept of honor had its impact in the years leading up to the Civil War. After his furious assault on the seated, fiery antislavery advocate Charles Sumner in 1856 on the Senate floor, Congressman Preston Brooks of South Carolina defied Northern criticism. He declared, "Any man who held his honor above reproach would have acted, under similar circumstances, precisely" in the manner he had.[10]

Apart from the first two chapters, this study highlights military, rather than civilian, male honor, about which Paul Robinson has written an important work, *Military Honour and the Conduct of War*.[11] While this study focuses on military honor, however, it also considers the concept of honor within society in general, especially in terms of the role race and military duties played in both advancing and holding back African American self-respect. Honor is far more complex in a nonmilitary context. Not surprisingly, then, the recent and more general historical works on honor as a cultural and ethical scheme have grown to a small library, relying in part on the fine work of anthropologists.[12]

The honor ideal has served as justification for the rich and mighty to dominate others. In its most primitive form, honor has been a source of power. For instance, in American street gangs an ethic of honor applies so that to be "dissed" or disrespected can lead to violent confrontations. On the West Coast, for example, inner city members of the Blood gang identify themselves with tattoos. Wearing their symbol establishes their honor and standing in the neighborhood, and it challenges other gangs to respect their tattoos—or else: "Ash to ash, dust to dust, bloods I trust; Crabs we bust, kill a crab, win a prize; Kill a blood your whole family dies." Murder can indeed be the result. In April 2011 in California, two gang members were convicted of killing a male juvenile for disrespecting their gang identification.[13]

Closely related to honor, humiliation may produce a variety of responses including obeisance, sullen reaction, and violent vindication by force of arms or other means. In the context of this study, winners humiliate losers. Certainly the early Greeks knew this. In Homer's *Iliad*, the half-god Achilles begins as a noble, magnanimous spirit who is also merciful. In the course of the war, he becomes tempered in the flames of his anger and turns from his former enemy Agamemnon to the Trojans and their hero, Hector. After Hector kills Patroclus, Achilles' beloved comrade in arms, Achilles slays Hector and drags his body in the dust around the walls of Troy. By dirtying and scarifying the body, by showing no courtesy and respect for the fallen foe, Achilles seeks to obliterate Hector's very soul. The humiliation he inflicts on the corpse was not only to demonstrate his own heroic prowess, horsemanship, and superiority but also to humiliate the Trojans in their terrible loss.[14] It was myth, of course, but it reflected the social order in Homer's day. From that time forward, the employment of humiliation against an enemy or defeated party appears in almost all wars as well as in civilian circumstances. Similar atrocities to Hector's fate will even appear in some of the situations in America at a far later time.

✠ ✠ ✠

A further confession: I am a nineteenth-century Southern historian who has concentrated much work on the theme of cultural honor in that period. Inevitably the book provides somewhat more detailed information about the period from the Revolution to the Spanish-American War of 1898 than it does about events following. Nonetheless, in these pages, the purpose is to turn the historical spyglass on the later years as the concept of military honor, exclusively male, and its serious deficiencies played out in those wars. Civilian attitudes regarding race naturally affected the men at arms, prejudices that emerge in the larger national landscape described herein. The primary aim, however, is to treat the conduct of war and the relationship of honor and dishonor to those conflicts. The passions at home were bound to affect the morale of those in service, for better or worse. Yet, the focus is on those in war and in harm's way.

While race and to a lesser extent honor have received scholarly examination, humiliation has only a thin bibliography. Two landmark studies, Evelin Lindner's *Making Enemies: Humiliation and International Conflict* and William Ian Miller's *Humiliation and Other Essays on Honor, Social Discomfort, and Violence,* have informed this text. Lindner notes that the word "humiliation" did not enter dictionaries until 1757. Yet, the age-old order of hierarchies in all countries established a lower and upper caste and stratifications in between. In her opinion, the notion of human rights and human equality, while long proclaimed in Christian and Islamic teachings, did not catch hold until the middle of the eighteenth century. Lindner writes, their adoption, at least as an ideal, "eroded the old *age of honor (with fear as defining negative emotion)* and gave way to the new *age of dignity (with humiliation as defining negative emotion)*."[15] While the statement has some validity, the continuation of honor, not dignity alone, remains a current but largely unspoken and even unrecognized phenomenon.

William Ian Miller, a well-known specialist on Viking history, offers a different interpretation. He points out that humiliation figures in the lives of all human beings, including scholars. Yet, it has had virtually "no scholarly life." Part of the reason, Miller argues, is that it fell behind shame and embarrassment as negative factors in explaining psychological difficulties. In the 1960s, shame became almost a synonym for guilt.[16] But guilt and shame are altogether separate. According to Douglas L. Cairns, an ancient Greek specialist, guilt, instead, "relies on the internal sanctions provided by the individual conscience, one's own disapproval of oneself, and shame is caused by fear of external sanctions, specifically the disapproval of others." Gabriele Taylor's perception of shame stresses the indispensability of subjection to the assessment of the public.[17] Shame occurs when the shamed recognizes the offense, whatever it might be, and feels responsible for it, regardless of the validity of that judgment. A negative response to some act or words forces the shamed to take to heart the critical judgment of others.

Humiliation can have a devastating effect on the psychological well-being of anyone. It may be imposed by an unthinking individual seeking to ridicule or by a powerful authority or massive group regardless of any violation against themselves personally, real or imagined, in order to humble, scarify, or even incite the death of the victim. Consider the fate of Jamey Rodemeyer of Williamsville, New York, a suburb of Buffalo. Bullied owing to his homosexuality, at age fourteen the middle-school pupil killed himself in September 2011. Rodemeyer had literally been bullied to his death. His North High School classmates, both boys and girls, inflicted the most hateful language on him. "I always say how bullied I am, but no one listens," he mourned a few days before taking his life. "JAMIE IS STUPID, GAY, FAT AND UGLY. HE MUST DIE!" appeared on the internet. Another statement declared, "I wouldn't care if you died. No one would. So just do it. It would make everyone WAY more happier!" His sister was informed by her female classmates that they were glad he had ended his life.[18] Obviously, the power of humiliation is such that the outcome can be catastrophic. Humiliation can also lead to fierce revenge, sometimes just as deadly as suicide.

The first chapter of this book deals with the complexities of slave humiliation but also the sense of honor that African Americans brought with them as a legacy from their homelands. In some respects, this analysis differs little from the late Eugene Genovese's classic *Roll, Jordan Roll*. The findings here confirm much of what Genovese wrote about slave attitudes, but my view focuses on the continuing desire for honor as well as liberty, which persisted over the course of centuries. Genovese describes a world in which the slave owners had total control of the physical world of the slaves. In this analysis, however, the physical control did not eliminate the slaves' continuing desire for honor as well as liberty. Slaves might exhibit compliance, but their inner thoughts had to reconfirm their own identity and convictions.[19]

Most West Africans belonged to warrior cultures and knew the exhilaration and deadliness of wars and the uses of humiliation of enemies, even their enslavement. Humiliation knows no national, provincial, or tribal boundaries. It is found in the African societies from whence came the American slaves. Chapter 1 shows how the struggle to overcome that loss of dignity via enslavement persisted under the worst possible conditions of oppression. But it was at least partly recovered during the Civil War, which enabled newly confident former slaves and free men in the Union Army to demonstrate their prowess in battle. The use of black troops in the course of the conflict seemed a further insult from the Confederate perspective. Yet, the 180,000 blacks in uniform not only were indispensable for victory but also gained a renewed measure of honor and self-confidence for the black veterans themselves.

Chapter 2 is devoted to the ways that whites adopted the honor scheme from their British heritage and employed it to enhance their status in the community. It examines the role that honor played in fashioning the Way of Living in the Old South. Some readers will find this chapter's contents rather familiar, but the rule of white men over black men (and women) as well as fellow whites has to be explored. Chapter 3 begins the narrative of American wars and the role of military honor in engagements before the Civil War. Chapter 4 explores the role of honor in bringing on that lengthy, bloody sectional conflict. While slavery was the root cause, honor demanded a vindication by force of arms when Southerners felt humiliated by Yankee insults.

The postwar period, as described in chapter 5, delves into the matter of Confederate reactions to loss of honor after Appomattox and the revenge that dedicated whites in the South found in guerilla warfare against the new regime of freedmen and their Northern allies in the Republican Party. In chapter 6, this discussion turns to the Spanish-American War and World War I in which American atrocities were even more appalling in the Philippines than the treatment of prisoners, black and white, in the Civil War. The next chapter sketches the racism and black response in World War II and Korea.

The final chapter examines the issues of honor, race, and humiliation in Lyndon Johnson's Vietnam War and George W. Bush's war in Iraq. It would be foolish to go beyond 2005, as the historian must yield to the journalist. More exploratory than definitive, this pioneering study shows scholars how worthwhile it is to further advance the themes of honor, race, and humiliation in their own work.

I hope that readers will take from these pages a fresh understanding of how honor, race, and humiliation have tragic, perhaps irreversible, consequences unless the national mood is somehow amended toward more peaceful decisions. Nations like ours, with seeming dominance in world affairs, act belligerently in response. They sometimes react far too hastily in response to real or imagined threats to that position of power.

President Dwight D. Eisenhower in a famous address in 1961, referring to a growing military and industrial complex, warned the American public not to rely on the use of warfare to respond to dangers real or imagined. Rather than promoting democracy, security, and freedom, such bloody undertakings may prove a threat to those very ideals. The nation must respect the cultures and aims of other nations. Our power, he insisted, did not lie in the development of still greater destructive technological advances but in fostering "the liberty, dignity and integrity among people and among nations." A failure to recognize our own "arrogance, or our lack of comprehension or readiness to sacrifice would inflict upon us grievous hurt both at home and abroad." The president continued, "We must guard against the acquisition of unwarranted influence, whether sought or unsought, by the military-industrial complex. The potential for the disastrous rise of misplaced power exists and will persist."[20]

What Eisenhower observed during the height of the Cold War remains no less valid today. Historians may trace the origins of our national fighting spirit. But the past does not offer useful precautions, it appears, if policymakers and indeed the public at large ignore its lessons. As a result, needless wars are blithely launched with tragic outcomes in lost lives and treasure. In the case of preemptive wars, a soul-wrenching dread of dishonor induces leaders to make hazardous decisions. Fear of appearing weak and indecisive in the face of a judgmental electorate can warp better assessments.

It should be clear from the outset that this work diverges from previous probing of Southern and American character. Nevertheless, this study is built on the shoulders of some formidable predecessors. They include such thinkers as W. J. Cash, C. Vann Woodward, John Hope Franklin, Fred Hobson, Clement Eaton, and others. With the exception of humiliation as a historical touchstone, all of them deal effectively with matters of race and race prejudices. John Hope Franklin, for example, engages the topic of honor. But no prior writer has offered the thesis proposed in this text.[21]

The world we live in has changed since many of these historians were writing, with Americans operating in an increasingly tightly connected, global environment. As a result, this book seeks to highlight the complex interdependence that the United States and its people face when addressing issues of race, humiliation, and warfare in this new reality.

1

AFRICAN AMERICAN MALE SLAVES' HONOR

LOST AND REGAINED IN WAR

Over the last twenty-five years, studies of honor in the Old South have dwelled on the peculiarities of that ancient code among white Southerners. The subject of black slave honor in that same period has scarcely been touched, despite the great advances made in African American scholarship over an even longer period. But that neglect must be rectified. After all, slaves imported to the United States came from African honor societies themselves. That heritage was mostly lost during the antebellum period of enslavement but retrieved when prospects of liberty emerged in the Civil War years. Moreover, it appeared in the resistance that slaves developed to challenge white overrule, however hidden it might be. Even when traditional forms of honor were no longer possible within the stigma of bondage, slaves found other means to assume self-identification as honorable individuals.

The goal in this work is to be sensitive to the psychological aspects of slave life, which is a formidable and perhaps controversial effort. This approach is in contrast to Stanley Elkins's discredited argument that confined black reactions to the "Sambo" image. While his investigation of concentration camp inmates was innovative, he overlooked the myriad ways by which the Nazi prisoners still found other means of preserving integrity. The same error appeared in his depiction of American slaves. The comparison of slavery and Holocaust victimization was also flawed in that the camps were designed to kill whereas the goal of plantations was to get work done.[1] Clearly, slaves found pathways to self-expression despite a lack of autonomy.

The term "honor" is used here chiefly as the expression of how human beings perceive themselves, which in turn involves how they fit in the social rankings of their culture. As a result, slaves did assert themselves within their own world apart from that of whites. But it is also important to understand that resistance, a far more popular term than honor, includes the concept of honor within it. Ordinary slaves may have lost their original honor via social status, but they still sought to regain the freedom that their forebears had taken from them in the horrors of the Middle Passage and sale. Thus, liberty involved not just the goal itself but also a push for self-respect. Once rendered nearly naked, herded aboard ships, and sold on the auction block, slaves were all dishonored in their own eyes and their captors'. Their continued humiliation was passed on through the oppression of their progeny in perpetuity.

A desire for liberty is a state of mind that transcends the shackles—but that remained a hidden goal. It should come as no surprise that black slaves and freemen fought alongside white colonials in the Revolution against British rule. The yearning for freedom is not exclusive to one class or race, as it was to become in the Old South. As slaves saw it, that right belonged to them as well. The mutual aims of liberty and honor, so tightly chained for slaves in the Old South, were essential to their personal fulfillment. For slaves, the quest for liberty and honor buttressed their sense of self—their inherent value as men despite their condition. The shame of slavery cruelly dissolved so much of what men, white or black, expected of themselves and their society. Yet, sparks of that spirit of manhood remained.

Indeed, because of the harsh, unforgiving, universal nature of slavery, American or otherwise, and the code of white honor imposed upon its antebellum victims in America, the values of personal integrity that the enslaved once possessed were necessarily suppressed from the sight of the outer world. This resulted from the disparity between the powerful and the powerless. Still, slaves used a wide variety of means to reestablish that feeling of self-regard. But their efforts did not always meet the criterion for projecting self and receiving confirmation before others. Instead, as will be discussed later, some slaves turned to outright resistance and rebellion to move beyond self-regard and gain public regard.[2]

None of this analysis can be proved beyond all doubt. In that age and place, introspection was scarcely recognized. Slaves could not record their feelings on paper, but their behavior speaks to what lay in the heart. Action must necessarily illuminate emotional life. There is no other choice.[3]

To explore the various ways in which black manhood under slavery survived the outrage of lost liberty, it is essential to discuss the character of African bondage as it existed in the centuries of the Atlantic slave trade. This chapter begins with the sketch of a valorous figure, Abdul Rahman Ibrahim Ibn Sori, an African noble imported in the eighteenth century from his own slaveholding state of Futa Jallon, now part of Guinea. In many ways he was atypical of the new human properties, but he symbolizes a style and dignity that many other slaves exhibited. Next, the chapter offers a brief account of the honor that African masters held. From thence the topic broadens to the ways slaves managed to achieve a degree of inner confidence.

The troubling issue of slave submissiveness must also be examined, but not because it conforms to the "Sambo" stereotype. Rather, it was an unfortunate although understandable way for men (as well as women) to handle their owners' demands and manage their own vulnerability. Race, however, has nothing to do with this submissive reaction toward the powerful. It is found in other societies and circumstances, indeed wherever a systematic intent to humiliate and destroy a victim's free will exists. Finally, the chapter shifts to the methods employed by slaves to resist the slave regime. These methods ranged from feigned servility and deceitful speech scenarios to overt acts of violence.

All these factors, even the role of playing the subservient soul, demonstrates the buoyancy of the human spirit in the face of degrading humiliations. W. E. B. Du Bois observed that few slaves in America or Africa fully relinquished their sense of honor. However, masters' "'honor' became a vast and awful thing, requiring wide and insistent deference." He further deplored, "As the world had long learned, nothing is so calculated to ruin human nature as absolute power over human beings." Still, there were also actual rebellions, often led by members of the warrior class from Africa. The Stono Rebellion in South Carolina was a case in point. Some twenty slaves on a plantation near the Stono River began the attack. They killed their master and seized his weapons. Marching to round up others, their numbers reached nearly one hundred, making it the largest rebellion in the colonial period. They fought lustily, and twenty-one whites died in battle. The leaders of the rebellion were probably from Angola, but, in any case, they knew the warrior culture of their African homeland according to historian John K. Thornton. There, wars and skirmishes were a constant activity so that they had much experience in warfare. In response to the rebellion, the South Carolina authorities passed in 1740 the Negro Act, which prohibited the importation of slaves directly from Africa. Presumably, officials believed that seasoning elsewhere would lessen the perils of slave insurrections.[4]

✠ ✠ ✠

We can never know entirely how warriors from other African cultures that were contemporaneous with the Fulani system reacted to the humiliation of defeat and complete subjugation. But for an attempted, if only partial, answer, we should explore the story of Abdul Rahman Ibrahim Ibn Sori, who eventually arrived in Natchez, Mississippi, as a slave in the 1780s. At age twenty-six, Ibrahim had been an officer in his father's Fulani Army, which ruled the mountainous lands in present-day Guinea, West Africa, called at the time Futa Jallon (also spelled Fouta-Diallon). As the son and heir of the *almami* (Muslim leader), he stood high in the ranks of the Fulani elite. The kingdom was relatively recent. At the beginning of the eighteenth century, *almami* Karamoko Alfa established a Muslim theocracy and appointed an *alfa* (or religious leader) for each of the nine provinces under his rule. After Karamoko's death, his cousin and Ibrahim's father, Sori Mawdo (meaning Sori the Great), assumed the headship. Sori, though, was beset with uprisings from the ranks of the conquered "unbelievers." The latter group had disrupted the lucrative selling of non-Muslim captives and foodstuffs to the shippers and traders on the coast. Sori did not permit fellow Muslims to be sold, and the animists deeply resented the discrimination as well as enslavement. "The people on whom we make war," one of Sori's aides explained, "never pray to God." Sori's army, he insisted, did not make war on "people who give God Almighty service."[5]

The Muslim Fulanis were, on the whole, a literate people. Their mosque at Timbo, the seat of power, was quite sizable and well-attended. According to a French slaver, Theophilus Conneau, they would not sell others Muslims into slavery, only pagans.[6] And there was a degree of sophistication in Futa Jallon to put some western countries in the shade. Conneau found that women, even elderly ones, could often read the Koran. The young women of Timbo were noted for their exceptional beauty and grace.[7] Devout young men of the elite class attended the Arabic University of Timbucktu, and Ibrahim was no exception. He was well-educated in Arabic and the Islamic faith, having studied law and philosophy at the university in the sub-Saharan Mali city. Although he largely hid his faith during the period of his enslavement, Ibrahim refused, in the spirit of the Koran, to touch alcohol.[8]

On a fateful mission to suppress the rebels against the Muslim rulers, Ibrahim Ibn Sori headed a cavalry detachment of 2,000. The animists had turned from resentment to full-scale war. Ibrahim's force won the battle, but he and a small contingent were ambushed on their journey back to Timbo to proclaim the victory. Fearing reprisal from Sori's army if they slew his son, Ibrahim's captors sold him to *slattees*, native African slave traders, in 1788.[9]

Although Ibrahim must have stood out from other captured Africans by his commanding demeanor and self-control, he was most likely given no special privileges. In fact, after he had been seized, his kidnappers took away his shoes so that he had to march barefoot in chains all the way to the coast. He saw his horse just ahead of him but could not ride. He and the other captives passed through Mandingo country on the Gambia River and from there to the coast. With fifty others he was shoved aboard the British ship *Africa,* possibly at Banjul. The *Africa,* which held three hundred captives, sailed to the island of Dominica in the Caribbean. Ibrahim never elaborated in writing about his experience on the Middle Passage. Either his silence was owing to the suppression of traumatic memories or he retained the stern reticence of his people. The Fulanis found it difficult to air personal matters.[10] From Dominica, the former army officer found himself in New Orleans but soon was shipped upriver to Natchez, Mississippi, then under Spanish governance.[11] There, one Thomas Foster, a dirt farmer from South Carolina, bought him and another from Futa Jallon named Samba (meaning second son in the Fulani language). Foster paid $930 for the pair: *"dos negros brutos."*[12]

Ibrahim Ibn Sori was doubtless mystified about his location and the circumstances. He thought perhaps he could do as other defeated warriors did in Africa: win freedom through a customary redemption process. Ibrahim promised his new master a large ransom in cattle, goods, and possibly even other slaves from Futa Jallon if he would be permitted to return to his native land. Foster, of course, knew what a prize he had and was not about to send Ibrahim home. Because of his imperious, dignified style, Foster dubbed Ibrahim "Prince." But to indicate his new position in life, Foster had Ibrahim's hair, a symbol of his warrior masculinity, cut off. It was intentionally humiliating, designed to force him to recognize his degradation. Ibrahim manfully struggled against those holding him down for the barber. But Foster had deeply discredited his black antagonist. In Ibrahim's eyes, he, a Fulbe (another term for "Fulani") warrior, had sunk to the level of a tribal youngster, honorless and vulnerable.[13]

Other and worse debasements occurred when Ibrahim contemptuously refused to follow commands about work. His Fulani tribe was pastoral as well as agricultural, so the lowest ranking herdsman or field hand looked on manual labor as a woman's obligation. Such demeaning demands were not fit for a man of war, especially one with the high status that Ibrahim once held. Hard work in the fields belonged to the animist *Jalunke,* whom the Fulani had conquered and enslaved. Women, too, were sent to the fields, although they also wove cloth, fixed meals, and did the other activities universally common to their sex. Newly arrived female slaves knew how to manage the agricultural tasks, but at home, they had done so on their own; now, a planter or overseer directed their labor.[14] Field work was a greater source of shame for the African male, who never willingly would stoop to that level. Outraged by the whippings he suffered for refusing to work, Ibrahim escaped in 1788 into a nearby swamp fed by St. Catherine's Creek. It took weeks for the new slave to realize that survival depended on his return to the small farm, later known as Foster's Fields.[15]

Ibrahim's Islamic faith prohibited suicide as an alternative. Some imported Africans, however, did kill themselves in the hope that their spirits would return them to their homeland. For instance, in 1776, William Dunbar, a wealthy and prominent planter and neighbor to the humble Fosters, recorded his outrage upon apprehending a new slave recently brought from Africa and Jamaica, who Dunbar thought was planning an insurrection. Under severe torture, another slave had named him as the leader of a plot, though the confession was likely tragically false. Adding to Dunbar's fury, the apprehended slave then had the unconscionable temerity to leap from Dunbar's skiff and drown himself to avoid further humiliation and imminent execution. Of course, the owner assumed that the slave's action was out of shame for his subversive conniving and remorse for betraying Dunbar's trust.[16]

As the local story goes in the Natchez community, Ibrahim suddenly materialized at the door of the crudely built Foster cabin. Thomas Foster was not there, but his wife, Sarah, was. Seeing the tall, bedraggled, half-starved African with piercing eyes, she might have been unnerved by so startling an apparition. But Sarah was a remarkable woman. Instead, she smiled. Sarah put out her hand in greeting. Then the most surprising thing occurred: The new Foster property dropped to his knees. With his hand, he placed her bare foot on his neck. What he meant was no obsequious gesture. This was the custom in West Africa when a tribal chief had to admit defeat. The victor then had the option of either beheading his foe or granting him life. If the victor so decided, he would consider the battle loss a sufficient demand.[17] Under the African honor code, this would have been a magnanimous gesture because it lent the victor the prestige of full power.

Thereafter, Ibrahim Ibn Sori did what he thought was in keeping with the Koran and Allah's will. According to one of the Foster family's neighbors on St. Catherine's Creek, Ibrahim became "a faithful, loyal servant." Bowing to the importuning of his American slave wife, Ibrahim even stopped his Islamic praying openly and put away his prayer rug. He joined the Methodist Church to which she belonged. He was, in fact, the first newly imported African to be admitted to fellowship in the church. Secretly, however, he kept his faith alive but only for his own satisfaction.[18] Although humiliated to some degree, he had adopted the role of faithful bondsman but never lost hope of a return to his native land. Despite his obedience to whites and to Allah, as he saw it, Ibrahim retained his deep-seated sense of honor. It never let him relinquish his self-regard, in Fulani, his *pulaaku.* Fulbe warriors used that term to mean valor, pride, and dignity, the highest principles they could achieve. As a result, he was known locally by whites and blacks alike for never smiling. That sternness probably reflected his submission to Allah's will, not to man alone.[19] It was also characteristic of his people—reserved, formal, and even sullen. To him, smiling would have represented a full acceptance of his subservience to whites.

As a distinguished man of African honor, Ibrahim Ibn Sori decided to do as Allah apparently had commanded by making the best of the situation. He rose in Foster's estimation to the point that he became the foreman. Knowledgeable about raising cotton in his native Futa Jallon, Ibrahim soon proved himself an excellent advisor on matters agricultural. He oversaw all the work on the plantation, which grew to 16,000 acres. His master gave him permission to sell produce in Natchez and walk about the area as if he were free. Aware of his lucky purchase, Foster became one of the wealthiest men in Adams County, Mississippi.[20]

Ibrahim's success was the result of his own proud character, natural ability to lead, and the good fortune to have a fair-minded but unlettered owner who recognized and rewarded his skills—to Foster's own great advantage. Unfortunately, few other newly imported Africans could enjoy the relatively comfortable position that Ibrahim had earned. The slave system relied on the patriarchal mode that had existed for thousands of years before the Roman Empire. The authority of the head of household was the paramount figure. Its antiquity and its continued connection to the uses of honor made it particularly appropriate for the management of American slaves. "Patriarchalism rationalized the severity that lay at the heart of the slave system," writes historian Philip D. Morgan. It was "an austere code."[21] Masters could themselves punish or could order overseers to punish those deemed rebellious, sullen, malingering, or deceptive.

✢ ✢ ✢

We turn now from the origins of slave honor to more positive themes, which, though circumscribed, kept the tradition of honor and human dignity from total loss not only in the slave quarters but in relations among slaves and others. By no means were slaves so demoralized that they could not find various ways to assert their manhood through their physical appearance and style. How a slave dressed could matter in their ranking among their compatriots no less than it did in the hierarchy of whites. Of course, in those days there were still vestiges of earlier European sumptuary laws that stipulated what each rank of society was permitted to wear. In America, a democratic spirit had partially changed Old World customs to allow for more informal wear. Yet, what a dress or coat was made of still counted a great deal for both races.

Among whites, the better classes signified their honor by covering themselves in silks, expertly woven cotton called chintz, and finely made wools.[22] When John Bartram, a well-known naturalist, prepared for travels in the South, a friend advised him about his attire. When Bartram was to introduce himself to the wealthy planter Isham Randolph, he must appear as the model of a self-assured gentleman: "These Virginians are a very gentle, well dressed people, and look perhaps, more at a man's outside than his inside." "Small clothes" (knee-length breeches with hose and buckled shoes) went out of fashion by the end of James Monroe's presidency. But rich gentlemen continued to wear well-tailored suits of fine wool and velvet breeches, which differed markedly from workmen's outfits of loose shirts, jackets, and pants. As a rule, slaves wore cheap linen dubbed *osnaburg*.[23]

The transition in clothing for newly arrived Africans was likely upsetting, a shock to have to relinquish one's own clothes and fit into the apparel of a new and alien society. The aged former slave Chaney Mack recalled in the 1930s her father's mortification. He had arrived from Africa when eighteen years old. "It went purty hard wid him having to wear clothes, live in houses and work."[24]

For many slaves, though, how one looked was important in achieving greater status. Those noticing slaves in eye-catching attire could be other slave women, other African Americans, or even white people. A most interesting example of the last concerns Oliver Cromwell Kelly, a slave belonging to a succession of Watkins family members of Clarksville, Maryland. A precocious young man, Kelly escaped to the North in 1848. Adopting the last name of Gilbert to honor an antislavery supporter, he worked in various Northern cities. By 1876, he had settled in Philadelphia and had saved enough to implement a long-held plan. Gilbert wrote his former master, Dr. William W. Watkins, enclosing a newspaper account about his earlier work helping New York blacks to vote. Watkins's son replied since his father was too ill to do so. "Father told me to say that he was much gratified to learn that you still remember him and how well you must have educated yourself to have been able to have written such a fine letter." The Watkins family, Gilbert learned, would be happy if he came for a visit. To demonstrate his achievements and retrieve his honor from the bonds that had enslaved himself and his family, Gilbert went to a high-toned clothing store and bought "a fine suit of clothes." He had left slavery in "very coarsely dressed rags." Then he visited Wannamaker's store to complete his sartorial needs before boarding the B&O Railroad to Ellicott City, Maryland. On arrival, Gilbert went to the best stable and ordered the hostler's finest carriage. It included "silver mounted horses" whose equipage "shone so bright you could see your face" in their reflection. The Watkins family greeted him warmly and were no doubt amazed at his transformation from lowly slave to dignified gentleman. The experience had depleted his funds, but it had been worth the trouble. Curiously, he did not seek out the families of his former friends in the quarters but only the members of the Watkins and neighboring Warfield families.[25] He may have felt that his grand appearance among other former slaves would be too easily thought a vulgar ostentation.

As time passed, slaves adapted dress to suit themselves whenever possible. To raise their standing and self-regard, slaves in city clothes could hold their heads higher than those in humbler surroundings. Frederick Law Olmsted, later famous for his landscape innovations including Manhattan's Central Park, was a New York journalist who undertook a tour of the slave states in the 1850s. Olmsted's observations were acute. He wrote to his newspaper readers about the "dress, language, manner, [and] motions" of the slaves. These differentiations marked them as separate from whites. There were also whites whose poverty was immediately observable in their rough clothing. Some were "a mean-looking people, and but meanly dressed," wrote the New York reporter.[26]

Indeed, dress was a means of differentiation in the quarters and even in the public arena. The historians Shane and Graham White offer telling details about how slaves managed to equip themselves with raiment that separated them from fellow slaves lacking their assertiveness. Given the opportunity, enslaved men could look quite like their overlords. The Whites cite a Charles Alexander Warfield of Anne Arundel County, Maryland. Warfield offered a good reward for the return of fugitives Dick and Lucy. Dick had left in a "green cloth coat, with a crimson velvet cape, a red plush do [i.e., ditto], with blue cuffs and cape, a deep blue camblet jacket, with gold lace at the sleeves, down the breast and round the collar, a pair of Russia drab overalls, a white shirt, two osnabrig do, a pair of pumps and buckles, with sundry other cloaths." He was quite the dandy.[27]

Lucy was similarly adorned with fine raiment: "two calico gowns, one purple and white, the other red and white, a deep blue moreens petticoat, two white country cotton do, a striped do, and jacket, and black silk bonnet, a variety of handkerchiefs and ruffles." In addition, she had "two lawn aprons, two Irish linen do, a pair of high heel shoes, a pair of kid gloves and a pair of silk mitts, a blue sarsanet [fine silk] handkerchief, trim'd with gauze, with white ribbon sew'd to it, several white linen shirts, osnabrigs for two do, hempen rolles petticoat." These items, her master thought, she was likely to sell rather than wear. These slaves not only owned a surprising quantity of clothing but also items that carried the mark of gentility.[28] In a rural society, to sport flashy attire would intentionally be an affront to the white elite. But it also would differentiate the wearer from other slaves in their drab outfits — attracting slave women and displaying the wearer's self-respect to the men.

Dress could become significant in cases of alleged slave insurrections. During the uproar in Charleston when the slave Denmark Vesey was supposedly organizing a plot against whites, a youthful slave owner brought two slaves into the court. He had suspected that they were conspirators. They appeared in "country rags," and they acted in the unsophisticated way of field hands. The magistrates immediately rejected the conspiratorial claim and let them go. Later on, the same pair were summoned again. This time they were wearing well-tailored clothes, looked and smelled clean, and had a distinctly citified manner. The officials "pronounced these very men participants in a scheme of the contemplated conspiracy."[29] Clearly, the magistrate assumed that urban blacks, more than country slaves, would be the ringleaders of an uprising.

Although treated as useful but deeply flawed workers, male slaves found creative ways to maintain their self-esteem and local repute. One social marker involved a seldom historically discussed matter — body smell. It was a most unfortunate discrimination. From first encounters with Africans, Europeans held their noses against what they asserted was rank black skin odor. In 1769, a Philadelphian remarked, "The negroes . . . stink damnably." Plantation slaves had little time to wash themselves after sweating in the fields all day. Yet, they tried to keep themselves clean unless too depressed or bone-weary. Masters did not ordinarily provide adequate housing, and the wells or streams available for washing might require too much time for worn-out hands to reach. Predictably, the slaves, not the conditions, were blamed for the odors they carried.[30]

The historian Mark M. Smith offers a telling story about an Alabama slaveholder who was seeking an addition to the household staff. Young Paul stood out in the line-up. He had high hopes of rescue from the cotton rows. He was proud of his "tidy and cleanly habit," and after being selected for the post, he assumed that was how he obtained the coveted position. The owner's wife told him to discard his old field clothes because he would be given a more appropriate wardrobe. "Have your old clothes burned. We can not allow the smell of the plantation to invade the house," she told him imperiously. Such smells were thought to be so strong that they were "absolutely capable of being *weighed* and *seen* as well as *tasted* and *smelt*," she complained. Smith concludes, "The notion that black space was identifiable by a tenacious, unyielding odor lasted long after slavery ended."[31]

Yet, Paul's example shows that some slaves themselves had a strong consciousness about the possibility of giving offense to whites' noses. Ambitious slaves did manage to surmount such nasal objections as the slaveholder's wife described. They bathed, found sweet smelling herbs or liquids, and changed their rough clothes as best they could. Food, however, presented a special problem. Many planters refused them decent meat rations. Slaves had to boil rather than fry stolen bacon because the odor could reach a master's nostrils, either on the slaves' persons or in their cabins. To prevent dogs from locating them, runaway slaves made up potions of turpentine and onions or splashed cow dung on their feet. If too demoralized to escape or maintain an odor-free state, slaves might show indifference to the fundamentals of cleanliness, losing their sense of dignity. Sadly, that also happened in the German concentration camps.[32]

Another way to win the favor of fellow male slaves and white planters was through language and self-presentation. To speak the grammar of white men or to swagger a bit in the street was to assert the honor that slaves inwardly felt, though expressed by mimetic means. The point was generally not to win favor from the masters. American slaves liked to boast about the high standing of their owners and families in their competition for honor with other slaves. They took some pride in their relative superiority derived from that source.

In the course of his Southern travels, Frederick Law Olmsted mentions the differences in speech. Black English, more recently called "Ebonics" or African American Vernacular English (AAVE), seemed a parody to white ears well before the Civil War and long thereafter. Black speech in minstrel shows and, later, on radio (such as *Amos and Andy*) and in Hollywood films, solicited many a guffaw from white audiences.[33]

Of course, the African heritage left its signature on the tongues of slaves. Yet African-based English, far from being a parody of language, had its own grammatical rules, syntax, and meanings that could easily be misinterpreted by whites, then and even now. Some African imports may already have known a pidgin English, as it was the lingua franca for some slave dealers and shippers. Indeed, according to a recent analysis, new findings supposedly indicate that the early imports from Africa spoke a dialect "not appreciably different from that of post-colonial European-American varieties." But that may not have been the case. Instead, scholars now stress, more accurately I believe, the African, not Western, origins of AAVE.[34] Regardless, how one spoke mattered significantly in the American assessment of who stood where on the social and racial ladder.

While dress, odor, and speech counted for much, religion played an even larger role for many slaves in establishing their humanity. It provided a major source of black strength and resilience. As a group of plantation worshipers in Georgetown, South Carolina, so sang, "We'll soon be free, / We'll soon be free, / We'll soon be free, / When de Lord will call us home."[35] Whether Muslim or animist, slaves shared the common African view that there was a High God and lesser deities, who, along with progenitors, helped the living in matters of love, health, and well-being.[36]

Secret worship services were quite prevalent in the Old South, their numbers creating a respectable population of worshipers. As historian C. Eric Lincoln writes, "This 'Invisible Church' met deep in the woods and swamps, as far as possible from the suspicious eyes of the master or his overseer."[37] Likewise, "In perceptions of time, in esthetics, in approaches to ecstatic religious experience and to understanding of the Holy Spirit, in ideas of the afterworld and of the proper ways to honor the spirits of the dead, African influence was deep and far-reaching," observes Mechal

Sobel.[38] As a slave in Red River County, Texas, Mose Hursey recalled, "I heard them [slaves] get up with a powerful force of spirit, clapping they hands and walking around the place. They'd shout, 'I got the glory. I got the old time religion in my heart.' I seen some powerful figurations of the spirit in them days. Uncle Billy preached to us and was right good at preaching."[39]

While accepting and even embracing Christianity, Africans forced into bondage by and large believed that their forebears were still present in the world. Muslim slaves had their *gris-gris*, or amulets, one of the few personal items allowed aboard slave ships. These pieces of jewelry, zealously guarded, were designed as good luck pieces and remembrances of ancestors. They could be beautifully wrought and were especially popular in Louisiana. For Africans, Muslim or otherwise, progenitors were to be honored as guardians of the living and revered along with other spirits.[40]

Early slaveholders, however, paid little attention to African customs and still less made efforts to convert slaves. After all, the Old and New Testaments were full of stories of righteous rebellion and vengeance against cruel regimes. That sort of message was certainly inimical to white dominance. (Indeed, in 1831, Nat Turner based his rebellion on biblical grounds.) In the course of plantation settlement, though, sentiment changed. Some masters felt guilty if they did not allow their hands the blessings of grace. Christian missions to the slaves became acceptable, but the stress in the pulpit was always on the duty of slave obedience. St. Paul had written about "servants" obeying their masters and other indications of God's so-called acceptance of holding others in bonds. Moreover, devout slaves, who might incline toward a submissive role, would find the Gospel of Matthew consoling: "Blessed are they who mourn; for they shall be comforted; / Blessed are the meek, for they shall inherit the earth" (Matthew 5:3–4). That was indeed the moral and spiritual understanding of the evangelical novelist Harriet Beecher Stowe in creating the courageous and devout character of Uncle Tom.[41]

Other biblical passages surely appreciated by slaves were those that presented Christ as the Comforter. "There is a balm in Gilead / to save the sin-sick soul," as the spiritual offers. "But the Comforter, which is the Holy Ghost, whom the Father will send in my name, he shall teach you all things, and bring all things to your remembrance, whatsoever I have said unto you" (John 14:26). Moreover, Christ was the source of hope. "Be strong and let your heart take courage, all you who wait for and hope for and expect the Lord!" (Psalm 31:24).

In the nineteenth century, Christian masters had their black dependents attend religious services. While receptive to the Gospel, slaves interpreted the scriptures in a spirit that differed from whites' expectations.
Slaves, for instance, found innumerable passages confirming the significance of honor, a fundamental element in their own lives, in the Old and
New Testaments. Throughout the latter work, for instance, Jesus defies
the Pharisees and Scribes by healing the infirm on the Sabbath, reversing
the order of seating at table, washing the feet of those deemed dishonorable, throwing money-lenders out of the temple, and treating tax collec-
tors, prostitutes, lepers, and others as equals. All these defiant acts violated
the honor of the Hebrew leaders who hated the teaching and defiance
of Jesus as much as they feared his preaching about a new freedom from
soul-constricting traditions. For instance, in Luke 13:10–17, on a Sabbath
day, Jesus healed an old woman, crippled perhaps by arthritis. At once she
stood straight and praised the Lord. An elder in the synagogue denounced
him for breaking the Sabbath rule against work. "You hypocrites! Does not
each of you on the Sabbath untie his ox or his ass from the manger, and
lead it away to give it water?" Here, the authority, or the master, as the slave
might translate the story, would lose esteem if he were no longer publicly
seen as the sole arbiter of the law.[42] Such a challenge would simply not do
in ancient Palestine nor in the heart of the plantation South.

The heretical ideas provided in the sacred account gave some gratification to Southern slaves who dealt daily with a system hallowed by tradition but no less rigid than what the orthodox Jewish authorities upheld.
How could such New Testament knowledge and beliefs be reconciled with
bondage even in whites' minds? On the other hand, blacks would find the
teachings of Jesus comforting and inspiring. To be sure, whites claimed that
proslavery theologians and literal readings of the Bible supported the holding of blacks in bondage.[43] But, as the religious historian Charles Reagan
Wilson notes, the African Americans' Jesus "seemed to circulate in the dark
nights of camp meeting preachings" and appeared almost visibly at their
prayer sessions "to offer hope."[44]

We do not know exactly how slaves interpreted particular biblical passages that demonstrated nonviolent resistance, such as the servant parables. But it seems likely that those slaves with serious aspirations for freedom would see the parables' subtexts of honor. That may help to explain
how quickly slaves incorporated their new faith with those compatible beliefs, rituals, and songs of African origins. It is hardly a wonder that slaves

thought God was their savior from the miseries of thralldom. If God could free the Israelites from bondage, the same could happen to the slaves. It was not only a matter of hope, which was paramount, but also a means to restore a full-bodied sense of honor. Through prayer and supplication, release from bondage might occur at any time, they believed. African Americans had a trust that Jesus, the figure of a far higher form of honor, was powerful enough to work for their emancipation.

Thus, through their worship of God and Jesus, slaves were able to obtain a new meaning in their everyday lives. The credo, inspired by Christian faith, included a warning that slaves should not inform owners of any act that could help their masters. It was that spirit of hidden defiance that inspirited the camp meetings in neighboring woods or wilderness. There they could sing, worship, and enjoy fellowship with little fear of discovery or disruption.

In addition to the Christian faith, African Americans had regard, too, for an older heritage from the West African coast. Hoodoo (the preferred term of blacks; whites tended to use *voodoo*), with many of its African customs, rituals, and formulae, was transported to the New World from Africa. Hoodoo practitioners, the "root doctors" or conjurers, enjoyed a special status. Even whites occasionally went to them for cures and potions, and the medicine they practiced was, in some cases, more efficacious than the white doctors' administration of leeches and blood-letting.[45]

That was evident in a Virginia court trial in 1802. John, a slave of one John Hopson, stood charged with trying to poison a Mrs. Lewis Ragsdale. The prosecutor introduced so-called evidence consisting of "palma-cristal seeds, dirt-dauber nests, with dead spiders and snail shells." These were found in John's box of conjuring materials. In his defense, John declared that the contents that he applied to the woman's arthritic joints eased the pain and also had the advantage of helping Mrs. Ragsdale's female house servant retain the good graces of her mistress's husband. The witnesses against conjurer John included General Carrington, a physician named Dr. Walter Bennett, and others not named. They told the court that they had taken other items from John's box and fed them to a cat, which promptly expired. The court took no time to convict and sentence John to death by hanging. Then, much to the outrage of the citizens of Halifax County, Hopson, convinced of John's innocence, petitioned the governor for a pardon for his slave. Fearful of reprisals from his neighbors, Hopson did so from another county. The supposition was that the prosecution's witnesses had planted the poison. John won the appeal and was deported as the alternative to hanging. Dr. Bennett must have been pleased to have this conjurer leave the county, as John was Bennett's rival in the medical field.[46]

In 1899, the Southern scholar Philip A. Bruce described what he called a "trick doctor" as a man who "is invested with even more importance than a preacher, since he is regarded with the respect that fear excites." His standing among blacks, Bruce asserted, was greater, in fact, than that of the slave preacher. An old school Southerner, Bruce meant that this reliance on magic was a sign of black inferiority. That is not true.[47]

The leading scholar of the subject, Jeffrey Anderson, has discovered three main strands of influence in the creation of this special class of healers. The practitioners from central and western Africa dominated the hoodoo enterprise in the sections of the South originally controlled by the British. Here, the Kongo tribal groups and Igbo and Mende people developed their version of spiritual enhancement. The Louisiana form was largely the consequence of slaves coming from Haiti. The Spanish, through Cuba, inadvertently imported *Santería*.[48]

To enhance their public esteem, some Christian slave preachers also performed as conjurers. Uncle Aaron, a West African slave in eighteenth-century Virginia, would preach on Sunday and carry out hoodoo rituals later that day. He was much feared in the community for undertaking the latter role. Using a title also helped to win customers. Root doctors were entrepreneurs who charged for their services. "Doctor" was a favored term to add to one's name, and some called themselves "Reverend" or even "King." Other practitioners added a totemic figure to elevate their standing, such as "Dr. Buzzard" of Beaufort, South Carolina. These professional slave spiritual leaders liked to stand apart from their fellows, thus creating a sense of mystery and awe.[49] All these various roles, which slaves could adopt as their skills or inclinations directed them, meant an enhancement of status that elevated them from the social depths.

Another factor to which whites were ordinarily oblivious was the slaves' sense of family and community, a tie of great intensity in Africa brought to America. Melville Herskovits studied this issue and concluded that in Africa, kinship ties were all important, with lineages readily identified and revered. He studied a collection of Mississippi blacks and found 141 were linked and recognized by all the kinspeople. "A feeling of kinship as widespread as this exists among a group whose ancestors were carriers of a tradition" that embraced more than simply immediate family members.[50]

Some slaves were less lucky with regard to family ties than others. While he was growing up, Frederick Douglass had little connection with his mother because she was forced to live elsewhere. After she died, the great autobiographer recalled, "My poor mother, like many other slave-women, had *many children* but NO FAMILY! The domestic hearth, with its holy lessons and precious endearments, is abolished in the case of a slave-mother and her children. 'Little children, love one another,' are words seldom heard in a slave cabin."[51]

The memoirist Harriet Jacobs, on the other hand, spent nearly a lifetime in slavery but was fiercely loyal to her immediate and extended family—father, mother, brother, and the older generation of a grandmother, along with aunts, uncles, cousins, as well as her own children. She lost her mother as a child but was not separated as Douglass had been. Jacobs was herself a loving mother although she despaired to think her children would always be slaves.[52] As Caroline Hunter recalled, "During slavery it seemed lak yo' chillun b'longed to ev'ybody else but you. Many a day my ole mama has stood by an' watched massa beat her chillun 'til they bled an' she couldn' open her mouf."[53]

The risks that slaves sometimes took to reunite with loved ones were formidable. Sadly, their efforts often failed, and even some whites recognized the tragedy of this. Elizabeth Fox-Genovese recounts instances of collaboration and concern among whites and blacks that certainly did not conform with the horrifying portrayals free-state abolitionists drew for polemical purposes. Fox-Genovese's book *Within the Plantation Household* narrates the story of Sarah Gayle's remorse over the selling of her father's slaves, Mike and his family, after the death of Sarah's father, their original owner. It was an example of how ties of affection could draw servant and owner together. Sarah sought to possess these favored slaves once again, and Mike felt the same way. "Mike had heard rumors," Sarah recorded after he had come to her, "that they might be moving and begged that they not think 'of leaving me, for I should be a lost man,' and the poor fellow really was choked into silence." To Sarah Gayle, these slaves represented a living tie to her parents, both dead, but she also had enough humanity to want to see the family held together for its own sake. John Gayle, Sarah's husband, also wanted to comply but apparently was too short of cash and thus refused to buy the slaves. Sarah was distraught, but there was no changing John's mind.[54] Such were the complexities and melancholy consequences of slavery. But these examples demonstrate the bonds of love slaves forged in the crucible of thralldom, just as their ancestors had in Africa.

Occupational skill was a potent source of slave esteem. Expertise at fishing, hunting, trapping, sailing, or some other occupation won the approval of other slaves and sometimes whites as well. Solomon Northrup built a fish trap, made a curved ax handle, and seems to have been ingenious and inventive. Some slaves played the fiddle and gained special privileges as entertainers. We learn from slave accounts, usually published by abolition societies or antislavery publishing houses, how slaves might be given substantial duties. They achieved these skills usually without any encouragement or assistance from whites, and generally had no access to formal education. Some pious slaveholders, often female, allowed rudimentary study so that a slave child might be able to read the Bible. Naturally gifted artisans, of course, did receive instruction that would profit a master.[55]

Masters were not altogether indifferent about the possible accomplishments their slaves might offer. After all, masters, too, would be honored and respected by their white neighbors if they could boast about the unusual talents of one of their slaves. William Elliott, a renowned South Carolina sportsman, was the proud owner of a slave named May, who was an accomplished harpoonist of devil fish.[56] Lovers of horses bragged about the achievements of their stable help and the slave jockeys who won races with their wealthy planters' Arabians. In such instances, master and slave alike could take pride in the slave's achievements and skills. Charles Tait, one of the wealthiest slaveholders in the state of Alabama, owned a slave whose mathematical skills made him a valuable accountant, reader of stock market transactions, and general factotum for his master. So shrewd was his mind that when he went on his owner's business to Mobile, he was invited to stay in local planter homes so that he could provide his hosts with financial advice.[57]

Honor was evident in the slave quarters. Male slaves who had a capacity to think, talk, and act fast gained status. This was a subtle way of assuring survival when a crisis arose. A fast-spoken lie might have a better chance of acceptance by the master than if there were hems and haws. To sharpen their talents, slaves might prepare themselves by taking up the game of "playing the dozens." The object of this game was to insult another slave who then had to retort with a greater insult, with onlookers clapping and groaning over the words exchanged. Those with the greatest gift for the exercise could win the respect of their fellow slaves, especially when they sought to fool the master or overseer. The game originated in the honor cultures of West Africa. That attitude of mind was not just a casual matter:

It was handed down from parent to child to prevent disaster. The trickster stories and "playing the dozens" instructed as well as entertained. The word games presented subtle ways to manipulate and outsmart the powerful.[58] It proved most useful in black relations to their owners. In particular, as Lawrence Friedman observes, the skill could quietly counter the white effort to instill abject docility in slaves.[59]

Nearly all slaveholders asked for more than was possible of their slaves, but they could be hoodwinked, even when the issue was not a matter of insurrectionary plots, real or imagined. A Mr. Whitehead owned a slave named Dick, who knew how to play the fiddle and sing. Dick complained all the time of being ill when work was about to begin. Finally, Whitehead sent the slave back to the quarters where he was to remain for some seven years. Finally on one occasion, "Old Master say to the overseer man, 'Let's slip up there and see what Dick doing.'" They found him fat and happy, "a-playing the fiddle and a-singing." His song was satirical: "Fool my master seven years. / Going to fool him seven more. / Hey diddle, de diddle, de diddle, de do." Whitehead, though, overheard from the doorstep and angrily shouted, "Damn if you will. Come on outen there, you black rascal, and go to work."[60]

House servants, who had frequent contact with the master class, were shrewd when it came to eloquent fabrication. They knew how to talk to white people. Out of a fear that paralyzed the tongue, an unprepared slave would have difficulty mastering the technique. That failure might cause the black community real trouble from an irate white man.

A curious example comes from eighteenth-century South Carolina. A dramatic case in Charleston in 1749 might have ended in a slave execution for plotting rebellion. During an interrogation, some slaves fingered other slaves, out of fear of a scheming master. The accusing slaves claimed that the suspects were insurrectionists, but their confessions were totally false. One of the imprisoned slaves, Cyrus, eventually recanted. He told his inquisitors that prior to his first appearance, Agrippa, the alleged leader of the plot, warned him to allow Agrippa alone to make the best case for their defense to the authorities. Agrippa claimed to have overheard a slave named Scipio say that another alleged conspirator, Kent, "was a Fool and did not know how to Talk before White People." Scipio had stood next to Kent and "Pinched him." Otherwise, Kent might "have told all & blown them." Another slave pointed out that Kent had been frightened and "hunch'd" so that he would "speak out as he ought to." This incident shows that much depended on how a deception was uttered. Those who worked daily with whites were more likely to develop trickster skills than those who spoke chiefly to their fellow slaves. Others, unable to learn these talents, were thought, like Kent, to be fools.[61]

But the story did not end there. A sudden development interrupted the interrogations. The alleged conspirators were actually victims of their master's plot to hide a local crime of his own, the burning of a barn. A doctor disclosed the master's offenses, leaving the slaves free to tell the truth. George, another slave, opened his new testimony by stating, "Sir I am in your presence, my Master tells me that you are head of the Country. It is true I am not a white Man, but I have a soul as well as others, and I believe there is a Heaven and a Devil." He was now relieved to confess "because he had been afraid of God's displeasure if he had not."[62] The relatively smooth transition from lies to truths, the exactitude with which the tales were adjusted to meet new revelations, the precautions by which the bondsmen protected themselves from targeting any whites, especially their master, were all demonstrations of a power over words that set these slaves apart and lent them the admiration of other slaves. The distinctions drawn between the inarticulate and the eloquent also separated the slaves within their own hierarchy of honor.[63] Such linguistic maneuvers illustrate how slaves could overcome their vulnerability, their powerlessness in a white-dominated world. By using their carefully constructed tactics, they could achieve a sense of dignity.

The more obvious form of developed honor was in actual rebellion, infrequent though the opportunities were. A number of insurrections and plots occurred as early as the seventeenth century, such as in Gloucester County, Virginia. The most famous revolts, of course, were Gabriel Prosser's rebellion near Richmond, Virginia, in 1800; Denmark Vesey's plot in Charleston in 1822; and Nat Turner's uprising in Southampton, Virginia in 1831.[64]

The rebellion with the largest number of participants, however, occurred in St. John the Baptist Parish, Louisiana, in early 1811. This revolt has not received as much scholarly attention as the others, but it was a telling example of black desire for freedom. Some 500 slaves fought for the cause. The leaders managed to create an army divided into companies, each with its own commanding officer, some even on horseback. The objective was the capture of New Orleans. As best they could, the slaves had armed themselves with a few muskets, knives used for the sugar cane harvest, hoes, lances, and pikes. They drew inspiration from the recent uprising in Haiti, which had ended in victory for black freedom. The effort in Louisiana grew stronger day by day with fresh recruits joining from various plantations. The rebels fashioned flags to wave and had drummers announcing their advance. The motto for the insurrectionists was "Freedom or Death." According to one source, "the sacrifices of these brave men and women were not in vain. They redeemed the honor of their people and extended the tradition of revolutionary struggle, which set the stage for the eventual end of chattel slavery." Some of those who fought were recently arrived slaves from the busy market in New Orleans. Such new imports would not yet have been integrated into the oppressive life that fellow slaves had to endure. Most, however, were native black Louisianans. In the end, the leading militants, including the chief rebel, Charles Desmonde, were executed, usually after short trials over which the owners chiefly presided.[65] All violent attempts to win slaves their liberty, save of course the Civil War, failed. Furthermore, many completely innocent souls were arrested on false testimony and hanged. The hopeful prospect of using weapons was simply illusory. The leaders may have been brave and honorable, but their cause was bound to fail.

✦ ✦ ✦

We cannot ignore the problem of submissiveness in the slave world or, as mentioned, wherever an authority seeks to obliterate resistance by a process of "brainwashing," as it were. Being placed in the grip of another human being might make most of us cringe. We would seek release from pain and even survival in acquiescing to the demands of a master. For instance, in the so-called Stockholm phenomenon, robbers of a Stockholm bank manipulated their hostages to the point that they began to identify with their captors and do what their captors commanded.[66] Similarly, Nazi guards so manipulated some inmates—whether Slavs, Jews, or other targets of annihilation—that some prisoners adopted an obsequious manner.[67]

In another example, North Korean intelligence officers notoriously brainwashed prisoners to gain information of military use. As a result, some prisoners gave away U.S. Army positions, strategies, and tactics. This sort of mind control sought to induce captives to adopt the desires of their manipulators as their own, to follow directives that were detrimental to their own best interests.[68]

George Orwell explored this issue of complete subservience with special acuteness. Humiliation and shame dominate the ordeal of Winston Smith, Orwell's main character in Nineteen Eighty-Four, in which Smith makes a final, sad capitulation to the love of Big Brother. More than many other writers, Orwell translated personal experiences of humiliation into fiction. He himself had been disillusioned and nearly assassinated by communists during the Spanish Civil War. Orwell, too, greatly admired and was influenced by Arthur Koestler and his mordant classic, *Darkness at Noon*. Both writers, formerly communist sympathizers, were struck by the horror of Nicolai Bukharin's false confession of guilt in the Stalinist show trials and eventual execution in Moscow. Orwell's understanding of the psychology of submission has entered into everyday discourse.[69]

These forms of subservience, fictional or historical, bear resemblance to the slave experience, albeit imperfectly. The common characteristic is the facility of all powerful regimes to coerce populations using a particular ethos—the superiority of the ruling group, race, or ideology over a singled-out, inferior people. All these cultural, religious, or racial differentiations mark how the powerful may overwhelm the minds and actions of the powerless. The reaction of the privileged is to accept their role of superiority; for the oppressed, it is to seek ways to survive under the vicious system imposed. There was really no logical or scientific reason to insist on black inferiority, but it gave status and honor to those on the other side of the color line. In American culture, almost from the start, white people assumed that African Americans, free or slave, enjoyed their place in life and glorified their owners and other whites as they were expected to. Generation after generation of whites reenforced that collective, time-hallowed understanding. Some slaves and free blacks may have agreed with the tragic imposition, but was it ever fully internalized? That we cannot know.

The assumption of black inferiority was not peculiar to the American slave experience, but in other instances, a racial element might not be involved. Submissiveness can occur anywhere, anytime, in any setting so long as those in authority choose to exercise full mastery of their victims. The German people under Adolf Hitler enjoyed and even relished the Aryan myth of Nazi propaganda, and Jews became the scapegoats for all of the country's economic miseries. Only the most courageous dissenters objected. The rest acted submissively out of fear or actual pride in the glorification of the "master race." Totalitarian regimes, the most likely users of this technique, too often succeed in this kind of effort. But there can also be a cultural dimension in which, over the course of centuries, one group dominates and compels obedience and deference from another until that dominance becomes a part of the culture. So it was in the region below the Mason-Dixon line.

White Southerners fostered slavishness in ways perhaps too unconscious to have made it into an all-pervasive and systematic policy. Yet, the purposive and all-encompassing humiliations to which slaves were subjected affected some of them with the desire not to avenge wrongs, but rather to submit to them. To be sure, the examples from Germany, Stockholm, North Korea, and Orwell differed considerably from the slaves' situation in the antebellum South. Still, the resemblance of the so-called Sambo phenomenon to these other forms is not coincidental.

As a different slave situation from the American scheme, Africa itself offers another example of this lamentable mode of policing. There, race and color were not factors; religion alone separated the Islamic ruling class from the non-Muslims at Ibrahim Ibn Sori's Futa Jallon. These slaves were called *machube*. They, too, took on the appearance of faithful, obedient followers of their masters. That was a constant, persistent requirement, and it took a brave soul to challenge it.

The anthropologist Bernd Baldus discloses that the *machube* so internalized their low place in the social order that the slavish role was permanently imprinted in their minds, and they did not resent or rebel against their masters. So palpable was their state of utter humiliation, they hesitated to discuss or question their enslavement. The historian John Iliffe records that "to be born into slavery could foster acquiescence. 'I know that as often as I have been in the world I have been a slave, and as often as I shall come I must be a slave.'" This was the declaration of a slave on the Gold Coast in 1739.[70] When asked why such quick obedience was forthcoming, the *machubo* replied, "If you have a cock, then you do with the cock what you want, don't you?"[71]

Other tribes also compelled their slaves to accept their status by following prescribed rituals. Observing "a prescribed code of conduct," an English trader recounted how Mende slaves followed a prescribed ritual. They would "cringe up and place their two hands one on each side of their master's hand and draw them back slowly . . . while the head is bowed." Likewise, some American masters made a ceremony of humiliation. Jacob Stroyer, a former slave of South Carolina, recalled that "the [slave] boys were required to bend the body forward with the head down and rest the body on the left foot, and scrape the right foot backwards on the ground while uttering the words, 'howdy Massa and Missie.'"[72] What resentments the slaves felt inside can only be guessed.

For thousands of years, the oppressed of every land and culture have been told that their situation was as good and as happy as they deserved, that their status was a dictate of one or more gods, that rebellion or complaint was forbidden, that their lot benefited society as a whole. Even their suffering was alleged to be a therapeutic cure for the soul. Martin Seligman writes of "learned hopelessness" and "identification with the oppressor." By those means, the lowliest of the low might create their own social order based on their situation. So argues Johan Galtung, who writes of "implanting the top dog inside the underdog." In *Black Skin, White Masks,* Frantz Fanon identifies colonial subjects who keenly felt this kind of pressure not only to conform but to imitate their overlords.[73]

How much does this brief exposition have to do with the situation in a white, democratic American South? It is possible to argue that conditions in the slave South were not as dire as those of Jews in Nazi Germany, that the state alone was not the source of oppression as in North Korea, and that white Southerners by no means sought to obliterate their so-called inferiors as in Nazi Germany. Yet, it is appropriate to use analogies, however broadly, if they shed light on a mysterious phenomenon.

Slaves in the deepest reaches of the South were more autonomous than those in populated areas such as Virginia and Maryland. They could form their own hierarchies and, living mostly apart from white life, deal with interior matters in the slave quarters without constant oversight. Differences thus developed within the slave community between country and urban blacks. Frederick Douglass remarked on the sad state of the rural slave who had so little knowledge of the outside world beyond the confines of his small world. "Life, to them," he wrote, "had been rough and thorny, as well as dark." Douglass was both brilliant and lucky. He had the advantage of being partially raised in Baltimore, which widened his horizons considerably. It even prompted his repugnance against slavery itself. Country-bred slaves had less opportunity to carry themselves with an air that whites would deem "impudent."[74]

At the same time, even the most oppressed slaves still held a sense of integrity that belied their conditions. Although writing at a different time and place, the playwright Lorraine Hansbury remarked on the purpose of her classic *Raisin in the Sun* in a letter to her mother in 1954. The African American hoped that the play's pre-Broadway opening in New Haven,

Connecticut, "will help a lot of people understand how we are just as complicated as they are—and just as mixed up—but above all we have among our miserable and downtrodden ranks, people who are the very essence of human dignity."[75] Her thoughts equally applied to African Americans of an earlier time.

The desire for slaves to be like their white overlords in as many aspects as possible was an effort to claim a degree of honor from that association. Some slaves, like Ibrahim, gained a high standing by doing as white men did and used his master's methods to do so. This process could be called *collusion*, but a more preferable term is *accommodation*. As Frederick Douglass wrote, "A representative could not be prouder of his election to a seat in the American Congress, than a slave on one of the out-farms would be of his election to do errands at the Great House Farm. They regarded it as evidence of great confidence reposed in them by their overseers; and it was on this account, as well as a constant desire to be out of the field from under the driver's lash, that they esteemed it a high privilege, one worth careful living for." The cleverest of slaves thus achieved a sense of personal integrity, but this did not alter their status as black men and slaves in the eyes of whites. Such a dynamic bondsman, wrote Douglass, was thought to be "a most trusty fellow, who had this honor conferred upon him the most frequently." Like young white politicians currying favor with their high-standing patrons, these "black Governors" imitated their owners, Douglass observed.[76] A dread of possible harm could lead to efforts to please or imitate whites and meet their expectations. The role of "Uncle Tom"—a terrible misnomer, as Harriet Beecher Stowe's character was not subservient but a full figure of a man—was probably not fully internalized.

This approach was a very human response. Booker T. Washington, an expert on black survival "in the Lion's Mouth" and the president of Tuskegee University, once remarked, "The Negro is a born imitator; whatever the white man does the Negro will do." He meant this as a sardonic compliment. The "Negro" might take up arms or rob "a bank in Texas." This same imitative approach could also be found in Nazi concentration camps, prisons, and other institutions of coercion and control. It does not mean, however, that all was done to please the slaveholder or prison guard. Nor does it signify a diminishment of the slave's sense of identity. Primo Levi, the Italian Holocaust survivor, observed, "The need for *lavoro ben fatto*—'work properly done'—is so strong as to induce people to perform even slavish chores 'properly.'" The reason for such efficiency was "not out of obedience but out of professional dignity." That was true on the plantation no less than in the Nazi camps.[77]

Yet occasions did arise that undermined black confidence. Frederick Douglass himself felt inadequate speaking before a white audience at New Bedford, Massachusetts, where he had settled after escaping from Maryland. "It was a severe cross, and I took it up reluctantly. The truth was, I felt myself a slave, and the idea of speaking to white people weighed me down. I spoke but a few moments, when I felt a degree of freedom, and said what I desired with considerable ease." He went on to do his courageous work for those still in bonds.[78]

The culture of coercion had for many slaves an overwhelming power. Josiah Henson, a country-raised slave, offers an example of how slaves might succumb to white demands and seek to win favor as a result. All his life, Henson regretted that, as a young man, like others in the slave quarters, he had scarcely wondered about the rightness of his enslavement. Bankrupt, Mr. Amos, Henson's owner, put Henson in charge of moving Amos's human property of eighteen souls from a Virginia estate to Trimble County, Kentucky. "My pride was aroused in view of the importance of my responsibility, and heart and soul I became identified with my master's project of running off his negroes," Henson recounted. The little band sailed by barge past Cincinnati. Watching their progress, freed blacks along the city wharves shouted for them to come ashore and gain their freedom. Henson refused—to his later deep chagrin. In his mind at that time, he had felt that he would violate his "sentiment of honor on the subject." Often, slaves given unusual responsibilities would do as Henson did. Used to the dictates of absolute obedience and "too degraded and ignorant of the advantages of liberty to know what they were forfeiting," Henson realized, the eighteen slaves made no protest about his wrong-headed, even stubborn, rejection of liberty. The boat traveled on to its destination.[79]

The incident was appalling, as Henson later anguished, but was it not comprehensible? We can barely grasp that tragic scene, so alien is it to our way of thinking. But it demonstrates the reality of honor's existence, even if misplaced. Plantation slaves did not know what autonomy was. That conservatism was a study in humility, a psychological state that preserved their lives, but it did not enhance notions of honor and self-protection.

Long acculturated American slaves held concepts of liberty that were far more sophisticated than those of *machube* slaves serving the Fulani. Yet, like them, the isolated slave field hand in the Old South held to a peasant caution, which had its own sanctions and rituals of allegiance. Even after emancipation, as Leon Litwack has observed, country blacks found it hard to break old habits of deference—much to the gratification of previous masters. Georgia planter Louis Manigault, Litwack records, was gratified that former slaves were still "showing respect by taking off their caps."[80]

Not surprisingly in a world based on patriarchy, the sense of masculine proprietorship was also true within the slave cabin and marked its occupants. A slave caught flirting or more with another's woman would most likely be assaulted or even killed by the woman's husband. Male slaves ruled their women and children and expected deference to their decisions. Families were too often broken up by sale to other parties, and fear of that possibility was a serious deterrent to slaves' individuality and sense of wholeness. The late Herbert Gutman offers the most telling explanation for the integrity of black households, derived from familial traditions in Africa—even under the burden and sorrows of bondage. Inevitably, slaves adopted some aspects of white traditions as well, but they also acted in opposition to that source. Some customs, such as the offering of "bride wealth," could not be used as an inducement for an arranged marriage as it had been in Africa. Nor could slaves maintain their African lineages, traditionally an important part of their identities. Parts of West Africa calculated family through the maternal line, whereas other parts, including Mali and Futa Jallon, were patrilineal. The security that extended families provided could hardly be sustained under Southern slavery, either because of the break-up of families in sales by owners or local sheriffs or because of the wholesale movements of planters westward. The "supernatural sanctions of kinship," as Melville J. Herskovits puts it, was lost to a degree.[81]

Given the many different tribes and clans that were brought to America, there is a difficulty in teasing out levels of patriarchal control and the influence of mothers. As Herskovits notes, "Even in Dahomey, a society as strongly patrilineal as any to be found, the relation between a person and the mother's family is warm and permissive, in contrast to the harsh discipline exacted by the patrilineal kin."[82] But it is likely that Muslim slaves in America were determined to rule their households and permit little dissent from wives and children. Slaves possibly adopted the African code of honor similar to the ones followed by Ibrahim. He followed it when he returned from the woods and put his mistress's foot on his neck to indicate subservience. But, as mentioned, slaves also, as occasion permitted, asserted a sense of "I am a man" that could end fatally in light of white people's overwhelming power.

Clearly, the ability of slaves to control their own lives was severely limited. The memoir of Henry Bibb of Trimble County, Kentucky, for instance, tells a sad but not untypical story. Under his master, William Gatewood, Bibb lived with his wife, Malinda, and had to witness daily the "insults, scourgings and abuses" that she endured. It was more than he could bear, and he fled to Canada. What else could he have done? Three years later he came back to retrieve both Malinda and their young daughter. A freedman in Cincinnati, however, betrayed him, no doubt for a good reward. Gatewood packed Bibb's wife and children off to New Orleans for sale, and the family was never reunited, though Henry was able to return to Canada. His persistence demonstrates not only his love for his wife, but also his determination to retain, if possible, his honor as a protector against an evil system and what it licensed. Tragically, circumstances overwhelmed his resolve. After a final attempt to bring his wife to freedom, Bibb discovered that she had, by necessity, become the mistress of her new master. Bibb went back to Canada alone.[83]

At the same time, Bibb's account also reveals that the control of human property was never quite as secure as owners would have preferred. At great risk, Bibb escaped bondage several times. Slaves sometimes asserted themselves in ways that defied their owners even more directly. As a teenager, Frederick Douglass decided no longer to submit to frequent whippings from a cruel farmer named Edward Covey. Douglass struck back to retrieve his own sense of honor. The pair fought for over two hours, but Covey lost blood and the battle, while Douglass was unscathed. After that, Douglass reported, he felt no more the sting of the cart whip. He would no longer be shamed and ridiculed by white onlookers but was respected for his dignity and sense of resolve. Covey wanted no repetition of his former fate nor dared risk becoming the subject of local white mockery. Both whites and blacks had a strong dread of being shamed. Douglass's brave defiance restored his faith in himself: "This battle with Mr. Covey was the turning-point in my career as a slave. It rekindled the few expiring embers of freedom, and revived within me a sense of my own manhood."[84]

⁛ ⁛ ⁛

The moment for slave honor to emerge whole and ready for fulfillment occurred during the Civil War. For both races, honor provided an opportunity for service with unusual significance. Death in battle conferred an immortality in the eyes of the people just as the "divine blessing" of eternal life in the presence of God was thought to be the reward of religious faith. That dual linkage of grace and honor had always been a part of the warrior ethos, in non-Christian as well as Christian societies. At the time of the Civil War, slave men could decide to spy for the Union Army, serve as guides for Union troops, mislead Confederate soldiers, or join the invading forces. The latter was the best choice for advancing slave honor, but it could only occur when Lincoln's army came within a reasonable distance. Indeed, in the early part of the war, the Union Army was sharply divided with many Southern-born and conservative Democratic Union soldiers and officers despising blacks and excoriating abolitionists and antislavery Republicans. Even some members of the Republicans entertained vicious prejudices. General Robert C. Schenk, for instance, though a former Free Soiler, confided to his daughter that blacks were "mere animals, little above the brutes."[85] When opportunity beckoned, male slaves left the fields and headed for wherever they thought their thralldom might end. Others were still bolder, defying slave patrols, irate planters, and whites in general, and found freedom behind the Yankee blue coats.

If claims for honor are ever to be awarded to these real heroes, Robert Smalls should receive the first accolades. In May 1862, Smalls, an experienced seaman, commandeered the Confederate steamer *Planter*. Knowing all the signals to circumvent watchful rebel lookouts in the bay, Smalls sailed the ship into the Union blockade lines. He and his crew also brought useful military information about Confederate positions. His exploits caught the attention of President Abraham Lincoln.[86]

Similarly, the African American members of the all-black 54th Massachusetts Regiment engaged the enemy at heavily armed Fort Wagner, outside Charleston on Morris Island. They proved splendid warriors, as valorous as their African ancestors. The assault on the fort, however, was a military blunder for which senior Federal commanders were responsible. The troops were under the command of New England abolitionist Robert Gould Shaw who, fatally wounded, fell before the ramparts. The regiment, though, fought on but ultimately lost. Despite the unfortunate outcome, the example of bravery the black troops displayed encouraged a host of new black recruits and provided the Union Army with still greater numerical advantage.[87]

In another example, a small, undermanned fort stood on Milliken's Bend, situated north of Vicksburg, during Ulysses Grant's siege of this vital

Mississippi port. There, former slaves proved their mettle. Although poorly armed with decrepit muskets and limited ammunition, and unsupported by more experienced white troops, two brigades of newly arrived "contrabands" fended off repeated Confederate assaults until the arrival of two Union gunboats scattered the enemy. In reporting on the engagement, Grant was highly complimentary. He wrote that the raw enlistees had shown uncommon courage. "The bravery of the blacks," Grant reported, "completely revolutionized the sentiment of the army with regard to the employment of negro troops." Even formerly skeptical white officers found themselves to be new enthusiasts for the further use of freedmen in the army.[88]

During the election crisis in 1864, Lincoln was attacked, even by fellow Republicans, for having issued the Emancipation Proclamation in 1863. Democrats viewed the act as a stumbling block to a truce with the secessionists. But the president had a ready retort. To be sure, he denied that slavery's abolition was the chief aim for which the Union armed services fought. Yet, he quickly added that some of his critics were ignoring the moral aspect of the issue: "There have been men base enough to propose to me to return to slavery the black warriors of Port Hudson and Olustee [a Florida engagement]. . . . Should I do so, I should deserve to be damned in time and eternity. Come what will, I will keep my faith with friend and foe." In a letter drafted around the same time, he commented, "As a matter of policy, to announce such a purpose would ruin the Union cause itself. All recruiting of colored men would instantly cease, and all colored men now in our service would instantly desert us. And rightfully, too." In an address to Congress, he was equally forceful about what the proclamation meant: "In giving freedom to the slave, we assure freedom to the free—honorable alike in what we give, and what we preserve."[89] Had the blacks in uniform not fought and died for the Union, the outcome could well have resulted in a permanently divided nation.

In conclusion, it should be noted that the code of honor, as Southern whites imagined it, was losing its preeminence even as the storm clouds of war approached. A growing town life; an upsurge of civic institutions, especially churches; and a growing middle class were transforming the Southern economy during the midcentury years. These factors were replacing older notions of honor to a degree. Yet, in the slave states, the national crisis over slavery and abolitionism required the full assertion of rights and symbols of honor. That was particularly true when news arrived of Lincoln's election to the presidency.

Little did white people suspect that slaves, too, had their own version of honor, which included a burning desire to shake off the shackles that bound them. War was destined to make that possible. Black manhood was vindicated, ironically in a way that white slave owners brought upon themselves in their bloody striving to create a permanent slaveholding nation. But the nation paid a drastically high price in blood and treasure through the grime, stench, and horrors of warfare. All this misery occurred to preserve a labor system facing worldwide condemnation and a slave-supporting culture that embraced an outworn code of honor. The exaction came inexorably due at Appomattox. How and why proud, even reckless secessionists considered themselves civilized, Christian, and constitutionally sound will become evident in the next chapter.

2

WHITE MALE HONOR, SHAME, AND SHAMELESSNESS IN THE OLD SOUTH

A sense of discomfort lay beneath a longstanding Southern belief in the honorableness of the white race in the antebellum period. What caused the undercurrent of doubt? The previous chapter offers at least a partial explanation. There existed a suspicion among the white population that the hundreds of thousands of African Americans they controlled were not as compliant and submissive as their masters and others might wish. Any sign of slave dissatisfaction or open resistance stimulated a sense of anxiety. These cracks in the armor of honor and the security of self-esteem were not a matter of everyday discourse—far from it. Yet, the rhetoric of the day revealed the intensity of the social and racial division. Southerners proclaimed liberty the sword of the honorable man.

The Founding Fathers and others in the patriot elite all assumed that liberty and honor were virtual twins. Liberty was the great reward of honor, but might well be enhanced by the ownership of more than a few slaves, although it was not a necessity to achieve that status. Honor rested on the community judgment of character, and that could include reputation for wealth, whatever its form. Poor men seldom would be considered members of the gentlemanly class. Those with much honor stood at the top of the social order, with gradations following below that privileged few. Some were not included at all—women, Indians, slaves, indentured servants, and other menials. (White women, of course, had honor within the system but not equivalent to that of men's when it came to the functioning of personal liberty. Female honor had its gradations with regard to wealth in money or land, and it was dependent on parentage and marital ties.)[1]

The hierarchy traced its origins deep into the social realm of the Old World. But, in America, liberty was more fluid. Class distinctions were not bound as tightly by tradition and means of wealth as they were in Europe. As William Shakespeare wrote in *The Merchant of Venice*,

> To cozen fortune and be honourable
> Without the stamp of merit? Let none presume
> To wear an undeserved dignity.
> O, that estates, degrees and offices
> Were not derived corruptly, and that clear honour
> Were purchased by the merit of the wearer!
> How many then should cover that stand bare!
> How many be commanded that command!
> How much low peasantry would then be glean'd
> From the true seed of honour! and how much honour
> Pick'd from the chaff and ruin of the times
> To be new-varnish'd![2]

The playwright's words imply a clear distinction between the worthy and unworthy. He conveyed the proposition of the Renaissance humanists that noble birth was not necessarily the sole criterion for honorableness. At the same time, honor and liberty were not expected to be universal; servants, menials, slaves, and others of the lower classes were not eligible, and few thought they ever would be.

Most seventeenth- and eighteenth-century thinkers—John Locke, Thomas Hobbes, Adam Smith, Thomas Jefferson, and others—seldom drew clear lines regarding who was eligible for honor, and therefore who might enjoy the entire and inviolate attributes of liberty. That idea needed no expression any more than would singling out particular sunbeams from a flood of light. Thomas Hobbes in *The Elements of Law* (1640) argued that men's grasp of power was not absolute but restricted by the power of others. This imperfect world required, it would seem, differentiations in the realm of honor and the exercise of power. Yet, there remains ambiguity because, at least in the American setting, the phrase "all men are created equal" obviously glosses over that problem. It certainly gave pause to those patriots who felt uncomfortable about enslavement.[3]

The fear of white enslavement, the overthrow of the sanctified order, was a steep precipice that surfaced publicly in times of political and racial crises. Real or supposed slave insurrectionary plots, domestic wars, the Revolution, and the Civil War all occasioned such moments. The idea may have lingered in the back of white Southern minds whenever white domination was thought to be threatened, though to the modern reader, such fears seem to be exaggerated fantasies.

Of course, masters insisted that everything was well-ordered, the under-race deliriously happy with their state, and the society safe and headed for still greater things. During the sectional turbulence of the 1850s, Southern intellectuals, theologians, and politicians took heart from a tribute given by Edmund Burke when he addressed Parliament, hoping to reconcile the mother country and Americans. He spoke on the theme of liberty within the monarchical order. These ideas, Burke thought, were difficult to combine, but both had merit, and slave ownership was no obstacle. Royal power, of course, no longer applied in the 1850s, but Southern orators and politicians often quoted Burke in defining their aims of independence. "Britons' Gothic ancestors," like other nations, ancient and modern, had held bondsmen and their families, he reasoned. Senator Robert Toombs of Georgia, the Southern Baptist leader Basil Manly, and others cited Burke's speech as a defense of their cherished institution against abolitionist onslaughts of words and hostile actions. John Drayton, governor of South Carolina, referred warmly to Burke, who had declared that the American slaves were happy and contented, a sentiment shared by most Southern whites.[4]

Four aspects of this ethic of honor require separate consideration, though they were intimately connected to each other. First and most important was the distinction between the white ideal of liberty and slavery, liberty's opposite. That lowly ranking was reserved for the unworthy, the dishonored, the African Americans upon whose labor planters depended. The second concern was the emphasis on how the honorable individual should conduct himself, not primarily to defend against discomfort and disorder, but to fulfill the Stoic tradition of ethical presentation. Many gentlemen of the Old South were devoted to the ideals of gentility, prudence, truth-telling, and dignified courtesy, all of which were part of the Stoic and Aurelian styles of honor. The thinking slave owner and other men of wealth were well acquainted with *The Meditations of Marcus Aurelius*. Inculcated from childhood, these attributes gave those in the Southern elite who exemplified them a standing and platform for the rest of the world to admire and even romanticize. In this connection there were two icons of Southern culture — George Washington and Thomas Jefferson. To contemporary outsiders and modern observers, their performance of upper-class decorum was the best characterization of honorable conduct that the South could provide.

The third issue, however, exposes the darker side of the ethic. In contrast to the more peaceable North, Southern society had always struggled with an unusual level of ferocity. Duels, fights, eye-gougings, tarring and feathering, mob rioting, and other forms of mayhem demonstrated the fissures of the society. Honor in the lower orders took the informal and brutal forms of ear-biting, cudgel beatings, and other violence, but the motives for such behavior usually and spontaneously resulted from verbal disputes. Alcohol further stimulated such troubles.[5] Over and over the impulse arose, whether in the upper or lower ranks, to prove the superiority and prowess of one man above another and thus uphold a claim to honor and community approbation.

Finally, the role of shame and shamelessness was closely tied to this issue of savageness. Some men, even those who considered themselves above such behavior, could act at times outside the boundaries of accepted honorable conduct. Such men risked a serious loss of reputation, but some seemed not to care.

⬩⬩⬩

Liberty was the most important ingredient in the realm of honorable standing. Possession of that privilege in America depended on one's own merit more than on a proper birthright. Even before the settlement of the Virginia colony, at the trial of Robert Devereux, 2nd Earl of Essex, in 1601 for treason, prosecutor Robert Cecil defended his humble lineage against the rebellious, overly proud defendant's slurs by saying, "I am not noble, yet a gentleman; I am no swordsman—there also you have the odds; but I have innocence, conscience, truth, and honesty, and to defend me against the scandal and sting of slanderous tongues, and in this Court I stand as an upright man, and your Lordship as a delinquent."[6] This emphasis on personal merit as the source of honor, too, could be found in America.

According to the hierarchy that the ethic upheld, slavery represented the most disgraceful, humiliating, and pitiable condition known to man. In the eighteenth century, slavery was only the most extreme form of social alienation. People facing other types of involuntary subordination—indentured servants, redemptioners, apprentices, landless laborers—were also situated within the accepted social order. The notion of freedom implied some minimal social standing; the freeman was one capable of self-provision or who enjoyed an autonomy from subservience to someone higher in rank. Class distinctions were important in America, as they were in the Old World. Yet, they carried less weight, less expected obligation. Deference to the wealthy and powerful was part of the unwritten code but forelock touching and deep, abject bows were not required as they were with English aristocrats. Slaves alone should tip their hats and drop a knee.

John Adams, who was known for his biting criticisms of so many of his contemporaries, knew Thomas Jefferson from their association in the Continental Congress of 1774–75. To the New Englander, he was a man "of deep reflection, keen sagacity, clear foresight, daring enterprise, inflexible intrepidity, and untainted integrity, with an ardent zeal for the liberties, the honor, and felicity of his country and his species."[7] By Adams's reasoning, liberty took the form of a hegemonic right to rule rather than a universal principle. Liberty in this era was multifaceted, not our modern version of its meaning. Instead, there were gradations based on a hierarchical system. The elite were scarcely prepared to relinquish power to those of less wealth and status, and fewer social connections. The historian Michal Jan Rozbicki argues that "Revolutionary liberty was a social relation between unequals, distributed according to rank, and that the patriot elite had a deep investment in preserving it that way."[8] Of course, by today's standards, the assumption might be that slavery in the presence of liberty was corrupting to both master and servant. But such an idea was still relatively new, one that Quakers might have entertained, but few others took seriously.

✢ ✢ ✢

The second aspect of honor focuses on the ideals of truth-telling, honesty, gentility, and civil manners. On this score, Southerners themselves saw the ideal of honor in a variety of ways. As the historian Stephen W. Berry II observes, "All Southerners had to determine what the word meant to them, and they did so with considerable variety and finesse."[9] There was no motive more elevated, many thought, than that of desiring to merit the love and respect of one's fellow men. Honor, Southerners believed, could be deserved only by a truly moral and virtuous course of conduct, undertaken with indefatigable application and perseverance. Appearing honest and being known for a rigorous adherence to truth were part of a gentleman's moral equipage.

In the Old South, as in the Old World, to pledge orally the fitness and strength of a horse for sale, for example, was to place before the buyer a gentleman's word of honor. Such a gesture carried no less weight than if a written contract had been drawn up. The English philosophers all believed that honor required openness and truth-telling: "What is a man but his promise?" And presumably, that man was a gentleman, not a commoner.

James Cleland, author of *The Instruction of a Young Noble Man*, argued that the dispensing of power and the moral imperative required faithfulness on this score. "The authoritie," he wrote, "puissance, and safety of al Princes dependeth upon faith, & promise-keeping."[10] Honesty and honor were synonymous.

The grounding of truthfulness as a primary virtue lay in the general understanding that outward and inward honor were one and the same. To lie with malice aforethought strikes at the heart of a gentleman's sense of honor. Since the late medieval and early modern eras, truth-telling among gentlemen was a sacred obligation. That moral excellence encompassed both Christian and ancient virtues of faithfulness, bravery, and fortitude. When a demonstrable falsehood proved to be a gross insult or detriment toward another, it could initiate a violent encounter in the antebellum South. Demands for truth-telling enabled duelists to challenge the alleged deceiver, and provided the insulted party with the right to vindicate his integrity and courage and enhance his social worth in a hierarchical culture. Posting a challenge using the words "liar, poltroon and coward"—all common terms of the day—required a response on the field of honor. A statement charging an opponent with lying or smearing the offended party's character would appear in a newspaper column or on the courthouse door. The purpose of dueling was to prevent feuds from arising by establishing rules for engagement and providing witnesses to assure fairness in the exchange of pistol fire.[11]

Virtuous behavior in truth-telling and other criteria would testify to a gentleman's right to esteem and deference. This was especially significant in a republic. Monarchies used the pomp and circumstance of court ceremonies and kingly parades before the people to reinforce the notion of the ruler's superiority over all others. The stability that such certainty elicited was supposed to induce lesser folk into obedience to the king's laws. Republics were more likely to be turbulent and even quixotic given the freedom of anyone to speak his or her mind. As a result, truth-telling and honesty in dealings were all the more necessary.

The honor of honest men would prevail. Jefferson's ideals of an egalitarian society, entirely white no doubt, also combined the virtues of honesty and honor with an agricultural order. Certainly that was the understanding of such prominent exemplars as George Washington and Thomas Jefferson.

A charming example of the way a gentleman should demonstrate his attention to civility arises from the pen of sixteen-year-old George

Washington. He did not mention honor but instead dwelt on the attributes that honor was supposed to stimulate. Copying from a manners book, he listed 110 maxims of dos and don'ts including, "42d. Let thy ceremonies in Courtesie be proper to the Dignity of his place with whom thou conversest for it is absurd to act the same with a Clown and a Prince. . . . 108th. When you Speak of God or his Atributes, let it be Seriously & wt. Reverence. Honour & Obey your Natural Parents altho they be Poor. . . . 109th. Let your Recreations be Manfull not Sinfull. 110th Labour to keep alive in your Breast that Little Spark of Celestial fire Called Conscience."[12]

Throughout his life, Washington had no doubt that fortitude and military valor were the marks of a gentleman and officer. Danger and suffering did not matter. Duty required pressing on. When he formed his circle of aides-de-camp, Washington assured himself that, as David Hackett Fischer writes, they possessed "character, manners, efficiency and courage under fire, where they had a major function." They became what their general liked to call his "military family." The task of leading other men into battle also required that the officer, imbued with a sense of honor, be reliable and careful in judgment. Although sickly as a youth, Washington worked at gaining strength and stamina. He forced himself to ride at a fast clip and hunted as often as he could. In the prerevolutionary campaign against the Indians, Washington proved fearless and enterprising. These exploits would add to his sense of living an honorable life.[13]

When Washington learned of British depredations and the shedding of blood on Lexington Green in 1775, he exclaimed to George William Fairfax, "Unhappy it is to reflect that a Brother's Sword has been sheathed in Brother's Breast, and that the once happy and peaceful plains of America are either to be drenched with blood, or Inhabited by Slaves. Sad alternative! But can a virtuous man hesitate in his choice?" But when he was unanimously selected to head the Continental Army, he was scarcely elated. He wrote Patrick Henry, "Remember, Mr. Henry, what I now tell you: from the day I enter upon the command of the American armies, I date my fall, and the ruin of my reputation."[14] That commodity—his reputation—Washington, as well as most other gentlemen, prized as his first principle.

A noteworthy example of Washington's sense of honor and duty occurred when, as commander of the Continental Army, he crossed the Delaware River in treacherous weather in December 1776. He marched his troops toward Trenton where the Hessian mercenaries for the Crown were stationed. After a brief battle, the Americans won a decisive victory.

On his visit to the fallen garrison, Washington comforted Colonel Johann Rall, a proud German officer, as he lay mortally wounded. Rall begged that his men be allowed to keep their possessions, a request that Washington duly honored. That evening, Rall died. Rall's aide remarked that he had been "satisfied that it was not necessary for him to outlive his honor." In addition, Washington ordered his troops, officers and men, to treat all prisoners, British or Hessian, with decency. That was not merely a matter of kindness but a practical decision. Any ill treatment would reach royalists' ears. Retaliation on American prisoners would soon follow. At the same time, it was honorable as well as humane and practical.[15]

Many other examples exist showing the importance of military and civilian honor in Washington's life. Nonetheless, quite surprisingly, Washington's reputation, which he so highly valued, was not always as lofty as it later became. He had many critics, including Jefferson, who thought Washington had given himself over to the monarchist style when president. The press was often negative if not downright vicious and insulting, too. Partisanship was at the root of the reaction to this godlike figure. Jeffersonian Republicans hated the first Federalist in the office of president, and journalists attacked him ferociously. The turmoil in France caused by the French Revolution created further controversy with the Republicans, who hated the British more than the French.

In contrast to Washington's moral style, Thomas Jefferson offers an example that illustrates the different meanings that honor might have. No president of the United States was more sensitive about his devotion to self-regard and honor than Jefferson. Sometimes it served him well, but not always. When governor of Virginia during the Revolution, the patriots captured British prisoners, including the royal governor, James Hamilton, and handed them over to the Virginia government. Hamilton had previously ordered the murder of Virginia civilians, including children, and subjected Indians in his hands to ferocious brutality contrary to the rules of military engagement.

In Hamilton's case, however, Jefferson and his Council of State showed no mercy. The Virginians imprisoned the governor under conditions worse than were used for ordinary prisoners of war. General Washington understood why the Virginians were violating accepted wartime standards, but he urged a change as being in the patriots' best interests lest the British retaliate against American prisoners. Jefferson, however, would only move in begrudging steps. When Washington requested, in no uncertain terms, that the captured troops be accorded prisoner of war safeguards, Jefferson took umbrage but complied up to a point. He resented the British in their attempt, as he put it, "to bully us" into submission when the patriots held many more prisoners than the British command did. He felt his honor was compromised in this affair. Although long requested, it took him a year to agree to having Hamilton paroled to New York, which took place in October 1780.[16]

Far more serious a problem was Jefferson's relationship to his slave mistress, Sally Hemings. His handling of the public charges stood in contrast to the actions of Alexander Hamilton and his scandalous affair with Maria Reynolds, a married woman in Philadelphia. The same angry, tabloid-style journalist, James Thomson Callender, would be instrumental in tarnishing both these politicians' reputations. Callender had been a loyal Republican newsman whom Jefferson had defended when Callender was arrested for sedition against the state over the Hamilton situation. Callender had exposed Hamilton's adultery with Reynolds but also accused Hamilton of corruption for allegedly giving James Reynolds, Maria's husband, a sinecure in the Treasury Department. The charge was never verified and, given the malevolent source, likely specious. In this case, honesty—Hamilton's admitting the affair—was synonymous with honor, as the ideal required, even though the scandal was bound to distress Hamilton's wife and injure his reputation.[17]

On the other hand, Jefferson, always touchy about his possession of public esteem, took a different course. Chagrined at Jefferson's refusal to appoint him postmaster in Richmond, Callender brought charges of sexual misconduct against the president for events in both Jefferson's early and later life. As a young man, Jefferson had made unwanted advances to a married Virginian. Jefferson was highly embarrassed about the matter. It was, in the words of a biographer, "a private one that touched Jefferson's personal honor to the quick." Jefferson never denied his attempt to make love to Betsey Walker. He did assert, however, that the whole story was highly exaggerated. A Jefferson expert, Dumas Malone, believed that Jefferson's secretive compartmentalizing of his private life grew from an unwillingness to "gratify the curiosity of posterity."[18]

Apparently, Callender did not know about Jefferson's relations with Maria Cosway, a married Englishwoman when Jefferson was the American representative at the court of Louis XVI. Having lost his wife four years earlier and a daughter Lucy, more recently, Jefferson welcomed in his loneliness a romantic attachment to the accomplished Italian-English artist and beauty. In a famous 4,000-word letter called "The Dialogue between the Head and the Heart," he expressed his feelings. After a separation for some months, however, Maria Cosway on her return to Paris found Jefferson's attitude much cooler. Perhaps his taking up with Sally Hemings had quenched his ardor.[19]

More distressful than Callender's other charges was his exposure of Jefferson's possibly fathering as many as seven children by Hemings, his light-skinned, handsome, and favorite housekeeper and mistress. In this case, Callender was on firm ground. DNA tests in 1998 of Sally Heming's descendants gave unmistakable evidence of the liaison. Annette Gordon-Reed demonstrated the strong case for the relationship in her prize-winning book *Thomas Jefferson and Sally Hemings* a year before the scientific discovery.[20] Throughout America, attitudes about such issues as "miscegenation" were rapidly changing, and the practice was roundly condemned for religious and racially prejudicial reasons in the Old South.

The relationship with Sally Hemings had begun when Jefferson was the minister to France in Paris in the 1780s. She was just fifteen years old but handsome and winning. She had the spunk to confront her master when he wished to return her to Virginia. The teenager had enjoyed the freedom that life in Paris afforded a black woman, and she initially refused to return without promises from Jefferson. Her son Madison recalled being told that Jefferson pledged to accord her special favors, including the emancipation of her children when each of them turned twenty-one. As a result, she complied, and on landing home she gave birth to a baby boy. Other progeny followed. Her children, as promised, were later freed and sent to the free state of Ohio. Until recently, historians either ignored or denied the liaison. Merrill Peterson, Dumas Malone, and others refused to countenance even the possibility, for fear that it would detract from the image of Jefferson as honorable and honest. The canonization of the Founding Father and author of the Declaration of Independence held firm until recent times.[21]

How was the president to handle Callender's exposure of his liaison? His approach was the one often used by gentlemen—a refusal to provide an answer. Thus, he neither lied nor confessed. This tactic was hardly extraordinary in the Old South. There, a man's honor accorded its possessor the license to act in the bedroom as he pleased. Sally, on the other hand, could not demand her freedom without losing her privileged status and distinguished lover. Neither party wished to separate from the other. In

most matters, Jefferson, though he never fought a duel, was quite conscious
of preserving his claim to public regard.

The importance of violence in the affairs of men is undeniable. Defense
of one's honor during the antebellum period required such truculent vindication because the outer shield of reputation was part of one's sense of
identity. As a result, an insult, verbal or otherwise, damaged the psyche
as surely as a slap on the face, and required a violent response. In 1896,
B. J. Ramage outlined this vexing Southern problem of using violence to
defend honor: "The two men meet," he explained, "and since it is almost
universally customary in many sections of the South for the average man
to carry at least one revolver in the hip-pocket—elsewhere in the Southern
States significantly called the 'pistol pocket'—the trial by battle occurs."
If, as happened every so often, a criminal case for murder arises, the defendant has his attorney plead his "self-defense." In nine cases out of ten,
that plea is sustained. Among local residents, the exchange of fire may be
judged as fair as long as the outcome was in doubt until one or the other
fell. The loser's defenders then have no grounds to complain in the eyes
of the public. Thus, "long before the trial occurs friends of the murderer
are ingeniously working in the community to create sympathy in his favor." To be sure, Ramage continued, homage was gratuitously conferred on
the dead man's allegedly unblemished virtues. But that sentiment scarcely
mitigated the crime itself.[22]

What astonished Ramage and many other observers like Alexis de Tocqueville, the great French interpreter of American democracy, was the casual
response to such violence. The visiting aristocrat in 1830 heard directly
from an Alabama lawyer a most curious statement. Those who killed the
other party, in a duel or otherwise, the attorney explained to de Tocqueville,
were "always acquitted by the jury, unless there are greatly aggravating
circumstances." In the individual juror's mind, "he might, on leaving the
court, find himself in the same position as the accused, and he acquits." As
historian Randolph Roth observes, "the need to dominate others was what
led to murder."[23]

Both before and after the Civil War, violence in America was ubiquitous
throughout all classes and races. Special attention by the general public was
usually given to upper-class violence. In most cases, the motive for confrontation, often broadcast long in advance of the actual fatality or assault, was

dread of honor lost. Duels were necessary as the honorable way to resolve the insults exchanged. Otherwise the parties might resort to lower-class methods of reprisal. Historian Richard Bushman observes, "Ours is not the first age to feel pangs of anxiety about the decline of civility, refinement, and manners." After the founding of the republic, the Founding Fathers worried that the upper classes were losing their sense of proper decorum. The famous Philadelphia physician Benjamin Rush proposed that "'the principles and morals' of the people had declined." Like others, he attributed it to young upstarts and blamed the lower orders for mayhem, but actually all ranks of society engaged in swift reaction to insult.[24]

This state of affairs was analogous to what the late Lawrence Stone discovered about the intemperateness of noblemen and gentry in Tudor and Stuart England. Many decades before, Francis Bacon, the English philosopher, had lamented that dueling was nothing more than a regrettable response to some trivial cause. He contended, "My lords, it is a miserable effect, when young men, full of towardness and hope, such as the poets call 'auroræ filii,' sons of the morning, in whom the expectation and comfort of their friends consisteth, shall be cast away and destroyed in such a vain manner."[25] Duels were always the prerogative of the gentry and noble classes in England and the elite in the American South, following European and British example. "I was educated to believe," recalled Charleston physician Marion Sims, "that duels inspired the proprieties of society and protected the honor of women."[26]

In contrast to the learned Bacon, the homicide expert Randolph Roth contends that the rise of dueling in America was the result of increased democratic practice with political figures as the chief participants. He notes that attorneys, newspaper editors, officeholders, and military officers were the leading duelists. But Roth overlooks the intimate connection between duels and patron-client relations in the Old South. This verbally pledged bond between two men was based not on democratic equality but on the inequality of their status—"lop-sided friendship," an anthropologist calls it.[27] Yet, with the practice came practical and mutually rewarding advantages. "Most clients," writes a historical specialist of the subject, "rendered faithful service to their patrons and most patrons reciprocated by looking after the clients' interests."[28]

This arrangement was as ancient as honor itself. The Old and New Testaments reveal its importance in the Middle East. In the ancient Mediterranean world, writes a biblical scholar, "a patron's social status was measured in part by the number and status of his clients." Roman men of wealth and high standing used that connection to assert their public status. The tradition arose because of the rigid social rankings of society.[29] All European and British cultures used this basic scheme, and the example traveled to America where, too, the number and sometimes status of clients conferred prestige on the patron. The client owed his vote and political work to the patron. In exchange, the patron protected the client and his family, gave legal advice, and helped the client financially or in other ways. It mattered most if the clients were themselves men of good local standing, as that lent further honor to the patron.

The historian Joanne B. Freeman explores the matter with effective detail in her work. She discovered that the patron-client arrangement in politics required young, ambitious men to become loyal followers of a master guide from the upper ranks. The aspirant would seek to please his patron, and the patron was obliged to advance the career of his client within the political faction to which they belonged. The result was often the shedding of blood to defend the reputation and honor of one or the other. It was a military code that guided this political practice.[30]

Dueling provided one way for an individual to demonstrate loyalty to the leader of a political faction, often a man with military experience. Patrons sometimes defended their clients, and clients, in turn, took up the cause of their leaders in political disputes about honor, duty, loyalty, and other civic virtues. But dueling was not usually a sign of democracy at work. The lower classes were excluded from this practice, which established the preeminence of those educated and generally wealthy men who could win applause and prove their mettle to voters of all classes. In rare situations, however, a man of inferior status could gain a higher ranking if challenged by a gentleman. Political factors in so many duels arose because the duelists thought it necessary to demonstrate their willingness to die for their own and their group's honor. Not to meet a challenge was more perilous to career and reputation than to risk death on the field. George McDuffie, an uncommonly bright young man of humble origins, was the protégé of John C. Calhoun of South Carolina. McDuffie's patron paid for his education. In later years, as a rising politician, this faithful client defended the good name of his patron in a nearly deadly duel with William Cummings. McDuffie remained loyal even though Calhoun broke with Andrew Jackson, who had passed him over in favor of Martin Van Buren as his vice presidential running mate in the 1832 election.[31]

Likewise, the duel between Mississippi Senator Sargent S. Prentiss and General Henry Foote, former state governor, illuminates the situation. They had quarreled over some political differences and decided to resort to a duel. To avoid the state's antidueling law, the pair crossed into Louisiana near Vicksburg. They agreed on ten steps' distance. Prentiss claimed that he had no intention of killing Foote. At the agreed ten steps, they both missed. Not long afterward, a second meeting took place, in which Foote was wounded in the shoulder. What set this affair apart was that Prentiss hailed from Portland, Maine, before moving to New Orleans and then Mississippi in the 1820s. According to a sympathetic nineteenth-century biographer, he had fought not solely for "his own reputation but that of New England." He "fancied that he was challenged because he was 'a *Yankee,* and would not fight.'" Guilt, though, followed this deviation from his Yankee heritage. Prentiss urged his brother not to tell his mother about his "foolish scrape." But, he continued, he had to fight because not to do so would have destroyed "my own self-respect, and life itself would have had no further objects for me." Whatever fellow New Englanders might think, "when a man is placed in a situation where if he does not fight, life will be rendered valueless to him, both in his own eyes and those of the community, and existence will become a burden to him; then I say he will fight, and by so doing, will select the least of two evils." But, in the future, he would try to avoid confrontations, "so long as I can do so, and retain my self-respect." In fact, he never raised a pistol against another duelist.[32]

Honor and the impulse to dominate, of course, appeared in other parts of the country as well. Nor were duels the only forms of murderous assault to arise. Not all confrontations were fought under the *code duello.* Almost as frequently men squared off by prior appointment without seconds, surgeons, or friends in attendance. Historian Christopher J. Olsen cites an example from Mississippi in 1856. A man named V. S. Stewart and another named Head met, as agreed, on the street of Yazoo City, Mississippi, each bearing double-barreled shotguns. Firing first, Head killed Stewart with a ball to the heart. Whether one or both were gentlemen is unclear, but sometimes, as in this case, the formalities went unobserved. That circumstance, in a case involving "murder by duel" from 2009, will find a parallel in chapter 8.[33]

Southern violence extended into the Southwest, to which region whites from the Deep South migrated before and after the Civil War. An example appeared in the ironically named Pleasant Valley, Arizona, in the 1880s. The

Graham and Tewkesbury families feuded and somewhere between twenty and fifty men died as a result. The causes were complex and loyalties were confusedly fluid, according to historian Daniel Justin Herman. To make the situation still more chaotic, the feuding Tewkesbury and Graham factions turned their fury on incoming Mormons. These quarrels thus pitted the advocates on honor against the Mormons, who placed conscience and guilt above the deplorable practices that they thought honor sanctioned.[34]

The manner of men's deaths often tells much about the values by which they lived. By that reckoning, Southerners in the nineteenth century were clearly guided by an ethic that hobbled self-control and incited resorts to knife and gun. The historian Sheldon Hackney has shown how much more likely the Southerner was to shoot someone else rather than put a bullet through his own head.[35] Quite apart from the homicide-suicide ratio, Southerners, white and black, killed one another at a remarkable rate compared to Yankees. The 1890 census shows that 106 Mississippians had slain one or more victims in that year. In Ohio, 61 did likewise but in a state with three times the population. Iowa, not so bloodthirsty, recorded 26 murders in a population of 1.9 million, whereas Louisiana registered 98 killings in a population of 1.1 million.[36]

Sensitivity to popular opinion, or a salutary sense of shame, had more peaceful uses, too. It was the chief method of enforcing community values. Excessive fun-making diminished a man's capacity as a defender of family and community, and thus diminished his reputation. As Southern Christian revivalists made their converts throughout the nineteenth century, their proscriptions against drinking, dancing, and gambling drew on this older tradition, a heritage that might be called a sort of country puritanism.[37] The South's teetotal evangelicalism, which developed in the mid- and late nineteenth century, was built on that foundation. Although conscience played an increasingly significant role, the crusade against social sins continued to rely also on gossip and shame.[38]

✠ ✠ ✠

The final topic concerns shamelessness, the fourth element in the ethical dimension of Southern distinctiveness. That term refers to self-aggrandizement in defiance of convention and respectability. There was a hierarchy in shamelessness as in honor itself. The higher one was on the social ladder, the more tolerant the community was about one's social offenses. Thus, to take an extreme example, Henry VIII could lie, cheat, and despoil in the name of royal honor when a more accurate term might be royal shamelessness. A monopoly of power, in other words, gave its wielder a degree of immunity from popular judgment. Such figures sought not the total obedience of those beneath them so much as the liberty to do as they pleased. As absolute rulers on their estates, how many slaveholders felt that way?

On a mundane level, however, the planter who cheated on his wife by nocturnal visits to the slave quarters lost no honor in the betrayal. But there were rules: He should not make a public spectacle of his faithlessness so that his wife and people heard of it. He could strut by the courthouse on his way to his slave mistress, and the male observers seated on the benches would wink, nudge each other, and smirk as he passed. So long as men whispered about it in their own circles or the women did so in theirs, all was well. But if the gossip became "promiscuous," that is, shared by all, then the planter was in deeper trouble for bringing open dishonor to his wife and her kin.[39]

The South, well known as a center for gambling, offered employment for the shameless, that is, the professionals who serviced the planters' appetite for cards and races. As early as the 1720s, in Virginia, a French observer found the gentry class addicted to gambling. They laid bets on almost any topic or event. "The more uncertain the result, the more likely they were to gamble," writes David Hackett Fischer. Dice, horses, cockfights, card games like "veint-un," and backgammon—even harvest results, women's sexiness, and upcoming weather—were all subjects of wagering. Colonel William Byrd, wrote the French visitor in Virginia, "is never happy but when he has the box and dice in his hands."[40] The rules of gambling were bound by a code of honor governing the making of bets and the paying of a loser's debts. The entertainment arising from the excitement of the play and the camaraderie it stimulated was increased for the winning party. He was the momentary hero. To lose, though, was not necessarily a disgrace but a brief loss of stature.

Gambling was not in itself shameless, and it was the male prerogative of all classes of the social order. Virginians were particularly addicted to horse-racing, as were people from Charleston. In fact, many a duel was fought on the racing grounds because of a dispute over the winner and possible cheating. Bertram Hoole, my Charleston ancestor, was challenged to a duel by a member of the powerful Ravenel clan over a bet on a horserace Hoole had won. Ravenel, rather than paying the $1,000 debt, proposed that he have Hoole's portrait painted by a traveling artist instead, a huge savings to Ravenel. If Hoole were to refuse, Ravenel threatened to challenge Hoole to a duel on the grounds that he had somehow won by underhanded means. Like Shakespeare's Falstaff, Hoole chose the better part of valor and accepted the portrait.

Those who arranged the racecourse bets and manned the card tables, faro boxes, and dice games, however, were "gentlemen of leisure" only when it suited the players. Members of the gentry class never brought home card-sharks to meet their wives and families. Evangelical clergymen, known as "fighting parsons," were hotly opposed to gambling and willing to fight for their beliefs. Their influence was growing at the time but not enough to change the mores of dedicated sportsmen.[41]

Robert Bailey, a professional gambler, was an early nineteenth-century Virginian. In his memoir, he noted that his favorite "sportsman," as he dubbed the type of partner he liked, was "a high-minded liberal gentleman, attached to amusements regardless of loss or gain; his motto is honor, his shield is judgment." But he admitted that his profession was based on desperation for money and that professionals like himself were "destitute of all honor and honesty." As with many others of his profession, Bailey claimed to have been the childhood victim of a vicious and mean-spirited stepfather who set him on the wrong path.[42]

In the 1830s, there was a swelling of opposition to gambling. In Vicksburg, Mississippi, in 1835, an infuriated mob routed and killed a number of professionals. The mob claimed that the gamblers were secret abolitionists as well as cheaters at cards and faro-box management. Soon the Southern states began to pass antigambling statutes. Legislation began to appear that prohibited gambling in North Carolina, South Carolina, and Georgia. They were, however, modified to make exceptions for "respectable gentlemen," who would be immune from arrest. Tennessee, Mississippi, Louisiana, Florida, and Kentucky did likewise, though all these states refused to invade private homes and only denied gambling in public places like steamboats and taverns.[43]

One center for gambling was Natchez, Mississippi. The local authorities attributed 30 percent of all crimes to professional manipulators of cards and games. And those caught cheating, if not punished through regular channels, might have ended up covered with tar and feathers. So it was for James Foster Jr. of Natchez in 1834. A wealthy planter's son, he had earlier fled from creditors and irate workmen in Louisiana when he manipulated his rigged faro box aboard the steamship *Calcasieux,* plying the waters of the lower Mississippi River. The cowboys and sailors had sued him for cheating them out of their wages after getting them drunk. He was arrested and jailed but allowed to go home a short time later. On return-ing to his family's plantation on St. Catherine's Creek, near Natchez, he beat his teenage wife, Susan, to death in a drunken rage and fled. Arrested in a neighboring county, he stood for trial. Judge Alexander Montgomery dismissed the case, however, because the jury had been improperly impan-eled. Both the prosecutor, Spence Monroe Grayson, and defense counsel, Felix Houston, permitted a mob to carry him off to a place specially used for frontier justice. There, Foster was treated to 150 lashes. After that painful baptism, he was covered in a coat of tar and feathers head to foot. The mob hauled him back to town in a cart, their humiliated victim facing backward. He survived the ordeal and fled to Texas but remained a bachelor until his death in the 1890s. He was punished not just for slaying his wife but also for his reputation as a shameless professional gambler.[44]

Shamelessness took other forms as well. An illustrative example comes from William Faulkner's novel *The Unvanquished,* as fiction can reveal a cul-ture more succinctly than some recitations of fact. John Sartoris—a former colonel in the rebel army eager to suppress the newly freed slaves and their hated Republican allies—had a poor white farmer killed for joining the Radical Republicans at a time when Mississippi whites sought to overthrow the hated Yankee-controlled, Carpetbag government. The victim's widow appears while Sartoris eats his supper in the dining room. Without a word, she throws down the twenty-five dollars that he had sent her in compensa-tion for the life of her murdered husband. Sartoris continues eating. He makes no gesture to indicate regret, remorse, or understanding. He did not consider any of his actions shameless: Rather, he felt he was using the only means available to preserve white honor against the black race.[45]

Not all aspects of the Southern version of honor were as unpleasant and uncivilized as those outlined here. Certainly military honor in the Old South, as always, had its own separate rules and merits within the culture that generally prevailed in that era. Self-discipline, deference to authority, faithfulness to duty, intense bonding of soldiers and officers in battle, and other necessary attributes were required. Honor has many faces, and those mentioned here are but some of them: the commendable, the puzzling, and the downright mean-spirited. The next chapter explores the role that honor played in the wars before the great midcentury conflict.

3

AMERICA'S ANTEBELLUM WARS, 1776–1848

RATIONALE AND CONDUCT

Afore I come away from hum I hed a strong persuasion
Thet Mexicans worn't human beans,—an ourang outang nation,
A sort o'folks a chap could kill an' never dream on't arter,
No more'n a feller'd dream o' pigs thet he hed hed to slarter;
I'd an idee thet they were built arter the darkie fashion all,
An' kickin' colored folks about you know, 's a kind o' national.
                                   —JAMES RUSSELL LOWELL, *The Biglow Papers*

The American Revolution, along with the wars that followed, from the Barbary conflicts through the Mexican War, exhibited the continued life of the honor code. This chapter is restricted to concerns about the pre–Civil War conflicts and the honor culture, motivations, and passions of those fighting. It does not dwell on the battles and their outcome, the purpose being to disclose how the ethic of honor figured into the minds of prowar politicians, officers, and oftentimes troopers. With regard to the origins of the Revolution, many excellent studies offer a clear picture of what the patriots thought. Yet, there is a curious irony in the study of the causes leading to that war, as historians have overlooked a major ingredient that animated the movement for independence. What actually gripped the angry revolutionary soul? The brilliant historian Gordon Wood and most other experts have noticed only casually the ubiquity of references to honor in the thousands of pamphlets, sermons, newspaper articles, and letters in which the patriots, as men sensitive about their honor and reputation, expressed their resentment of British insults and arrogance.[1] Wood's works recognize that the concentration of historical studies on the intellectual roots of the American cause have neglected the social character of the effort. Wood has observed, "The objective social reality scarcely seemed capable of explaining a revolution." My reflections argue, however, that the Age of Reason was also an Age of Honor.[2]

In dealing with the restive colonies, the British authorities undertook a disastrous policy that combined haughty condescension with military coercion, as if dealing with wayward, juvenile miscreants. Under orders from Admiral Samuel Graves in Boston, Captain Henry Mowat of the Royal Navy, in October 1775, warned the villagers of Falmouth, Maine, of his intention to raze their port. Mowat justified the bombardment as "the rod of correction." The people had too long defied "the legal prerogative of the best of Sovereigns."[3] American loyalists to the Crown adopted the same posture. In 1775, Thomas Chandler of New York warned patriots, "You must know, that singularity in right conduct will be an honour to you, and a shame only to them that act otherwise." In once more appealing "decently" and "humbly" to "King, Lords, and Commons of Great-Britain" following the bombardment, we must assure them, Chandler continued, "that we dread the very thoughts of an absolute independency; and that we see no prospect of security or happiness, but under the powerful protection and mild superintendency of the mother country."[4] Another Tory denounced the rebels as ungrateful children and worse—"detestable parracides."[5] Yet, such language only drove home to Whig patriots that the royalists at home and overseas haughtily denied Americans—whatever their place in society might be—the honor due them as morally responsible, respectable adults.

In response to such charges, American revolutionary pamphleteers seized the grammar, vocabulary, and style that bespoke the honor of their cause and the dreaded humiliation of submission. They did so with a regularity that suggests its salience in everyday colonial life. Since pride of male sexuality and the shame of its absence figured in the honor code, tract writers indulged in allusions that bordered on the scatological. Charlestonian John McKenzie raged that Britain had "insulted—bullied" and generally treated Americans as "emasculated eunuchs."[6] Likewise, Thomas Paine in *Common Sense* stressed the ideal of virility in defense of family: "Are your wife and children destitute . . . ? Have you lost a parent or a child by their hands. . . . If you have, and can still shake hands with the murderers, then you are unworthy of the name of husband, father, friend, or lover, and whatever may be your rank or title in life, you have the heart of a coward, and the spirit of a sycophant."[7] That the rhetoric wandered far from fact did not matter in this or any other polemical war.

Moving from secular depths to sublime heights, pious New Englanders, more than Southern patriots, tended to couple honor with lofty scriptural reference. They found the Old Testament especially appropriate. The ancient Hebrew nation, like the modern Middle East, was well versed in the dictates of honor.[8] The irascible John Allen, a Baptist minister of Boston,

in 1773 took Micah 7:3 for his text. He expounded on the right of a chosen
people to protest and even overthrow the tyranny of evil rulers. Allen thundered, "Have you not heard the voice of blood in your own streets, louder
than that which reached to Heaven, that cry'd for vengeance, that was, said
the Lord to Cain, the voice of thy brother's blood?"[9]

Peter Thacher of Malden, Massachusetts, became so overwrought that
he forgot to foreground the customary biblical text for explication. At once
he plunged into the heart of the matter. The preacher urged his flock to
"spring to action, let us gird on the sword of the Lord and of Gideon, and
determine to conquer or die! . . . Do not let us hear of any of you who behave like cowards." Only in the summation did he remember to insert the
requisite scriptural passage of 2 Samuel 10:12: "Be of good courage, and let
us play the men for our people." Dishonor entailed an unmanly spirit. Likewise, John Hancock noted in an oration on the fourth anniversary of the
Boston Massacre, Americans should reject "the soft arts of luxury and effeminacy" and sacrifice the pursuit of wealth to the cause of liberty. Those
who admire wealth alone, he warned, "almost deserve to be enslaved."[10]

Underlying these outbursts, of course, were just complaints. The list is
familiar: unfair taxes, official corruption, and unjust parliamentary reprisals against the restive colonies. As the anthropologist Julian Pitt-Rivers has
observed, honor is always the sworn enemy of taxation.[11] Coerced payment
involves a lessening of manhood and independence. From the dawn of history, defeated enemies and inferior people had to forfeit property as tribute
or tax. Free peoples, however, contributed to the king's treasury in terms of
subsidy, freely rendered out of affection and deference, real or feigned, for
the ruler. In earlier times, revenues for a head of state was more or less a
matter of gift exchange, as Marcel Mauss explained years ago. The expectation was that the payment of funds to the crown was a rendering for the
protection, justice, and mercy of the head of state.[12]

The outcry against British taxation without American representation
and voice in the process arose from this concept. It was based on the honor
of grant or subsidy versus the mortification of taxation. Ancient precedent
served to buttress the rationale. James Otis, for instance, pointed out that
in Periclean Greece, colonists were "obliged only to pay a kind of deference
and dutiful submission to the mother commonwealth." But, he insisted,
nothing more demeaning was required of them.[13]

As historians have long known, the parliamentary exactions on Americans to help reduce British indebtedness resulting from the Seven Years'

War were light by contemporary standards. But by the rubric of honor, cutting taxes is supposedly one of the highest acts of ethical conduct a ruler can perform. Colonists smarted under the affront of taxation with no means to bargain, modify, or persuade Parliament through colonial representation. In the Virginia Resolutions to Lord Frederick North in 1775, Thomas Jefferson argued that, "Whereas, we have right to give our money, as the Parliament does theirs, without coercion, from time to time, as public exigencies may require, we conceive that we alone are the judges. . . . *Because* at the very time of requiring from us grants of Money they are" planning war against us, "which is a stile of asking gifts not reconcileable to our freedom." Or, he might have added, "our honor." Likewise, the Continental Congress's resolution of 31 July 1775 spoke of taxes as "gifts" not to be "wasted among the venal and corrupt for the purpose of undermining the civil rights of the givers." The resolution further demonstrated the significance of the ancient prescriptions: "We consider ourselves as bound in Honor as well as Interest to share one general Fate with our Sister Colonies" and having in vain "appealed to the native honour and justice of the British nation," a new course of action is necessary.[14]

The category of involuntary taxpayer entailed reduced social and political status. Such exactions lessened a person's or family's independence— that is, freedom from the control of or obligation to another. Niccolò Machiavelli had long before warned that unwise rulers overtaxed their subjects at great peril, "for men forget more easily the death of their father than the loss of their patrimony."[15] In fact, by custom, those who gained the most glory and authority from either military victories or office-holding were expected to pay for such honorifics. They should not burden marginal folk. Taxing Americans, however, had become popular in the home country, argued one pamphleteer, because the British had drained themselves while Ireland had been "impoverished to almost the last farthing."[16] Even Ireland, which, in James Otis's opinion, had fallen into English hands as "a *conquered* country," deserved "the same right to be free, under a conqueror, as the rest of his [majesty's] subjects." How much more worthy then, Otis asked, should America be when at no time was it a defeated province, but one created by "*emigrant* subjects?"[17]

The second colonial grievance, bureaucratic malfeasance and venality, stimulated almost equal fury. Such vices violated the honor code in two specific ways. First, nepotism and favoritism in office-seeking put Americans, given their physical distance and longer times away from the center of power in London, at more of a disadvantage when competing for titles and posts that bore the marks of honor against placemen with contacts at Whitehall unavailable to the distant colonists. Second, corruption reinforced the sense of impotence that men of honor felt in the handling of political affairs. Their anger stemmed from the implied dependence and subordination that the indignity of open corruption flaunted in their faces. The imposition of the Stamp Tax, of course, was seen as a further opportunity for gross corruption.[18]

In thunderous response to the crisis, the Reverend Enoch Huntington of Massachusetts preached, "Already do the avaricious courtiers of *Great-Britain*, with the numerous train of their . . . hangers-on, with the whole tribe of dissolute spendthrifts, and idle deboshee's, feast themselves" upon "the spoils of our future earnings." John Adams echoed the sentiment: "When luxury, effeminacy, and venality" have reached "a shocking pitch in England; when both electors and elected are become one mass of corruption; when the nation is oppressed to death with debts and taxes . . . what would be your condition under such an absolute subjection to parliament? You would not only be slaves, but the most abject sort of slaves, to the worst sort of masters!"[19]

The third objection intimately connected with honor was the outcry against standing armies during the prerevolutionary period. Not only were these soldiers potential instruments of tyranny, but their presence also signified mistrust of the local elite and general populace. The use of professional forces created a conflict in which military inquisitors interfered in what members of a given locale believed were their exclusive affairs. Such an opposition to standing armies has been traced to the philosopher John Trenchard and earlier to James Harrington.[20] Public suspicion of occupying armies long predated the prerevolutionary years. Clearly, such armies violated a sense of local independence, the honor of the community. To the American colonists, the imposition of permanent forces, especially when quartered in civilian billets instead of barracks, signified humiliation and naked despotism.[21]

The famous words of Patrick Henry in the Virginia House of Delegates on 23 March 1775 were based on the revolutionary Virginian's sense of honor: "It is in vain, sir, to extenuate the matter. Gentlemen may cry peace, peace, but there is no peace. The war is actually begun. The next gale that sweeps from the north will bring to our ears the clash of resounding arms. Our brethren are already in the field. Why stand we here idle?"[22]

In the actual war itself, honor was a major component of the motivations of the officer class. For example, a Maryland regiment under the command of Colonel William Smallwood consisted largely of wealthy gentlemen planters, attorneys, and merchants, all high-toned. Likewise, soldiers under the name of the Baltimore Cadets wore startlingly bright uniforms, each resplendent with cutlass, powder, several pounds of lead, and a brace of pistols. They were not derelict about discipline and soon proved themselves highly courageous as one of the most effective regiments in the Continental Army in 1776. One of the captains boasted that the unit was "composed of gentlemen of honour, family and fortune, and tho' from different countries animated by a zeal and reverence for the rights of humanity." As Caroline Cox points out, the military community, such as this one, was "a complex and sometimes contradictory world."[23] It was a reflection of the larger community yet separate from it. Both arenas were ones where ambition for renown was intense.

A pursuit of glory particularly inspired the officer corps. Eager for promotion, for instance, General Robert Howe wrote a friend how he yearned to head an army in South Carolina: "I have been long on the Brigadiers list and pant to get higher."[24] Denied a chance to command a regiment but offered instead a staff position, Nathanael Greene ruefully moaned, "I am taken out of the Line of splendor."[25] An unhappy colonel who was passed over when another officer took a senior posting complained to George Washington: "It is impossible for a soldier, who is tenacious of his honor (the only jewel worth contending for) to suffer himself to be degraded by being superseded."[26] Similar disappointments threatened the honor of civilian office-seekers when defeated for election.

✠ ✠ ✠

After the Revolution, the new nation entered a period of great uncertainty in foreign affairs. The country lacked a sufficient tax base. It had an undersized army and a nearly nonexistent navy. Enemies, though, were not in short supply. The Napoleonic Wars affected American commerce severely, and relations with both France and Great Britain were tense. During President John Adams's administration, a conflict called the Quasi-War with France occurred. This episode demonstrated that honor denied despite peace restored could have a political downside. But that is not the way it looked at the start of the crisis.

In the late 1790s, President Adams and others were ready and eager for war with France. Adams and other Federalists feared the French revolutionaries, the Jacobins, with a passion only equaled in the 1950s by the fear of world-wide communism. The XYZ Affair, named for the French officials involved in the strained relations with the special commissioners whom Adams had sent to negotiate a settlement, was an insult to American national honor. The event nearly resulted in outright war. The riotous behavior of Republicans in opposition and the belligerent godlessness of the French regime all conspired to arouse panic and fierce outrage in Federalist circles. Adams roundly denounced what he called "this terrorism" abroad in the land.[27]

The aging Cincinnatus at Mount Vernon, George Washington, was called on to leave the plow, as it were, in order to head the land forces. Civil liberties fell by the wayside with the passage of the infamous Alien and Sedition Acts, a common American reaction to war scares as later patterns would prove, even up to the present day. High Federalists were sure that a declaration of war would silence and defeat the Jeffersonians as unpatriotic and cowardly. The slogan of the day was the cry: "Millions for defense, but not one cent for tribute!" It represented a demand for nationwide unity and the upholding of the country's self-esteem.[28]

Republican politicians, particularly ones from the South, were also convinced that war was the answer. The Federalist Robert Goodloe Harper of South Carolina argued that war was "the most manly and honourable course." Others, however, argued that building a home defense would suffice for the moment.[29] Congress dithered without acting. Meanwhile, France sent out strong peace feelers. This was all to the good, Federalist Alexander Hamilton wrote sarcastically, as negotiations with the perfidious French would soon and inevitably bring that nation's "friends into power."[30]

And so it did. Given Adams's close loss in the electoral votes in 1800 (Jefferson and Aaron Burr each received 73, Adams 65, and Charles Cotesworth Pinckney 64), a declaration of war could have led to his reelection. That decision would have overshadowed the blunder of Adams's signing the hated Alien and Sedition Acts, and the rift between Hamilton and Adams, the principal leaders of the Federalist Party. Instead, the Republicans won in 1800 and gradually drove the Federalists into oblivion. Adams had missed a grand opportunity to perpetuate Federalist rule for at least another four years, but his Yankee caution and common sense about the perils of warfare had prevailed. With the right wing of his party thoroughly disgusted and his party divided, Adams gained too little credit for leaving the "State with its coffers full," as he wrote shortly after defeat, "and the fair prospect of a peace with all the world in its face."[31]

Of course, other factors were involved as well. Yet a hue and cry for war usually unites a nation behind a leader in the short term by placing national security and national pride at the forefront. In 1979, Jimmy Carter also turned away from the rubric of honorable revenge for insult in the Iranian hostage crisis. A war to free the embassy hostages could well have furnished him a second term—whether it violated his moral principles or not. He was possibly one of the few Southern-born chief executives not to choose warfare. As a result, he sealed his fate as a one-term president. Americans, then as now, proclaimed their devotion to peace, but they worried that any sign of weakness in the head of state would lead to a sense of vulnerability in the eyes of other nations.

✧ ✧ ✧

The United States, however, was new to the world scene and uncertain of its strength. Adams's successor, Thomas Jefferson, knew that a well-timed war offered great political benefits. When Jefferson could locate a war that offered little expense and lots of glory, he moved as swiftly as a wildcat. That was the case in the honor-driven war against North African piracy. According to biographer Nathan Schachner, Jefferson was "hot for vengeance against the Barbary States."[32] Unlike the upcoming war with the British Royal Navy, this one would be cheap and most likely victorious.

Behind the First Barbary War was a history of American acquiescence to acts of piracy in the Mediterranean. In the closing years of the Washington administration, the United States was forced to pay nearly a million dollars in cash, along with other valuable commodities, to rescue over a hundred sailors from the Algerian dey, the ruler of Tripoli and Algeria. With an empty treasury and virtually nonexistent forces, the young United States was following European precedent. The United States was dependent on foreign trade and could ill afford its disruption. The impotence of the undermanned American navy was also a sign of dishonorable defenselessness. Britain and France were too preoccupied with their own rivalries and too powerful to let pirates determine policy. So, payoffs were the most convenient resource and least costly method to handle the serious vexation caused by the Barbary pirates. The pirates, who called themselves *mujahideen,* believed they were defending Allah and demonstrating their determination to resist further encroachments by European powers. The same would be true in recent times off the coast of Somalia until the action of a naval coalition finally patrolled the East African waters.[33]

In the late eighteenth and early nineteenth centuries, sailors and passengers—including in earlier times Miguel de Cervantes, author of *Don Quixote*—captured by the Barbary pirates were enslaved to work as galley oarsmen, miners, or in other back-breaking occupations. In the 1780s, after France had left America to its own weak and friendless devices, and the British were, of course, indifferent, some forty or so American sailors on merchantman ships were made slaves, stripped of their possessions, and totally humiliated in dank and dark dungeons with little clothing and minimal food. Those who tried to rebel were threatened with beheading or impalement on spikes.[34]

Jefferson, as U.S. minister to Versailles, tried to organize a coalition of European countries to patrol the North African coast, but even with the Marquis de Lafayette's lobbying for the idea, the plan went nowhere. In addition, the Confederation Congress failed to appropriate two million dollars for developing a navy. Even Jefferson at that time had worried about the expense of arming a navy and feared it would increase the power of the central government. When the states debated the formation of a new constitution with a stronger central government, state legislators spoke feelingly about the loss of honor when sailors were brutally mistreated. The ratification of the U.S. Constitution in 1787 owed something to the piracy issue.

Matters changed in the following decade. When war seemed imminent with France in 1798, President Adams, who had reestablished the U.S. Navy as a fighting force, oddly did not make use of it against the tribute-demanding North African pashas. Instead, Jefferson, Adams's successor, decided that national honor demanded a response to the hijacking of vessels and enslavement of American sailors. Americans, who had no quarrel with enslaving Africans, were horrified that fellow white citizens could be made into abject slaves. Fisher Ames, an ultra-conservative Massachusetts congressman, even worried that the Islamists might appear off the coast of this continent. While the navy was successful in its first encounter in 1801, the Jefferson administration still paid out sixty thousand dollars, basically as protection money, for American prisoners. The sum was called a ransom payment, not a tribute to the dey of Tripoli.

In a recent journalistic account of the Barbary Wars, Joseph Wheelan subtitled his work "America's First War on Terror 1801–1805." He points out that within days of Jefferson's inauguration, the new president had ordered four ships of the line to the North African coast without seeking a war resolution from Congress or giving any prior notification to European powers, in order to conduct what Wheelan dubs "Jefferson's War." As early as 1785, Jefferson had advised James Monroe, "The motives pleading for war rather than tribute are numerous and honorable, those opposing them mean and short-sighted."[35]

Clearly, a sense of national honor had prompted Jefferson to ignore his own commitment to a limited federal government. Even former president John Adams, who had paid off, albeit reluctantly, the Barbary States, admitted that a war would be "heroical and glorious" at a time when maritime Europe "has made cowards of all their sailors before the standard of Mahomet." Indeed, he wrote, "The resolution to fight them would raise the spirits and courage of our countrymen immediately, and we might obtain the glory of finally breaking up these nests of banditti. But Congress will never, or at least not for years, take any such resolution, and in the meantime our trade and honor suffer beyond calculation. We ought not to fight them at all, unless we determine to fight them forever." But Adams was inconsistent. The Marquis de Lafayette reported that Adams preferred peace and payment, whereas Jefferson, Lafayette wrote, "finds it as cheap and more honourable to cruize against" the pirates. Before he died in 1799, George Washington had remarked "that chastisement would be more honourable, and much to be preferred to the purchased friendship of these Barbarians," who were simply heaping up "the highest disgrace" on their own heads.[36]

As secretary of state in Washington's cabinet, Jefferson had earlier despaired of any easy settlement. After all, he wrote, "we have the example of rich and powerful nations, in this instance counting their interest more than their honor." A young, untried nation was hampered by financial weaknesses. What could be done? Yet, when elected president, Jefferson reaped the rewards of undertaking a war against a decrepit enemy without much loss of lives or treasure.[37] The fight against bribery and extortion certainly helped Jefferson's overwhelming 1804 presidential election victory.

In terms of honor, the Barbary Wars provided Americans with reason to take pride in the country's maritime victories and to celebrate its first naval hero since John Paul Jones in the Revolution, Stephen Decatur Jr. Even before the Barbary pirates harmed American commerce in the Mediterranean, Americans thought of the "Musselmen" as the "ultimate other," writes Michael B. Oren. They were "primitive, sordid, and cruel." Throughout the 1780s, the Algerians had seized American vessels; in one case, they enslaved twenty-one sailors. It was not until the 1800s that the U.S. Navy's strength had increased sufficiently to deal with the problems.[38] By then, heroes did emerge to lead the way. Decatur, from Worcester County, Maryland, was born to be a sailor like his father, Commodore Stephen Decatur. The commodore's son became the youngest captain in U.S. naval history. One of his friends declared him to be "chivalrous in his temper, courteous and amiable in his deportment, and adding grace of manner to rare attractions of feature and person." At the time a lieutenant, Decatur's role in the first Barbary encounter resulted in the brief recapture and burning of the disabled USS *Philadelphia*. This ship had previously been seized by Tripolitan corsairs in 1803, and its captain and crew enslaved. Along with other sailors from the USS *Intrepid* dressed in Arab garb to hide their intentions, Lieutenant Decatur boarded the grounded ship, which could not be refloated. The invading crew set afire the equipment and masts to render the *Philadelphia*'s cannons and stock inoperable.[39]

Decatur became an immediate national hero. The exploit earned him a high compliment from Horatio Nelson of the Royal Navy, who declared that it had been "the most bold and daring act of the age." President Jefferson had Decatur's rank elevated to captain. Decatur's later bold acts only added to his record as a major naval advocate and hero. In 1820, at the height of his career, he was killed in a duel with the former captain of the *Chesapeake*, James Barron.[40]

✛ ✛ ✛

The events surrounding the *Chesapeake* debacle, which ultimately led to Decatur's death, were a major contributing factor to the War of 1812. In this second conflict with Great Britain, honor was once again uppermost among the rationales for war: the insult inflicted by British Orders in Council and the impressment of American soldiers from both commercial and naval vessels, with the *Chesapeake* incident being the most demeaning. In 1807, HMS *Leopard* fired on the *Chesapeake*, forcing Barron to strike his colors and surrender three supposed deserters from the Royal Navy. The attack was seen by many Americans as a gross violation of national honor, requiring war.[41] In his 1878 account of the war, John Clark Ridpath concluded that, prior to the outbreak, the "insolence" of the royal Orders in Council would eventually have to mean "retaliation and war" or else a continuation of "humiliation and disgrace."[42] Ridpath's interpretation did not last, however. An economic and material approach followed in the interwar period. In 1961, Norman Risjord reopened the subject and offered another, more plausible explanation.[43]

Previous historians proposed economic motives—a western desire for land—as the chief rationale for war. Risjord notes, though, that only ten congressmen from the West sat in the House of Representatives. The thirty-nine Southern delegates were chiefly responsible for hostilities in the second war with England. The famous War Hawks—John C. Calhoun, Henry Clay, Felix Grundy, and others—were not concerned with territorial expansion as much as with the defense of national honor against seeming British arrogance. Jeffersonians fretted about the costs of warfare because it meant great outlays, higher taxes, and central government expansion at the cost of rural values. But when honor was at risk, Jeffersonians believed these problems had to become secondary. According to Risjord, with different economic and territorial aims influencing different parts of the Union, "the only unifying factor, present in all sections of the country, was the growing feeling of patriotism, the realization that something must be done to vindicate the national honor." Not to take up arms, warned Henry Clay of Kentucky, would stain the country "with shame and indelible disgrace."[44]

Shaking off his Republican doubts on taxes and expanded government only reluctantly, John Smilie of Pennsylvania echoed Clay's sentiments: "If we now recede we shall be a reproach to all nations." Risjord concludes his assessment with the idea that the Republican party, particularly its Southern members, had slowly reached the judgment that "war was the only alternative to national humiliation and disgrace."[45]

Federalists were outraged and, later, impatient for peace. Their radical wing, meeting at Hartford in 1814–15, even talked of secession, using a states' rights argument that is usually identified with Southern defiance of federal authority. Dismayed at the cost of the war, some New England states refused to surrender their militia to national service. Samuel Eliot Morison, the great naval historian, called the second fight with England "undoubtedly the most unpopular war that this country has ever waged." (He wrote before Vietnam.) A New Englander himself, Morison argued that the Hartford Convention leaders never meant secession to be their policy, but that is a matter of dispute. In the slave states where the war was popular, Federalists were hounded unmercifully long before the convention occurred. Baltimore Republicans rioted against a Federalist journalist on 20 June 1812 and shouted such curses as "We'll feather and tar every

damned British Tory. And this is the way for American glory." Robert E.
Lee's father, "Light-Horse Harry" Lee, one of their targets, was humiliated
and permanently injured in that riot. Caught in a second anti-Federalist
riot that followed a few days later, he was fingered as a hated partisan
despite his heroic cavalry effort in the Revolution. The Republican rioters
were eager to seize all Federalists—journalists and men of wealth—and
remove the alleged betrayers of the Republic. Hundreds of them roughed
up Lee and others. One rioter even slashed and stabbed Harry Lee's face
with a pen knife, wounding him severely. He was then dumped on a pile
of corpses and left to die. Even after a lengthy recovery, he was never the
same in mind or body.[46]

The war itself memorably produced one major hero—Andrew Jackson.
Without his victory at New Orleans, the nation might have had to accept
the humiliation of having its capital burned, its top leaders fleeing in haste,
and the loss of the Battle of Bladensburg. Much has been written about the
founder of the Democratic Party, the duelist, and the general, so little of his
tempestuous life need be reported here. It was his victory in the defense
of New Orleans that won him the acclaim that he expected and deserved.

The final example of honor's influence in American warfare prior to the
Civil War is the Mexican struggle of the 1840s. This conflict was the first
large-scale foreign war fought by the United States. The impetus for action
came largely from Southern politicians who were eager to expand the reach
of slavery and cotton. Their demands increased the pressure for Mexican
territory on the Polk administration after the president appeased Northern
Democrats by acquiring the Oregon Territory from British Canada. Like the
wars in Vietnam and Iraq, this war was not a response to outside forces but
a preemptive strike, couched in terms of national honor.

There were, in this case, some grounds for that position, as Mexico had
refused to recognize the Republic of Texas. The Texas struggle for independence produced, of course, the famous Battle of the Alamo in March 1836.
The commander of the besieged Texan revolutionaries, Lt. Col. William
Barret Travis, issued a proclamation. He announced, "I am besieged, by
a thousand or more of the Mexicans under Santa Anna." Nonetheless, "*I
shall never surrender or retreat. Then,* I call on you in the name of Liberty, of
patriotism, & everything dear to the American character, to come to our
aid. . . . If this call is neglected, I am determined to sustain myself as long as

possible & die like a soldier who never forgets what is due to his own honor & that of his country—VICTORY OR DEATH." The tiny garrison was overrun and the defenders mercilessly killed. Their bodies, soaked in oil, were placed outside the mission walls, "stacked like firewood," and burned. That atrocity and the massacre of three hundred surrendered Texas prisoners at Goliad not long after the Alamo alarmed the American public. The brutal incidents also fed into a virulent hatred of Spanish-speaking Catholics. In fact, according to one historian, the military policy in the conduct of the war suggests an unofficial discrimination against Catholics. Still, it was "Manifest Destiny," the enlargement of the American Union, that prompted war fever. Honor figured but less so than in the War of 1812.[47]

Sam Houston successfully avenged the massacre at the Alamo and Goliad and helped to establish the Republic of Texas. Its annexation to the United States on 29 December 1845 resulted in a complete break in diplomatic relations with Mexico. Thwarted by the Mexican government's adamant refusal to bargain, on 13 January 1846 President James Polk ordered Gen. Zachary Taylor's army at Corpus Christi to march to the Rio Grande. To Mexico this was a *casus belli*. A cavalry troop crossed the river at Matamoros and surprised an U.S. squadron. The incident moved Polk to send a war message to Congress on 13 May. In the course of the address, Polk announced that "after repeated menaces, Mexico has passed the boundary of the United States, has invaded our territory, and shed American blood upon the American soil." The nation was compelled "to vindicate its honor and rights." Almost at once, the House authorized the president to muster an army of fifty thousand men to pursue that aim.[48]

There was significant Northern resistance to the war after Polk delivered his war message in April 1846. Congressman Joshua Giddings of Ohio lambasted the Southern clamor for "an aggressive, unholy, and unjust war." In voting against funds to carry out the military mission, he declared, "I will not bathe my hands in the blood of the people of Mexico." The purpose of war, he argued, was to "purchase perpetual slavery" and advance "an institution on which the curse of the Almighty visibly rests."[49]

Initially the war had great popularity with the public, who were outraged by Mexican atrocities and intransigence. Urged by the president to form a volunteer army, 100,000 or more enlisted, overwhelming the tiny number of regular army personnel. The recruits soon discovered disappointment, however. They were largely poor, young, unskilled laborers with minimal prospects and no military experience. The regular army personnel maltreated them. As one historian puts it, the duties they had to perform, mostly building fortifications and the like, was "not the sort of work that brought honor to the individual nor bound him to the community." Meanwhile, the glory of warfare belonged to the professionals. Yet, even they were subject to harsh conditions. The regulars endured mind-numbing routines and found themselves housed in prison-like barracks. Not surprisingly, alcohol was a constant solace—with the attendant release of barroom brawls. Official whippings were frequent and kept both regulars and recruits in line. The inefficiency and inadequacy of the food rations, medical attention, and shelter were among the everyday discomforts. Desertion rates were high despite the threats of imprisonment or worse for those caught AWOL. During the fighting, tensions ran high between the various ranks of volunteers and regulars.[50]

Discipline in the military and the freedom cherished by civilians inevitably clashed. The lower-class volunteers entertained notions of ordinary advance through hard work, a little luck, and a carefree, youthful style. But later, as the historian Paul Foos notes, prospects of "conquest, military honor, loot, and land" took the place of notions of advance through hard work.[51] Few diaries and newspaper accounts discussed the possibility of land grabs or looting. Instead, they brought up the loftier sentiments of the concept of honor and the benefits of liberty.

Southern exhilaration over the acquisition of so much western territory in Mexico was overwhelming. Those who objected to the land grab, like Congressman Abraham Lincoln of Illinois, were branded as traitors in the happy fever of war and conquest. Lincoln introduced a resolution on 22 December 1847 requesting that Polk give a precise rendering of what parts of Mexico U.S. troops had occupied. Like other antislavery Whigs, Lincoln doubted that honor had been at stake, believing instead the war was an attempt to propagate slavery into new territory. Lincoln had barely taken his seat as a newly elected congressman when he had the temerity to offer this resolution. Democrats were indignant, and even fellow Whigs only half-heartedly agreed with the freshman representative.[52]

As the North became more worried about the disproportionate power of the slave states, the notion of a great slave power seeking to dominate the country became the conspiratorial view of many, not just Lincoln. On the other hand, the South, facing an ever-growing Northern population, feared a diminishing of their influence in Washington. Unless more land was opened to white migration and slavery, the South would have far less control over federal policies. Northerners were skeptical, but party loyalties of Whigs and Democrats, both in the North and South, kept this regionalism from breaking the country apart for the time being.

Prior to Lincoln's resolution, Congressman David Wilmot in 1846 gave his name to a proviso prohibiting slavery from any newly acquired lands — including California, the great prize. The amendment failed to pass, but it indicated that compromise on slavery was increasingly problematic. Lincoln declared that he voted for the Wilmot Proviso forty times during his brief term in the House.[53]

In the meantime, back east, young Henry David Thoreau of Concord, Massachusetts, was taking his stand against the war in a new, nonviolent way. On 23 July 1846, the authorities arrested him for not paying a local tax. Thoreau responded that his act of defiance was a protest of the Mexican conflict. A kinsman paid the tax after Thoreau had spent a night in jail, much to Thoreau's chagrin. Inspired by his decision, he wrote his famous essay "Civil Disobedience," which Leo Tolstoy, Mahatma Gandhi, and Martin Luther King Jr. greatly admired. He urged others to follow his example and believed that the power of the people would lead to a cessation of hostilities. "Any man more right than his neighbor," Thoreau advised, "constitutes a majority of one."[54]

Yet, despite the divisiveness of the war, romantic notions of death and glory flourished as never before. At the same time, demonizing the enemy was a common reaction of soldiers facing the possibility of death or serious injury. James Russell Lowell's satire, found in the epigraph of this chapter, gives some idea of what the foot soldier felt.[55] Humiliation was bound to accompany the fighting, particularly because events at the Alamo and other Mexican brutalities had conjured up desires for full-scale vengeance. Both the regular army and volunteers engaged in plunder and the humiliation of Mexican civilians. According to one historian, "The propaganda surrounding the war effort was nakedly opportunistic and expressly promised plunder as the right of the volunteer." Hopes of riches were soon dashed. By and large, the Mexicans were poor and had little to be seized. That only made the soldiers more bitter. Racism, anti-Catholicism, and contempt for the Spanish language all also encouraged disrespect for the enemy. "Manifest Destiny," it would seem, was a watchword for conquest for the sake of conquest.[56] Astonishingly, this war was the bloodiest Americans had yet fought given the numbers participating. The death rate was 13,283 from a total of just over 78,000 enlisted.[57]

Theodore O'Hara, a Catholic volunteer from Kentucky, penned once famous verses that later graced the archway entries to Union Army cemeteries from Gettysburg to Shiloh. As a brevet major, he had fought in the bloody engagement at Buena Vista on 22–23 February 1847. There, 4,759 soldiers serving under Zachary Taylor drove back some 18,000 Mexicans, whose chief was Antonio Lopez de Santa Anna, the butcher at the Alamo and Goliad. The Americans lost 267 men, and 456 were injured. It was the highest casualty rate of any battle in the war. O'Hara penned these lines:

On Fame's eternal camping ground
Their silent tents are spread,
And Glory guards, with solemn round,
The bivouac of the dead.
Rest on, embalmed and sainted dead,
Dear as the blood ye gave,
No impious footstep here shall tread
The herbiage of your grave;
Nor shall your glory be forgot
While Fame her record keeps,
Or Honor points the hallowed spot
Where Valor proudly sleeps.[58]

The Mexican conflict enhanced American self-esteem. It also offered a number of the Civil War generals and leaders—Robert E. Lee, Thomas "Stonewall" Jackson, Joseph Johnston, Pierre Beauregard, Jefferson Davis, Braxton Bragg, and John Pemberton for the South, and Ulysses S. Grant, George McClellan, Joseph Hooker, and George Meade for the Union—experience in the field. The tensions created over the expansion of slavery was a negative consequence. The looming threat of Southern secession posed another difficulty. It undercut the elation of military victory and territorial gain. The war was also an attempt at proclaimed nation-building—the absorption of a Catholic Mexican population, sparse though it was, into the beneficence of democracy, white freedom, and a Protestant hegemony.

If Polk had had his way, all of Mexico would have been folded into the arms of Dame Liberty. The war, however, lasted too long, as wars tend to do. Toward the end, public support started to wane. As a result, the Democratic Party, which had initiated and led the war, went out of power at the next election. The war's bold hero, "Rough and Ready" Zachary Taylor, a Whig planter from Louisiana, took office. At the same time, the war created tensions among Northern and Southern Whigs that were never to be resolved, and the party collapsed in the mid-1850s.

In the Mexican conflict, honor wore its most arrogant attire, a territorial victory over a poorly led, demoralized, humiliated, and divided neighbor. Yet that conquest precipitated the greatest crisis in U.S. national history. Indeed, military honor, as often it does, came at a high price. Promises of civilian support and firm but fair leadership proved elusive. Moreover, honor, in the nineteenth century most especially, seemed to be a commodity that only officers were well positioned to gain. Lesser men could share their commanders' esteem but benefited less individually than as members of a well-disciplined, motivated unit. The major test of honor came with the secession crisis and the tragedy of the Civil War.

4

HONOR, HUMILIATION, AND THE AMERICAN CIVIL WAR

War is cruelty, and you cannot refine it.
—GENERAL WILLIAM T. SHERMAN

The mid-nineteenth-century transition from the pinnacle of Southern honor, both in terms of its practice and its being embraced in the South, to abject mortification occurred remarkably swiftly over the course of less than a decade. The Southern secessionists, infuriated by the 1860 triumph of the antislavery Republican Party, never dreamed of such a reversal of fortune. In the antebellum years from 1800 to 1861, Southern whites gloried in upholding an ethic that sanctioned slavery, cultivated hierarchy, and exalted the martial virtues or "chivalry," as they liked to say. In fact, with the onset of the sectional war in 1861, honor, both Southern and Northern, began to play a greater role than in any other American resort to arms. As a result, the later fall from that apex of the practice of valor and manly reputation was all the more dismaying and frustrating for the losing side.

The topic of the Civil War is massively broad and has already been treated in thousands of books and articles. The purpose here is to sketch the major features of honor and humiliation as they were instrumental in the unfolding of historical events. First, of course, must be a study of the developing crisis. Then, the chapter treats some examples of honor on the battlefield and in the generalships of Robert E. Lee, Ulysses S. Grant, and William Tecumseh Sherman. Next, we consider dying "the Good Death," as Drew Gilpin Faust describes it in *This Republic of Suffering*, focusing on the ways people reverently proclaimed honor and glory over the fallen.[1] Finally, a review of atrocities and acts of unauthorized brutality follows, with special attention to black Union troops.

During the mid-nineteenth century, Southern disunionists insisted on the righteous necessity of an honorable vindication of slavery. It was an institution basic to the Southern social and racial order. Yet, it required, many thought, stout defense against a growing international movement opposing enslavement. In the inflammatory reaction to this opposition, honor was the ethical force behind that desperate defense of slavery. White Southerners felt honor-bound to repulse the Northerners' allegedly baseless antislavery assaults on Southerners' pride, power, and way of organizing their society. Anyone who dared to question the legitimacy of slavery earned immediate punishment in the slave states. The antislavery critic was subject to mob action, whippings, and even coatings of tar and feathers, all designed to humiliate the victim and warn others to fear a similar fate. In 1835, New York abolitionists' postal campaign, which sent tracts through the mail to leading Southern judges, clergymen, and local squires, set off an outbreak of violence. For passing out some abolitionist literature in 1834, the Reverend Amos Dresser of Oberlin College was whipped, tarred, and feathered in Nashville, Tennessee. Another victim, Aaron Kitchell, was accorded the same stinking covering in Hillsborough, Georgia, in 1836. In his newspaper, *The Liberator*, William Lloyd Garrison estimated that over three hundred white people were murdered because of their suspected or actual distribution of hated Yankee literature.[2]

Clearly, proslavery Southern whites acted out of fear of black emancipation and deep-seated loathing of blacks. Given freedom, Southerners assumed, African Americans would revert to a primitive, vicious state of nature. The African heritage, gossiped William Elliott of South Carolina, included the vile practice of cannibalism. Besides, some Southerners reasoned, if given liberty, blacks would quickly become extinct. They needed the guiding, benevolent hand of the superior race simply to survive. Apparently it did not occur to such thinkers that in Africa, blacks were hardly as lethargic, backward, and barbarous as whites liked to imagine. Southerners ridiculed the idea that African captives had left behind a rich cultural heritage. In the postwar period, the well-respected Richmond journalist E. A. Pollard grandly announced, "We, above all, . . . were guarding the helpless black race from utter annihilation at the hands of a bloody and greedy 'philanthropy.'"[3]

The North was scarcely of one mind about matters of race or even slavery. Throughout the postrevolutionary era, until westward expansion caused friction between white men of the North and Southern planters, Yankees were divided on these matters. Even some abolitionists were uncertain if members of the black race were up to the task of full public responsibilities. William H. Seward, a prominent Republican leader in the 1850s, sought black voting rights but also entertained the idea that people of color were exotic and incapable of "assimilation and absorption." It took years and wartime needs to bring Abraham Lincoln to a full understanding of black hopes for freedom and equality. Black leaders of the North, some of whom had escaped their Southern bonds, spoke eloquently for their compatriots before audiences in America and also England. Frederick Douglass was the most prominent of these.[4]

Despite these Northern divisions, slavery grew to be the central issue over which the sections contended. When the South Carolina secession convention met in November 1860, Fire-Eater (Southern disunionist) congressman Lawrence Keitt insisted that the rationale given for dismembering the Union should single out the issue of slavery's political, economic, and ethical viability. That was, he said, "the great central point from which we are now proceeding." Likewise, in 1861, Confederate vice president Alexander H. Stephens hailed slaveholding as the "corner-stone" of Southern wealth, security, and well-being. At the disastrous Democratic national convention in the spring of 1860 in Charleston, Stephen Douglas, the presidential nominee, had to watch helplessly as South Carolinians and others marched out in fury. Before they left, they had heard William Preston, a well-known orator, pronounce, "Slavery is our King, slavery is our Truth, slavery is our Divine Right." Such monarchical sentiments seemed a repudiation of the American dream as well as a bizarrely antique line of vindication.[5]

By the war's end, however, Southerners were denying this earlier *casus belli* and no longer unabashedly defending the four billion dollars' worth of human property that they had earlier deemed in jeopardy. The planters adopted a more ethically palatable defense, that of states' rights—as opposed to centralized unionism—and the protection of the "Southern way of life." After the war, Alexander Stephens implied that his earlier use of slavery as justification for armed rebellion was misunderstood. He had merely been commenting on public sentiment, he averred, not stating a principle to be defended at all costs. In his diary of 1865, written that summer while a prisoner at Fort Warren in Boston Harbor, Stephens asserted that "few sensible men of the South ever expected or desired a distinct Independent Nation embracing none but the slave States."[6] This denial of slavery's absolute centrality has long been used by neo-Confederates to explain their veneration of the Confederate flag, even today.

Whatever the official reasons for secession, the "speech acts" of honor, to borrow a linguistic term, became a fashionable way to articulate the

South's burning indignation at the Northern threat to slavery. As I once put it in another study, "The threat to slavery's legitimacy in the Union prompted the sectional crisis, but it was Southern honor that pulled the trigger."[7] Southern radicals began the fight certain that they had the proper martial temperament. In Nashville, Tennessee, a newly enlisted soldier wrote home that he expected a very short war because "the scum of the North *cannot* face the chivalric spirit of the South."[8]

Southerners also believed that, along with cultivating honor, the secessionist movement was a recapitulation of the American Revolution's goal to protect ancient liberties from the loathsome grasp of yet another imperial authority—the federal government. Like the New England ministers in that earlier contest, the Reverend James Henley Thornwell of South Carolina preached, "We are upholding the great principles which our fathers bequeathed us." The goal was to "perpetuate and diffuse the very liberty and the honor for which Washington bled, and which the heroes of the Revolution achieved." They argued that Christians should rally around their arguments for secession.[9]

But the Right Reverend James H. Otey, Episcopal bishop of Tennessee, entertained doubts. He predicted that the unplanned outcome of secession would be a "speedy inevitable extinction [of slavery], as certainly as the sun's rays fall upon the Earth." Despite Lincoln's election in November 1860, Otey thought that the moral certainties of honor and patriotism necessitated a continued loyalty to the Union. A stalwart former Whig, Otey saw extreme danger ahead. When South Carolina began preparations for leaving the Union, he denounced the radical step as "infamous. There is not a redeeming trait about the movement to save it from the just and deep condemnation of Posterity."[10] In similar fashion, a native New Englander, the Reverend George Henry Clark, rector of St. John's Episcopal Church in Savannah, supported secession but with such reservations that his use to the Fire-Eaters must have been small indeed. His text was from the book of Isaiah: "They shall look unto the earth, and behold trouble and darkness."[11] It was hardly a call to arms. Clark returned to the North in early 1861, no doubt because of concerns for his safety and the mistrust of his planter parishioners.

Apart from Whiggish antidisunionists in the clerical ranks, the white clergy of the South generally applauded the secession cause. In an ironic way, the concept of honor easily fitted into the religious traditions of the South. For instance, the Episcopal Right Reverend Francis H. Rutledge of Florida, originally a South Carolinian, came out boldly for secession. He rabidly pledged "five hundred dollars, towards defraying the expenses of government for the year eighteen hundred and sixty-one, whenever by ordinance she shall be declared an independent republic."[12] Rutledge "had himself already seceded, with his native state, & in advance of Florida," rejoiced the contentious Fire-Eater Edmund Ruffin of Virginia, then in Florida. Ruffin suffered severely from chronic depression. Nonetheless, his angry spirit took pleasure in Rutledge's decisive behavior. Ruffin recorded his feelings in his diary, declaring an admiration for the "venerable old minister . . . with his ardent & active patriotic sentiments."[13] Many of the Florida state politicians and militia leaders were Episcopalians with equally strong disunionist opinions. Despite that, Bishop Rutledge tried unsuc-cessfully to convert former Whig governor Richard Keith Call, an ardent defender of the Union. The ecclesiastical hothead Rutledge cheered when the state's secessionist convention decided on disunion. Ex-Governor Call replied to Rutledge's message of secessionist joy: "Yes, you have opened the gates of Hell."[14]

Rutledge was not the only ecclesiastical figure to display his radical convictions so publicly. Other clergy dissented. "Virginia's gallant sons," *The Central Presbyterian* proudly boasted in May 1861, "have sprung forward to the defense of their insulted Mother; assured that they are contending for the most sacred rights, and for the dearest interests for which patriot soldiers ever drew the sword."[15] In a fine essay, historian Edward Crowther concludes that a set of values had developed that he identifies as "a holy honor." Southern whites "cloaked their society" under this banner, and in the name of that cause, "they were prepared to fight and die."[16]

When the clergy eagerly advocated for war, honor, and military glory, politicians could be counted on to do likewise—and with greater vigor and emotion. Some referred to the glorious days of the revolutionary cause. Jabez Lamar Monroe Curry of Alabama waxed eloquent in a speech at Tal-ladega, Alabama: "The heroes of '76 encountered all these and more to pre-vent the domination of a foreign people. It was attempted to stave off the war of 1812 by dilatory restrictive and embargo measures, but the people demanded a declaration of war to protect New England men and New En-gland property, and preserve national honor." So, too, must the slave states. We must resist, he warned, "Federal coercion."[17]

A series of political events in the 1850s led to increased Southern desire for independence as a means to preserve the slave states' sense of honor and the institution of slavery. The Kansas-Nebraska Act of 1854, which permitted slavery in those territories, had been a sizable blunder for peace advocates. It had required the repeal of the Missouri Compromise, which had excluded slavery from the Northern territories. The compromise's repeal was a tragic mistake from the point of view of those in favor of peace. With abolitionist settlers challenging the proslavery territorial government in Kansas, the issue in Southern eyes was less a matter of free access for the spread of cotton culture and slavery than a question of honorable equality of the South with the more populous free states. Warfare broke out in the 1850s between the radical abolitionist John Brown with the majority abolitionist Kansas settlers and the "Border Ruffians" from slaveholding Missouri. Their battles led Horace Greeley of the New York *Tribune* to coin the term "Bleeding Kansas."

Fire-Eaters like William L. Yancey, an Alabama secessionist, demanded that Northern Democrats repudiate "popular sovereignty," agree to Kansas statehood under a proslavery constitution, and submit to slavery's territorial expansion. These moves toward reconciliation, Yancey assured them, would cost nothing, morally or politically. Outraged, Congressman Charles Pugh of Ohio replied, "You endeavor to bow us down into the dust. Gentlemen, you mistake us—you mistake us. We will not submit to dishonor." Pugh was not alone in his reaction to Southern demands. Even a supporter of Stephen Douglas from Michigan was pushed to abandon his leader's pro-Southern posture in rebuttal to Yancey's demands. If asked to "yield up a principle of honor," his reply would be "never, never, never."[18] After the firing on Fort Sumter, Democrats of this persuasion preferred war to passivity.

When Charles Sumner, a Massachusetts senator, fell victim in May 1856 to a caning by Congressman Preston Brooks of South Carolina, the crisis grew worse. Brooks repeatedly struck Sumner at his desk in the Senate chamber in response to a speech by Sumner that Brooks considered uncivil, demeaning, and contemptuous on "The Crime against Kansas." Sumner's denunciations of the South, slavery, and the half-disabled senator Andrew Pickens Butler of South Carolina went far beyond acceptable debating points. He mocked that the venerable Butler had "read many books of chivalry, and believes himself a chivalrous knight, with sentiments of honor and courage." For the Edgefield, S.C., congressman, such ridicule of a fellow statesman and kinsman placed Sumner far beyond the respectability and privilege of a formal duel. Over six feet tall and heavily built, Brooks came up to Sumner, who was signing copies of his lengthy speech. Brooks announced, "Mr. Sumner, I have read your speech twice over carefully. It is a libel on South Carolina and on Mr. Butler, who is a relative of mine." Then he struck Sumner repeatedly on his head and shoulders until the gutta-percha cane snapped in two. Sumner was caught in his seat and could not rise to defend himself. Finally, he fell to the floor unconscious. Senator Robert Toombs of Georgia, another Fire-Eating politician, saw the whole episode but simply stood by, secretly applauding and offering no assistance. Nor did Stephen Douglas, the Illinois Democrat, intervene. He had no use for the antislavery firebrand Sumner.[19]

The attack inflamed Northern hearts. According to William E. Gienapp, the attack on Sumner, perhaps more than the troubles in Kansas, aroused Northern opinion against the South. Even in conservative circles formerly hostile to the Massachusetts senator's course, concerns for Northern self-respect and free speech were evident. The Yankees' sense of honor and right behavior had been violated in the assault. Northerners believed that honor could have been satisfied with less forceful action. Yet, for Northerners, the notion of a national honor was bound to the ideal of a Union indivisible.[20]

The New England philosopher Ralph Waldo Emerson spoke for thousands when he wrote in his diary: "It is not Sumner who must be avenged, but the tree must be cut down. . . . But this stroke rouses the feeling of the people, and shows every one where they are. All feel it. Those who affect not to feel it must perforce share the shame, nor will hiding their heads and pretending other tasks and a preoccupied mind deceive themselves or us." Public protests, meetings, editorials, and legislative resolutions all denounced not only the cudgeling of the senator but the evil character of slavery. It was a major boost for the newly formed Republican Party.[21]

Henry Highland Garnet, an African American preacher, had already advocated violence to end slavery from Northern pulpits. In 1843, he delivered a "Call for Rebellion" during a meeting of the National Negro Convention in Buffalo, New York. In it, he urged slaves themselves to resist physically in order to win their freedom. It was, he insisted, the only way to bring down the hated institution. He did not, though, suggest armed rebellion. Strong criticism from white abolitionists greeted his remarks; black activists were more impressed, though Frederick Douglass thought Garnet's ideas were too radical. At that time, white and even most black abolitionists thought "moral suasion," as evangelical antislavery reformers called it, would be a more efficacious way to proceed. When that failed to move Southern planters to repentance, abolitionists created the Liberty Party in 1840. This move was the beginning of full-fledged political action by the abolitionists, which would eventually culminate in the effort to form the Republican Party. Garnet deplored the political strategy but supported the Liberty Party and later joined the Republican Party.[22]

Still more dramatic and disrupting was John Brown's act of terror at Harpers Ferry. He and his armed band at Harpers Ferry undertook a doomed but crucial mission. They believed a slave insurrection, which they would lead, was the quickest and best way to end slavery. His raid signified a new antislavery strategy of promoting slave insurrection, an aggressive move that stirred Southern outrage. In a curious twist, after his capture in the town firehouse, Brown became the agent of a violent chivalry. Southerners, it seems, had no monopoly on devotion to the masculine code of chivalry. Some Southerners marveled at Brown's intrepidity. In a review of a recent biography, Adam Gopnik writes, "Brown triumphed rhetorically and, in the end, effectively at Harpers Ferry because the slaveholder's code of honour . . . was not entirely a sham."[23] Governor Henry Wise of Virginia was among those who recognized in Brown a fellow spirit, albeit in the enemy camp. In a speech at Richmond, Wise declared that Brown is "a bundle of the best nerves I ever saw, cut and thrust and bleeding and in bonds. He is a man of clear head, of courage, fortitude and simple ingenuousness."[24]

In other words, Brown was a man of warrior honor, with all the virile attributes so greatly prized in the South. One of Brown's chief admirers was John Wilkes Booth. In 1864, the pro-South actor told his sister Asia that Lincoln was "walking in the footsteps of old John Brown but no more fit to stand with that rugged hero—Great God! No!" Just as ideologically driven as Brown himself, Booth anointed Brown "a man inspired, the grandest character of the century!"[25] Clement L. Vallandigham, later a wartime Copperhead (pro-Southern Yankee), praised Brown as a potential Southern gentleman of the old school. He might have become a "consummate commander" in a nobler and worthier cause than the freeing of slaves, the Ohio congressman mused.[26]

Yet, most Southerners were appalled by the audacious assault on the federal arsenal and the planned revolution. In the wake of these events, the Yorkville, South Carolina, *Enquirer*, for instance, urged the immediate need for "vigilance everywhere." The editor spelled out the type of skulking intruders that might be dangerous. "The roving mendicant, the tobacco-waggoner, the whiskey peddler, the sample trader may be honest

and reliable, but in such like disguise abolitionists have prowled about elsewhere and may do so here." Such fantasies led to the tarrings and feath-
erings, the hasty departures, the looks of suspicion of Northern visitors
throughout the South.[27]

Needless to say, John Brown's Northern admirers depicted him with
almost religious fervor. James Redpath penned these words: "That stern old
English sense of justice; that grand Puritan spirit of inflexible integrity—
how beautifully do they bloom out, thus early, in the life of this illustrious
man! Evidently, in honor of this bright trait, history will place John Brown,
in her American Pantheon, not among Virginia's culprits, but as high, at
least, as Virginia's greatest chief," George Washington.[28]

For all his valor, Brown was to proslavery Northern Democrats and
Southern whites a terrible portent of an abolitionist determination to erad-
icate slavery by force. The Northern electorate was permitting, according
to a reporter for the Democratic *New York Herald*, "the churches, the Sunday schools, the moral propagandist societies," to become "indoctrinated
with hatred to an institution which they know only theoretically." He then
raised the question of honor: This moral "condemnation of an institution
which, in a community of mixed races, is considered to be the most wise,
and consequently the most productive of high moral results, touches the
honor of every Southern man and woman, and leads to that blind resentment which discards all considerations of material interest." Lincoln and
his party are "looked upon as the embodiment of this moral slur upon
southern society." To surrender to it would be "an admission of inferiority
in the face of the whole world."[29]

According to a Virginia secession convention delegate, the Yankees
saw the slave states "as a running sore, and throw contempt upon us in
every way." Such hatred of the South and its ways was an insurmountable
obstacle against a continued union, he insisted. The South's sacred honor
was at stake. As the historian Daniel W. Crofts proposed, "Defense of honor
was 'far more precious' than protection of property rights." A proud people
could never accept "the stamp of inferiority for ever to be put upon" them.
"A horror of dishonor," Crofts continued, "prompted yet another secessionist to spurn the idea of remaining in the Union. Were he to agree to
that, the Virginia delegate asserted, "I should feel that I was base enough
to bend my knee to my oppressor, to take the yoke upon my neck, and to
present my own hand for the 'shackles of slavery'." Eager for a fight, young

Southern men applauded "the glorious little game-cock of South Carolina" and generally gushed over the white Carolinians' "lofty sense of honor."[30]

Southern virility was being drained, they claimed, by the constant barrage of Northern insults. Resistance to the federal government under Lincoln and defiance of the Republicans, the secession advocates endlessly repeated, was necessary to "save us from dishonor." What could be worse, believed Governor Henry Wise of Virginia, than submission to *"shame and dishonor."* "We may be shattered to pieces—we may be torn and rent asunder—we may be conquered—we may die," Wise fulminated. But, even so, the whites of the South would retain their firm grasp on honor and the moral rightness of their way of life.[31]

An underlying fear of black rebelliousness filled the speeches, newspaper articles, and letters of disunionists. Speaking to fellow Democrats at their acrimonious convention in Charleston on 28 April 1860, William Yancey, leader of the Alabama secessionists, sketched in dramatic terms the full horrors of abolitionism. If successful, that movement would mean total degradation and the rule of barbarous black freedmen for the submissive slave states. "Ours is the property invaded; ours are the institutions which are at stake; ours is the peace that is to be destroyed; ours is the property that is to be destroyed; ours is the honor at stake—the honor of children, the honor of families, the lives, perhaps, . . . all of which rests upon what your course may ultimately make a great heaving volcano of passion and crime."[32]

As the crisis grew more intense, worries about the restlessness of the slaves grew alarmingly. Observing the crisis with some detachment, William Tecumseh Sherman, then superintendent of the Louisiana Military Academy, wrote, "The mere dread of revolt, sedition or external interference makes men ordinarily calm almost mad."[33]

Southern women, too, joined in the growing chorus for secession using the language of honor. Susan Keitt, Congressman Lawrence Keitt's consort, defended Southern principles in a sexualized way, by which strategy she sought to demean Northern women. The Yankees were, she uttered, "a motley throng of San culottes and Dames des Halles [prostitutes], Infidels and freelovers, interspersed by Bloomer women, fugitive slaves and amalgamationists."[34] According to Drew Gilpin Faust in her brilliant study *Mothers of Invention*, Ada Bacot, a Louisiana widow in a state of deep mourning, found a new pleasure and raison d'être after the war began. She was certain of a new destiny: "Now I can give myself up to my state, the very thought elevates me."[35]

Added to this unflattering arraignment were aspersions cast upon Northern manhood. City-bred fops and limp-wristed reformers—and their fanatical congressional leaders—deserved contempt, Southerners insisted. Although reluctant to resort to war, the editor of the *Rome (Georgia) Weekly Courier* was certain of Southern military superiority and ultimate unity of purpose: "We cannot, and will not stand as idle and indifferent spectators and see noble and patriotic men fighting for *our* principles and our rights, beat down and trampled in the dust. As long as they fight faithfully, we will fight with them; and if they must fall we will fall by their side."[36]

Southern radicals like Yancey, though a minority at first, gradually won over the doubters. The *Charlottesville Review* was the foremost antisecession paper in Virginia. Like thousands of other journalists and ordinary white Southerners, the paper gave up opposition to secession: "There is a habit of speaking derisively of going to war for an *idea*—an abstraction— something which you cannot see. This is precisely the point on which we would go to war." Those who fail to battle for their ideals will not do so for any lesser cause. "Therefore, we say, for this *idea* of State honor—for this abstract principle of not bating her just claims upon threat of coercion— we would convulse this Union from centre to circumference."[37]

Meanwhile, the antislavery forces in the North were taking a far more acerbic and threatening line than in earlier years, when they had naively hoped that moral suasion would be sufficient to bring slave owners to repentance and commitment to voluntary emancipation. The ordinarily peace-minded abolitionist Gerrit Smith, a wealthy New York landowner and one-time congressman, resigned his seat. He wished to promote antislavery resistance against proslavery Kansas settlers. In his valedictory speech in 1856, Smith proclaimed in the House of Representatives, "I and ten thousand other peace men are not only ready to have [slavery] repulsed with violence, but pursued even unto death, with violence."[38] Such insults and dire warnings of abolitionist justice did not go unanswered.

There had always been tensions between the two regions. In more congenial times, national honor had been a term and justification for war against foreign foes and Indian tribes. Both sections shared the same view of nationality, but with the collapse of the transsectional Whig Party and divisions in Democratic ranks, there was little hope of reconciliation. Northerners, not necessarily abolitionists, were becoming increasingly aroused by news of Southern aggressions in Kansas, in the Senate chamber, and in the Southern streets where anyone deemed to be sympathetic about ending slavery was attacked. It was a humiliating affront to the people of Boston, for instance, when federal troops in 1854 carried off the fugitive slave Anthony Burns to return him to his master. Led by free black residents and such abolitionists as Theodore Parker and Thomas Wentworth Higginson, both clergymen, a riot ensued and a deputy U.S. marshal was killed. The attempted rescue of Burns failed.[39]

Beginning in the 1840s, there was already talk about a "Great Slave Power Conspiracy" undermining the comity of the states and the principle of a unified national honor. In 1864, an obscure writer named John Smith Dye published a book in which he claimed that for thirty years, a Southern clique had sought to break up the Union. Among other subversive crimes, Dye argued, agents of the so-called slave powers in 1853 had derailed President Franklin Pierce's railroad car, which was to carry him to his inauguration. The newly elected Democrat from New Hampshire survived along with his wife, but his son, age twelve, had died. So intimidated was the president that he was willing to do all that the Southern slave elite demanded of him, according to Dye. Pierce's successor, James Buchanan, presided over a banquet at a Washington hotel, Dye charged, where the guests were poisoned with arsenic, including the president. He recovered, but thirty-eight guests supposedly did not. Of course, Dye invented the entire scenario of the incident's being a plot of Southern partisans. Many others, even social and political leaders, came to believe that a slaveholding conspiracy was afoot.[40]

Chief Justice Roger Taney's words in the *Dred Scott* decision of the U.S. Supreme Court were further indications of a slave power conspiracy. The revelation that Taney, a Northern judge, had been pressured by President James Buchanan into joining the majority to declare slaves neither citizens nor even people was proof enough to satisfy any skeptic. So thought those who believed in an organized plot.[41]

The usually level-headed Charles Francis Adams, later American minister to London, in 1855 thought the membership in the plot numbered "three hundred and fifty thousand men, spreading over a large territorial surface, commanding the political resources of fifteen states." A Michigan Republican congressman believed that "a system of espionage prevails which would disgrace the despotism and darkness of the middle ages." William H. Seward, more radical in the 1850s than he later became, argued that the Southern aristocracy ruled the people in a conspiratorial way. Dissenters who questioned "rightful national domination of the slaveholding class," he proclaimed, were silenced and oppressed throughout the slave states.[42]

Closely connected to the slave power conspiracy was the issue of national honor as opposed to the states' rights ideal that Southern politicians argued limited federal power. On the floor of Congress, Yankee congressmen and senators began to urge both a condemnation of slavery and a recommitment to national honor. Senator Walter Lowrie of Pennsylvania, for example, announced in a raging congressional debate, "If the alternative be, as gentlemen broadly intimate, a dissolution of this Union, or the extension of slavery over this whole Western country, I, for one, will choose the former." Whether he meant that war would follow is not clear.[43] Lydia Maria Child, an early abolitionist with literary talent, argued against compromises as early as 1833. In her view, surrendering principle only emboldened the slaveholding powers to increase their menacing behavior. At the same time, she contended, the perpetuation of slavery stained national honor. She admitted that Southern whites entertain "a high sense of what the world calls honor, and that they are brave, hospitable, and generous to people of their own color." Nonetheless, such virtues rested on a deplorable foundation that shamed the whole nation.[44]

No less threatening, as Southern militants interpreted it, was the election of the "black Republican" Abraham Lincoln. His elevation to the highest national office, declared a New Orleans editor, was *"a deliberate, cold-blooded insult and outrage"* against Southern honor. A Virginia legislative committee proclaimed it "an offense to the whole South."[45] An amusingly garbled editorial in the *Bossier Banner* of Bellevue, Louisiana, announced on 27 January 1860, "Our institutions have been cinctured and defied resentment; our honor and integrity has been insulted and abused; until it behooves the spirit of resentment to encase itself from its dormant hiding place."[46]

Abraham Lincoln's understanding of honor was inseparable from his conception of national unity. At Springfield, having debated the Democratic candidate, Stephen Douglas, in a famous encounter in 1858, Lincoln claimed that, contrary to Douglas's interpretation of the Declaration of Independence, those who wrote it "intended to include all men." They may not have meant all men were equal in every way, but that they were equal in possessing the benefits of "life, liberty, and the pursuit of happiness."[47]

Lincoln's participation in Whig politics; his law practice, to which he was wholly devoted; and his growing maturity all contributed to a change in his view about the genuine value of honor. Like many other Northerners, he identified martial virtue with the nation and with the supremacy of the law over personal notions of justice. National loyalties should be paramount. He once declared, "let it [national loyalties] become the *political religion* of the nation." In 1847, the first-term congressman joined other Whigs against the honor-laden Southern clamor for war with Mexico. He thought the Southern congressmen, with their steady stream of demands to avenge national honor, full of so much empty bluster. In 1854, the passage of the Kansas-Nebraska Act drew the Illinois attorney back into the political arena. Lincoln, however, did not understand the true feelings of Southern whites despite his marrying into a Kentucky family and having many clients who were Southern migrants into Illinois. In the course of his drive toward the Republican nomination in 1860, he maintained that his first duty was to the Union and Constitution; that commitment and principle overrode any pride in his "personal honor."[48]

After Lincoln's election, the Upper South unionists, chiefly former Whigs, were hoping that his policies would persuade the seceded states to rejoin the nation. Instead, on 15 April 1861, he called for 75,000 men at arms, a demand that would require citizens of the Upper South to fight against their brethren—many of them direct kin in the Lower South. The reaction was almost unanimous, and even former advocates of peace fell into line. The Right Reverend James Otey of Tennessee pledged himself to the Confederacy. Most, if not all, Whiggish unionists in the South did likewise.[49]

Lincoln and the other Republicans really knew little about the Southern *mentalité*. Of course, they understood the whites' determination to hold slaves in bonds, but they did not recognize the depth of that commitment and how it was related to their innermost identity, their sense of honor as a dominant race. Lincoln did grasp the differences with regard to ideas of liberty. "We all declare for liberty," he observed, "but in using the same word, we do not all mean the same thing." For some, it signifies a man's right to do as he sees fit with himself or his labor, the president continued, but others "mean for some men to do as they please with other men, and the product of other men's labor."[50]

Just as honor was posed against shame, so freedom's opposite was slavery. The likening of their own system of labor to notions of humiliation and subservience meant that Southerners recoiled in revulsion and anger from any implication of themselves' being slavish, degenerate, and heathenish.

In the fighting of the war, honor played its customary role on both sides. Martial honor requires the suppression of freedom and individuality for the sake of group survival; self-sacrifice for one's comrades and fidelity to hierarchy and order are paramount. But in civilian life, especially in the slaveholding South, honor was deemed the ethical foundation of white male liberty—and sometimes license.

To achieve battlefield discipline, the principles of warrior honor must be firmly inculcated in the minds of all participants. Civil War officers on both sides were more likely to write of honor and duty than were their enlisted men. Soldiers and their leaders expected to achieve and often did gain the designation of hero, honor's reward. Commanders made a difference with regard to morale and fighting capabilities. Some had a special talent in that regard. Charles Russell Lowell, who led the 2nd Massachusetts Cavalry, possessed the "capacity of ruling men." He had had thirteen horses killed under him, and his men "never shrank from following him into any danger after they had seen him in one battle." Valor of this quality inspired those under such a commander. The men would have been "ashamed to do anything less than their full duty under his eyes." Captain Burage Rice of New York predicted eventual Southern defeat: "By the sacrifice and blood of our fathers was the Republic founded and by the treasure, faith, honor, and blood of their sons shall the same glorious flag forever wave over us."[51] Like many others, Rice identified honor and other high principles with the flag that flew over the fragile American structure.

The prize-winning historian James McPherson convincingly argues that young men went to war knowing why they did so—not for adventure, not for the pay or chance for booty, but chiefly out of one ideological conviction or another: Johnny Reb for defense of hearth and way of life, Yanks for flag and Union. Even at the start, some men went to war to free the slaves. Of course, motives are slippery commodities. But the prospect of glory and immortal recognition for valor was a component that officers encouraged. James F. Trotter, a Mississippian, commended the Southern cause: "We have won true glory, for our struggle for liberty has no parallel in the history of the world." At the First Battle of Manassas, the chief commander, General P. T. G. Beauregard, exhorted the troops, "Fight on, brave

Virginia boys; the day is ours everywhere else, and it must be here also."
In response, the soldiers, recalled Billy Woodward of Augusta, Virginia,
gave "a loud cheer, we rushed forward, determined to do as commanded
or die."[52] Battlefield bravery was undeniably a mark of Civil War soldiers,
whether Yankee or Rebel. At the Battle of Gettysburg, for instance, Colonel
Joshua L. Chamberlain, an abolitionist and former mathematics professor at Bowdoin College, led a regiment that defended Little Round Top
on 2 July 1863. After the Union victory, he praised the survivors for their
bravery and noted their "steady and gallant support," especially that of the
83rd Pennsylvania Regiment. "Our role of honor," he declared in an official report, was that the men had fulfilled all the responsibilities a soldier
should.[53]

Historian Gary Gallagher wrote that after the Battle of Gettysburg,
"Edgeworth Bird lauded the infantrymen who 'performed heroic deeds,
and died heroic deaths' in doomed efforts to dislodge the entrenched Federals. As the attackers 'rushed up into the very jaws of death,' noted an
appreciative [Union] artillerist, 'our men performed deeds of daring and
heroism which covered them with glory.'"[54]

In battle, where honor is the only "law" available, its mandate required
fidelity to one's fellow soldiers. To let them down was to court ostracism
and contempt. For instance, a wounded color-bearer asked Private William A. Fletcher to take the 5th Texas regimental flag. Fletcher promptly
refused, saying, "I am too cowardly for a flag-bearer to risk myself; and I
find the oftener I can load and shoot the better able am I to maintain my
honor."[55] A foot soldier in the 20th Georgia Regiment spoke for many when
he declared, "I had rather dye on the battle field than to disgrace my self
& the hole [sic] family."[56] That sense of familial pride was an integral part
of the ethic. But the horrors of battle soon revealed that fear, courage, and
excitement joined hands. When a Virginian named David Hunter Strother
came upon a disturbing sight, he was almost undone. There were some
forty dead Confederate soldiers lying in a thicket: "The bodies lay among
the bushes and trees just as they fell. . . . And were without exception shot
through the head with musket balls." The next day, he saw an "Ohio volunteer lay on his back, the brains oozing from a shot in the head, uttering at
breathing intervals a sharp stertorous cry." The soldier had been lying there
in agony for over thirty-six hours.[57]

Yet, the thirst for fame and a love of warfare could cloud an officer's judgment and prudence. Cavalryman J. E. B. Stuart, at age twenty-nine, seemed

an insatiable hunter for glory. His attire of cavalry boots, crimson-lined cape, and bright yellow sash with a black felt hat, to which he attached an ostrich feather, made him resemble "the dashing cavalier he aspired to be," writes James McPherson.[58] Stuart and his men, all experienced horsemen, played havoc twice with Union General George McClellan's Peninsula drive in 1862.

During the following year at Gettysburg, however, Stuart demonstrated the disaster that overconfidence, bravado, and irresponsibility, all in the name of honor, could generate. He and his men were galloping about the Pennsylvania countryside. Belatedly, the weary cavalrymen returned, but Stuart had deprived Robert E. Lee of his eyes for seeing where the Federals were located. Not all of the blame for the Gettysburg campaign's failure rested on Stuart's shoulders, however. Lee's plans were faulty: To attack the enemy that held the higher ground was a grave mistake. McPherson asserts that Lee was to blame for "mismanagement, overconfidence, and poor judgment." Richard Ewell and Jubal Early were supposed to take Cemetery Hill on 1 July 1863, but failed to do so either then or on the following day. General James Longstreet was also far too tardy and uninspired in his assault mission on the 2nd and 3rd of July. Asked years later why the Confederates lost the battle, George Pickett thought a moment and then sighed, "I've always thought the Yankees had something to do with it." McPherson, though, contends, as Lee did, that superior Yankee resources and manpower were the key to the Union victory. While partly true, McPherson says the explanation was self-serving. It enabled

> Southerners to preserve their pride in the courage and skill of Confederate soldiers, to reconcile defeat with their sense of honor, even to maintain faith in the righteousness of their cause while admitting that it had been lost. The Confederacy, in other words, lost the war not because it fought badly, or because its soldiers lacked courage, or because its cause was wrong, but simply because the enemy had more men and guns. As one proud Virginian expressed it: "They never whipped us, Sir, unless they were four to one. If we had had anything like a fair chance, or less disparity of numbers, we should have won our cause and established our independence."[59]

Yet, that famous charge of Pickett's men was a marvel of both futility and courage.

Pickett himself was another cavalier like Stuart. His hair was as long as any seventeenth-century Royalist against Oliver Cromwell in the English Civil War. He wore a drooping mustache and goatee almost in imitation of a hero out of a Victorian swashbuckling romance. While the cavalier affectation for sartorial display was almost ridiculous, it was consonant with the military culture of the Old South. Admittedly, such costuming was rare.[60]

Most ordinary soldiers fought simply because they wished to avoid the shame of not doing so. Others, though, fought for a cause—for or against slavery, for Union or secession. Still others battled to keep from getting killed by the enemy. A few fled from the field—often to their ignominy and peril. One Union ambulance driver, Jeff Davis, wrote to his sister Cornelia Hancock about a deserter who was executed before the troops: "He was in the 71st Pennsylvania—he was an awful brave man—he walked from the General's headquarters to where his grave was and then the officer in charge of the men who was to shoot him told the men to stand back then he put a bandage around his eyes then told him to get down on his coffin—he did so then the officer read the orders and asked the man if he was ready—the man said that he was, the officer told the men to fire. I fore wone do not want to see another man shot but I did not want to see him shot but I had to."[61]

Racism continued to be a barbarous and sad reality during the war. Southerners presumed that African Americans who wore the blue uniform were not human enough to deserve any acknowledgment of their courage, honor, or dignity. After issuing the Emancipation Proclamation of 1 January 1863, Lincoln authorized the arming of blacks and placing of them in Union ranks. Congress had already granted the chief executive the power to do so. That momentous change of policy was designed to save white lives, provide a stunning lesson to the Rebels about the foolishness of their cause, and give blacks a sense of national pride and respect. Confederates were naturally outraged at the sheer effrontery of such a mission. In response, Confederacy President Jefferson Davis promised to hand Union officers of black troops to the states to be summarily dealt with, even executed as if they were spies. The pledge did not, however, materialize. Yet, incidents of black prisoners' being executed without trial occurred all too often.

At the end of July 1863, Lincoln produced General Order No. 252 in which he stated, "The law of nations, and the usages and customs of war, as carried on by civilized powers, permit no distinction as to color in the treatment of prisoners of war as public enemies." If that policy had been enforced, the United States would have been justified in killing a Confederate prisoner for every black officer or foot soldier so executed by the Confederacy.[62]

The federal government only rarely carried out this threat of reprisal, even after the notoriously proslavery Nathan Bedford Forrest had all the black soldiers captured at Fort Pillow killed on the spot on 12 April 1864. Such atrocities were employed not only to send a threatening message to male slaves still under Southern control but also to humiliate these brave soldiers for the effrontery of fighting against their former masters.

Hundreds of thousands of men on both sides endured capture and expected to be given the customary standards of treatment for prisoners of war. Those sentiments, however, did not apply to their black mates. Dark-skinned Union soldiers were not considered by many Northern whites in the ranks to be worthy of that regard. As Michael Fellman observes, "When the fight was between white Americans, soldiers generally were willing to limit their killing in combat, not because they lacked firepower or because of tactical shortcomings, and not just because their officers enforced restraint, but primarily because they continued to act at least in part within the restraints of their implicit, shared, moral code."[63]

Union troops could be equally vengeful. According to historian Jack Hurst, African American units in Memphis, Forrest's home town, swore to "'remember Fort Pillow,' and they would make good the pledge. Taking a Confederate cue, they became less and less likely" to spare prisoners.[64] A soldier in the 105th Illinois recorded in May 1864 the seizure of a Rebel soldier who begged to be spared: "He had his shirt off, and on one arm was tattooed in big letters 'Fort Pillow.' As soon as the boys saw the letters on his arm, they yelled, 'No quarter for you!' And a dozen bayonets went into him and a dozen bullets were shot into him. I shall never forget his look of fear."[65]

African American troops performed surprisingly well in the Union Army. Thomas Wentworth Higginson, a regimental officer, observed that his black troops "have a great deal of pride as soldiers, and a very little of severity goes a great way, if it be firm and consistent." The desertion rate of the nearly 200,000 blacks, especially the former slaves who made up two-thirds of the total, was lower than that for whites: 8 percent for all black enlistees, less than 5 percent for former slaves, and 9 percent for all whites. Those who fought with their friends from the same plantation hardly ever deserted.[66]

Abraham Lincoln, Secretary of War Edwin Stanton, and General Ulysses S. Grant insisted that all prisoners, regardless of color, not be maltreated in any way. It took until January 1865, just a few months before the Confederate collapse, to assure fair handling of all prisoners. Grant heard that Confederate Major General Richard Taylor in Louisiana had under his command Rebel soldiers who had executed black captives and hanged a white Union captain. Writing the general, the son of President Zachary Taylor, Grant warned that the offending soldiers must be punished and in future "the same protection" be given to black prisoners along with other captives.[67]

The famous "Battle of the Crater" occurred in July 1864. The African American troops who served in the battle were eager to prove their mettle in an army still skeptical of their competence and courage. In the 48th Pennsylvania Regiment, under the command of Ambrose Burnside, some inventive coal miners had dug tunnels under the formidable bastions protecting Petersburg, Virginia. They placed four tons of explosives in the elaborate shafts. The detonation went off on 30 July. For days the Confederates had heard the noise of picks and shovels under their feet but failed to do much about it. Thus, they were only half-prepared for what followed.

The original plan was for Burnside's recently trained division of U.S. Colored Troops to rush up the slope to seize the Confederate defenses. General George Meade, however, changed the order at the last minute, causing confusion by demanding that a white division advance first. Unfortunately, that decision, coupled with weak leadership, demoralized the black soldiers. Still, they did their best. The result, however, was disaster. Nearly four thousand Union soldiers died with few enemy casualties. The black troops were caught in the crater itself when Confederate Brigadier General William Mahone retook the heights, and his men fired down into the gaping hole. The five hundred black soldiers who tried to surrender were murdered. It was another tragic breach of Rebel discipline.

When he learned of it, Mahone tried to prevent the massacre and may have saved a few of the defeated African Americans. His men, though, were in no mood to observe the courtesies of war and gleefully took revenge against former slaves. A North Carolinian recalled the feelings at the time. One of his mates declared, "'Ay, boys, you have hot work ahead—they are negroes, and show no quarter.' This was the first intimation that we had to fight negro troops." This news "seemed to infuse the little band with impetuous daring, as they pressed onward to the fray. Our comrades had been slaughtered in a most inhuman and brutal manner, and slaves were trampling over and mangling their bleeding corpses. Revenge must have fired every heart and strung every arm with nerves of steel for the herculean task of blood." Grant wrote to Chief of Staff Henry W. Halleck, "It was the saddest affair I have witnessed in this war." Later, before a congressional committee, Grant observed, "General Burnside wanted to put his colored division in front, and I believe if he had done so it would have been a success." But if they had, and the assault had failed, it would have been a catastrophe for recruitment of blacks. Some would say, Meade had told Grant, that the army was shoving "these people ahead to get killed because we did not care anything about them." Such complications left African American soldiers in a difficult position. General Robert E. Lee must have known about these unfortunate events from the battle. According to his biographer, Emory Thomas, he did nothing and said nothing. One South Carolinian wrote his sister that his unit had killed "500 negroes" but took only two prisoners. He regretted that horror, but his mates were too exhilarated to care for restraint.[68] On the whole, though, the black troops performed nobly at the Battle of the Crater and elsewhere.

In the aftermath of a bloody engagement, neither Union nor Rebel forces meticulously observed a respectful spirit toward the fallen. That omission was partly the result of bone-weariness, the trauma of war, and the heat, blood, and odors of the battlefield. Honor was thrust aside when it came to mass burial of the dead. After the Battle of Franklin in 1864, Rebels in desperate need even robbed the clothing and possessions of their six generals who had fallen. Bodies were sometimes dumped in common graves with Union and Confederate corpses lying side by side. A Union officer was enraged when he found that military hospitals were throwing the dead in common trenches with "no distinction between the graves of our Brave men who have died for our cause, and the grave of the worthless invaders of our soil." A Federal chaplain was equally appalled that farmers covered their potatoes better than those burying their dead mates. "Circumstances," he sighed, "prevent such tenderness from being extended to the fallen hero."[69] Glory and honor were postponed in the wildness of the fighting, to be resurrected only in postwar memorials, statues, parades, flags, and grand speeches.

Finally, the use of guerilla bands on both sides meant a reign of terror and recriminations in Kansas, Missouri, North Carolina, West Virginia, and Tennessee. Irregulars knew no limits and often acted shamelessly. Regular soldiers and their officers considered the undisciplined fighters to be barbarians who failed to observe the rules of war. But Union warriors also committed atrocities routing out rebel bands. In West Virginia, Union General Robert Huston Milroy responded to Rebel guerillas' successes by ordering Tucker County citizens, regardless of any evidence of guilt, to deliver cash for unionist families who had lost their houses to guerilla arsonists. If the citizens failed to comply, he threatened them with the gallows. Confederate protests and orders from Washington to desist did not halt the policy, and he was allowed to proceed.[70] In Kansas and Missouri, one pious New Englander, Sergeant Sherman Bodwell, became as terroristic as his enemies, the "Border Ruffians." According to the guerilla expert Michael Fellman, "he burned and killed on uncorroborated suspicions and celebrated himself as an avenging angel." Indiscriminate murders and destroyed properties escalated to the point of chaos in all these upcountry regions.[71] No less vicious was Rebel leader William Clarke Quantrill. With three hundred or so men, he attacked Lawrence, Kansas, an antislavery town. Quantrill may have been a psychopath who hated any form of authority, so that the war became a means to obey his demons. At Lawrence, he and his band of cutthroats destroyed the more substantial houses and stores and mowed down an estimated two hundred adults and boys.[72]

After surrendering his troops at Appomattox, to his credit, General Lee refused many requests to head irregular bands against the enemy. General Porter Alexander, Lee's chief of artillery, proposed that strategy after the Army of Northern Virginia was disbanded. Guerilla warfare would have meant war without any end, and Lee was bound to object. Douglas Southall Freeman, in his magisterial *R. E. Lee,* told what happened next, based on Alexander's memoirs, *Fighting for the Confederacy:* "Alexander proposed, as an alternative to surrender, that the men scatter through the woods with orders to report to governors of their respective states with their weapons. 'What would you hope to accomplish by that?' Lee queried. It might prevent the surrender of the other armies, Alexander argued, because if the Army of Northern Virginia laid down its arms, all the others would follow suit, whereas, if the men reported to the governors, each state would have a chance of making an honorable peace." But, as General Joshua Chamberlain, the hero of Gettysburg, remarked, he had given his word to lay down his arms forever.[73] Lee knew that a guerilla style of engagement was far too uncontrollable and could lead to outright lawlessness and piracy.

Despite these violations of military tradition, there were some redeeming moments at the end of the war. Consider what occurred on 12 April

1865 at Appomattox Courthouse. By nine in the morning, General Chamberlain had arranged his troops to accept the surrender of Major General John B. Gordon's corps. It was General Grant's policy to treat the Rebels as courteously as circumstances allowed, and Chamberlain was prepared to comply. In his postwar memoirs, Grant wrote, "I always admired the South, as bad as I thought their cause, for the boldness with which they silenced all opposition and all croaking, by press or by individuals, within their control. War at all times, whether a civil war between sections of a common country or between nations, ought to be avoided, if possible with honor." Once begun, however, soldiers are too human to "tolerate an enemy" entirely.[74] Yet, Grant and his officers could show respect for the defeated, recognition of a war fought, by and large, with honor.

Without stirring drums, blaring trumpets, or any music whatsoever, Gordon's emotionally drained soldiers fell into line and marched down the hill toward the courthouse. Meanwhile, Chamberlain, as he recalled the event, gave orders for the men to reach "the position of 'salute' in the manual of arms as each body of the Confederates passed before us." He did not command the officers to bark "present arms." That order would have inappropriately signified "the highest possible honor to be paid even to a president." Instead, the officers were to use the "carry arms" command, with the weapon "held by the right hand and perpendicular to the shoulder." Chamberlain signaled the bugler as Gordon arrived. While the notes filled the air, the Union ranks came to "attention," Chamberlain recollected. There rang out the crisp, chunky noise of the soldiers' hands as they grasped musket stocks in unison.[75]

According to Chamberlain, Gordon was in no mood for the ritual. "His chin drooped to his breast, downhearted and dejected in appearance almost beyond description." But hearing the bugle and "snap of arms," Gordon touched his horse "gently with the spur, so that the animal slightly reared, and as he wheeled, horse and rider made one motion, the horse's head swung down with a graceful bow and General Gordon dropped his swordpoint to his toe in salutation." Then, the war-weary Rebels draped their old and tattered battle flags on the piles of weapons or spread them reverently on the ground. Some Confederates "rushed, regardless of all discipline, from the ranks, bent about their old flags, and pressed them to their lips with burning tears," Chamberlain recounted. "On our part not a sound of trumpet more, nor roll of drum; not a cheer, nor word nor whisper of vain-glorying, nor motion of man standing again at the order; but an awed stillness rather and breath-holding, as if it were the passing of the dead!"[76]

In an interview with a Boston journalist in 1878, Chamberlain explained the meaning of the ceremony: *"Whatever was surrendered and laid down, it was not manhood, and not honor. Manhood arose, and honor was plighted and received."* The allusion to a marital love pledged and ratified by formal tie was appropriate to the reuniting of the temporarily separated sections of the Union. General Lee's officers, Chamberlain asserted, knew that the rules of honor required them never again to take up arms against the United States. *"They are men of honor, and they meant it, and their word of honor is good,"* the Union general then affirmed. He concluded, "God, in . . . his mercy, in His great covenant with our fathers, set slavery in the forefront, and it was swept aside as with a whirlwind, when the mighty pageant of the people passed on to its triumph."[77]

Of all the Union officers, Chamberlain may have been the most devout and the most eloquent on the expression of honor. According to Glenn Lafantasie, "Like the knights of old, he saw the two contending armies as representing good and evil, white knights battling black knights in epic duels that would determine the fate of the United States. . . . In his eyes, officers displayed knightly countenances as they rode by on noble steeds. He named his favorite horse Charlemagne and marveled that his mount suffered almost as many wounds as he did before war's end." Unlike later reactions in World War I to the horrible carnage and stench of war, Chamberlain's reflections were largely positive, even stimulating. War enlisted the "highest qualities of manhood," especially "sacrifice of self for the sake of something held higher." For him, overthrowing the slave institution was a task worthy of all the courage and grit the North could muster.[78]

In the South, the humiliation of defeat was hard to bear. Recent scholarship has proposed that the war harvested more deaths than had been calculated previously. While the Union dead can be figured with some accuracy, Southern records are faulty and incomplete. But the historian David Hacker has recalculated the numbers and argues that, rather than 618,222 losses on the field and in hospitals as traditionally stated, the reality was at least 20 percent higher—750,000. Drawn from a far smaller eligible pool of men, the Rebel dead came to 258,000, rather than the longstanding previous estimate of 94,000.[79] It is scarcely surprising, therefore, that the emotional impact of such a high proportion of working men—fathers, husbands, brothers—lying in the ground instead of rebuilding a land rendered poor and harried must have been extremely severe.

A sense of humiliation persisted for several generations thereafter throughout the former slave states. On a collective scale, demoralization had set in as early as 1864. Confederate politician Howell Cobb found Georgian civilians to be "depressed, disaffected, and too many of them disloyal." "Shall we indeed fight on against the decrees of God, to utter extermination!" a former secessionist editor wondered. "Was it 'the will of God . . . or the suggestion of the Demon of Pride' that kept the Confederate insanity afloat? I say 'Peace!'"[80] Such feelings were made worse by the actual surrender of the Rebel armies. One reaction to the great loss was a retreat to a psychological redoubt that might be called Fort Denial. Dr. Samuel Preston Moore denounced rumors that Lee had given up the fight as a "moral impossibility." "No one is willing to believe it," declared one Mississippian as late as 20 April 1865.[81] At first, the Reverend J. Henry Smith, minister of the Presbyterian Church at Greensboro, North Carolina, had half-disbelieved rumors of Lee's capitulation. When he discovered the truth, he declared it the *"Saddest of days!"* The clergyman found himself unable to leave his bed and made no entries in his daily journal. He groaned, "The doings & feelings, the disheartening, the gloom & burden & sorrow—no pen can describe. Oh is all gone? My bleeding, suffering country! Are all the prayers, the vows, the blood & lives & property of thousands & tears of many thousands in vain?"[82]

For many a veteran, alcohol was a solace but also a depressant that ruined lives and marriages. Former senator and then general James Chesnut was the despair of his wife, the famous diarist Mary Chesnut. He was too often in his cups. Still worse were those suffering from what we now call post-traumatic stress disorder (PTSD). Rebel private Albinus Snelson attempted to burn himself to death. Only moments before, others had prevented him from throwing himself out of an upstairs window. His nights brought on terrorizing nightmares, no doubt the reliving of war experiences. Captain William J. Dixon, an unmarried twenty-five-year old formerly in a Georgia regiment, returned from war deeply depressed. He took comfort in excessive amounts of spirits. The habit, some thought, explained his odd behavior, including mumbling to himself.[83]

With plantation slaves now free, the upper classes had to discover whether they could farm themselves, find enough labor, or take up another formerly unrespectable occupation such as selling insurance or opening a shop. General Pickett tried peddling insurance contracts. He constantly reflected on that foolish but memorable charge at Gettysburg. The deteriorating state of his wife's health and the loss of a beloved young son weighed on his soul. A cousin, responding to Pickett's news of his situation, sympathized, saying, "The[se] infernal hard time[s] are bad enough to make a man mad without having family afflictions to to[r]ment his feelings." In 1875, Pickett fell mortally ill from a "gastric fever." The former general was only fifty years old.[84] Early deaths had long been common in the South, but the effects of war and the humiliations of defeat and material and personal loss made that condition even more dire.

At least for a time, even the most pious found that their faith was shaken to the core. Ellen House, for instance, undertook to curb her bitterness and desolation over the defeat. "We have depended too much on Gen. Lee too little on God."[85] As the end drew near, the God-fearing General Josiah Gorgas, Confederate chief of ordnance, grieved, "What have we done that the Almighty should scourge us with such a war, so relentless and so repugnant?"[86]

The grief and shame of the loss was bound to have ugly repercussions almost equal to that of the fighting itself. If only the Union victory had been as complete as Joshua Chamberlain had implied. As the next chapter explains, the first disaster to undo the military triumph was Lincoln's assassination, an act based on Southern honor but, more importantly, a great national tragedy.

5

RECONSTRUCTION

SOUTHERN WHITE HUMILIATION
AND REVENGE FOR DEFEAT

John Lee, curling skyward
from the fire,
A town's worth of bullets
Searing white in the char
That was a man gunned down
And set ablaze. John Lee
will burnt til sundown.

—JAKE ADAM YORK, *Murder Ballads*

The Southern struggle to return power to the white population took years
to complete, with many complications. Yet, the eventual outcome became
tragically clear from the start: Whites would sooner or later rule, and African Americans, though no longer slaves, would once again be relegated to
the lower and most humiliated reaches of the social order. The hierarchy of
white honor would be resurrected. The assassination of Abraham Lincoln
was the first act in that mission. A brief exposition of the downfall of the
Republican Party's Reconstruction and the rise, through blunt violence, of
white domination are the twin themes explored in this chapter.

Some Rebels and sympathizers remained faithful to the secessionist
cause even after its fate was sealed. Among them was the flamboyant actor
John Wilkes Booth. Growing up in rural Harford County, Maryland, and
in downtown Baltimore, where slaveholding was a general practice, Booth
mingled with Southern-minded playmates on Exeter Street. In his mature
years, his devotion to the Southern cause and the ethic of honor became
paramount in his emotional and political life. It was no wonder that he
became a favorite performer throughout the slave states, known for his
athleticism and bravado on stage.

During the last months of the war, as Confederate fortunes eroded,
desperation to fend off the shame of defeat, a desire for vengeance, and
sheer outrage animated Booth's daily life. From any rational viewpoint, he
was scarcely oppressed by anyone. Yet, he identified with a beleaguered

Confederacy as if the whites themselves were soon to be enslaved to a brutal Northern juggernaut. Secessionists frequently referred to the prospect of Northerners' conquering and enslaving Southerners and setting ex-slaves over their former masters' lives, women, and livelihoods. It was a general article of faith that Yankee rule would mean the subjugation of white families—"wives and daughters to pollution and violation to gratify the lust of half-civilized Africans."[1]

Swept up in the fervor for retaliation and white purity, Booth reflected these ideals of the Southern slaveholding elite. In a statement for the Washington *National Intelligencer* shortly before the assassination, the actor lamented the fall of "Southern rights and institutions."[2] Seeking to retrieve an idyllic Southern past that had never existed, Booth despised modern and commercial innovations. In Booth's time, he specifically feared that Northern enterprises and industrial progress would obliterate age-old traditions and virtues, particularly those that upheld white domination. Following these themes of honor and resistance to impending catastrophe, Booth fantasized that, unless defeated, Lincoln would actually extinguish the Negro race with his false promises of freedom. Slaves needed their white masters' protection. "Witness their elevation in happiness and enlightenment above their race, elsewhere," he wrote. He had lived with slaves all his life and "have seen *less* harsh treatment from Master to Man than I have beheld in the North from father to son. Yet Heaven knows *no one* would be willing to do, *more* for the negro race than I. Could I but see a way to still better their condition. But Lincoln's policy is only preparing the way for their total annihilation."[3] Preserving the domestic institution, prohibiting racial mixing, and rescuing the South from "her threatened doom," as Booth framed it, required immediate, bold measures. For too long, the Union flag had waved above scenes of blood, "spoiling her beauty and tarnishing her honor." In closing, he referred to his favorite Shakespearean character: "I answer with Brutus: He who loves his country better than gold or life."[4]

For a number of years, Booth served the Confederate cause as part of a small band of conspirators in Washington and Baltimore. Booth belonged to the pro-Confederate Knights of the Golden Circle in Baltimore, where some of his schoolmates still lived.[5] Several joined his subversive circle. The original idea, hatched toward the end of the war, was to take Lincoln hostage and demand a settlement favorable to the South before releasing him. But the problem of where to hide him became more problematic. Nonetheless, Booth wrote in his diary, "Our cause being almost lost, . . .

something decisive and great must be done."[6] But the Union troops were everywhere. Robert E. Lee's army had surrendered five days before the fatal night of 15 April 1865. In desperation, Booth decided on a radical course: He moved comfortably through the crowds of theatergoers and crossed under the Ford's Theater stage, eluding close observation. With the muzzle of his derringer only two feet from the president's head, Booth fired. Major Henry R. Rathbone, a young member of the presidential staff seated next to his fiancée, quickly tried to grab Booth, who dropped the pistol but pulled out a knife. He cut Rathbone's arm just as the officer forced him toward the balcony. As he tumbled from the box, Booth snagged his left-foot spur on some patriotic bunting and fractured a bone in his leg upon hitting the stage twelve feet below. With hands upraised, Booth faced the stupefied audience and shouted, *"Sic semper tyrannis!"* Quickly Booth limped past the lone, benumbed thespian standing before the lights and staggered outside. He leapt on his horse and galloped off.[7]

Booth's act, he thought, would arouse, to his everlasting glory, the applause and gratitude of Southern whites. In the meantime, as he and his companion David Herold fled through Virginia, Booth grieved that he was pursued "like a dog" simply "for doing what Brutus was honored for." What a "degenerate people" his unmanly fellow Americans were. They had dubbed him "a common cutthroat." Booth thought himself a gentleman of unimpeachable reputation. If allowed to return to Washington, his station, dignity, and uprightness would be universally acclaimed. Once in the public eye, the former matinee idol pledged, "I have a greater desire to return to Washington and in a measure clear my name which I feel I can do."[8] For ideologues like Booth, reputation for valor is usually uppermost.

With Federal troops swarming everywhere, the fugitives were traced to Garrett's Farm just south of Port Royal, Virginia. On the night of 26 April 1865, Union cavalrymen surrounded Garrett's barn. They torched the building. Fearing for his life, Herold surrendered. Booth, however, decided to die with gun in hand. Before he could pull the trigger, however, Sergeant Boston Corbett shot Booth in the neck. He fell paralyzed. His final words were, "Tell my Mother I died for my country. I did what I thought was best."[9]

This was the first act, one might say, of the Southern response to defeat, a reaction that was to grow in strength over the rest of the nineteenth century. Still rebellious, Southern whites began guerilla warfare, though not under Lee, soon after most bluecoats had mustered out. The rise of whites against black freedom began during what was known as Reconstruction. The Union was once more whole, but building a biracial democracy in the conquered states was far more problematic. Republicans remained in power, but Lincoln's assassination, the first act of postwar Southern revenge, had been a devastating blow.

Southern attempts to regain control were aided in part by Yankee determination to return to regular pursuits; only some Republican politicians with abolitionist views saw the need to protect freed people. Nor did Andrew Johnson, Lincoln's vice president, help matters. A Tennessee Democrat, he had stood out as one of the few in the South to oppose disunion. Yet, after the war, he favored the Southern elite once the great slave power had been broken. As the antebellum governor of Tennessee (1853–57), he had been a favorite among Tennesseans. When he was approached to run for the office of vice president, the Democratic press was jubilant. "We believe—feel it instinctively," rhapsodized the Nashville *Union*, "that this nomination is the prelude to an overwhelming victory." From the mountainous east of Tennessee, Johnson, a once poor and half-educated commoner, the paper contended, was a politician whom the public would inevitably respect: "A self-made man—a man for the people and of the people—strong in intellect—pure in patriotism, and unsullied in honor, we are free to state that his superior could not be found." Truly, the editor concluded, Johnson was *"one of nature's noblemen."*[10] He moved from governor to the upper federal chamber, after which Lincoln plucked him from the Senate in 1862 to become the provisional governor of Johnson's home state.

After so many slaveholders expressed relief that they had been released from the burdens of slave ownership, Johnson was convinced that they could be trusted to handle racial matters themselves. Federal intervention could be held to a minimum without unduly injuring blacks. That fantasy was soon disproved. The state legislatures enacted black codes that hobbled any sign of African American advancement in economic and public terms. With roots in the old slave codes, these statutes were designed to assure planters access to cheap labor and reinforce the inferiority of blacks to whites. Presidential Reconstruction was a failure, at least as the Republican victors saw it.

In 1866, Republicans ran for office arguing against Johnson's opposition to the 14th Amendment, his belligerent outlook toward Congress, and his offering Southern whites too much leverage in running their affairs as they had in the antebellum period. For the Democrats and for Radical Reconstruction, the 1866 congressional elections were a disaster. At the national level, the Republicans gained a veto-proof majority to shape the plans for the conquered nation. Unfortunately, less radical members of the party, in conjunction with the remaining Democrats, restricted what Congress could do to guarantee the complete freedom of African Americans from Southern white majorities. Nonetheless, some aspects left a legacy upon which black Americans could regain, if many years later, their rightful place in the social and political order.[11]

The political aspects of Reconstruction did not survive, but some of the social ones did. For example, the Freedmen's Bureau, led by an evangelical abolitionist, General O. O. Howard, was effective in helping blacks in their labor relations. The agents, spread throughout the former slave states, dealt with problems of food, water, and health. Twenty-one million rations of food for the newly freed blacks were part of this massive effort, and $4.5 million was spent on this project. The bureau, however, was too understaffed and constrained by law to undertake a full-hearted mission of revolutionary change. The agency had no permission to let blacks remain on confiscated lands if the owners had received Johnson's pardon.[12]

Reconstruction enabled some blacks to go to schools established by such agencies as the American Missionary Association (AMA). In the Sea Islands of South Carolina, evangelical missionary Mansfield French announced his goal: "God's programme," he proclaimed, "involves *freedom in its largest sense—Free soil, free schools,—free ballot boxes, free representation in state and national*" seats of power. Despite long days in the fields, adult freed people flocked to schools for evening classes. Their object was to learn but also to avoid being "made ashamed" before their youngsters.[13]

With the generous help of the Freedmen's Bureau, both religious and secular institutions received some funding from the federal government. A secular agency, such as the American Freedmen's Union Commission (AFUC), and religious ones like the American Missionary Association, received federal funds under Howard's direction. The New York–based AMA founded Fisk University in Nashville and opened four normal schools in Georgia for black instruction. The AFUC took federal dollars for normal schools at Richmond, Virginia, and Raleigh, North Carolina.

Squabbles between the secular teaching organizations and the devoutly evangelical ones were a distraction, but by and large, much was achieved by both groups. The Oberlin College–trained and Quaker volunteers faced local snubs and worse. Despite many handicaps, these eager young pietists fanned out throughout the Old South to start African American primary education in whatever buildings they could find available. AFUC and AMA also opened primary schools. Classrooms were often overcrowded, so eager were children and parents for learning. In Athens, Georgia, one beleaguered schoolmistress tried to hold her primary class at no more than one hundred students. Parents came to her, though, begging her to let their youngsters in. One parent pleaded, "do let them come if you please, ma'am, and if you can't teach them even a little, just let them sit and hear what the rest learn; they'll be sure to catch it." Despite their financial limitations, black parents often organized their own schools with their own money. In 1867, when Northern charities were the most generous, the superintendent of the Arkansas Freedmen's Bureau had to deal with a great number of requests for teachers in places where the parents had managed to scrape up the funds for salaries and schoolhouses.[14]

The whole educational situation was both heartening and disappointing. Too many freed people were unable to gain even the rudiments of literacy. Still, many did, despite the handicaps. Along with facing inadequate diets, long distances to walk, and meager schoolroom supplies, some pupils would arrive to discover their schoolhouse burnt to the ground by disgruntled whites. As early as 1863 in Memphis, Tennessee, a black Baptist church that had been used for schooling purposes was destroyed. Samuel Glyde Swain complained in 1864 that Southern whites "are bitter against every thing that is northern, and, espiecially [sic] against everything that is done to advance the condition of the freedmen." They "do everything they can to try to break" the schools up. Schoolhouses were set ablaze—four in Maryland in 1865. Eighteen teenagers were killed in Virginia in school fires between September 1865 and September 1866. Placing black schools within proximity to some valuable property was a somewhat helpful strategy in discouraging white vandals from starting fires that might spread beyond their intended targets.[15] It was a remarkable educational effort that bravely proceeded in the face of all the obstacles. In the 1880s, white attitudes, at least among the cognoscenti, shifted. Southern industrialists realized that working-class literacy might be of economic advantage. One told his fellow industrialists, "Wherever public schools have been established . . . the industrial classes, becoming more intelligent, have proved more skillful and efficient; and all competing countries must likewise establish public schools, or be supplanted in the markets of the world." Many other whites, however, remained unconvinced and preferred an illiterate and malleable labor force.[16]

Philanthropic work with freedmen of any kind aroused the fury of Southern whites. Guerilla activity against the Republican's Union League, organized and largely led by white Northern Republicans, and other suppressive efforts occurred before the Ku Klux Klan became the symbol for all the various fancifully named units of armed whites including the White Cross, White League, and so on. Younger men rather than the old-timers were in the forefront of the battle for white honor against the despised black population. As Steven Hahn points out, all the first Klan members in Pulaski, Tennessee, in 1865 were battle-tried, young Confederate soldiers. An Arkansas Republican governor complained that, in suppressing the Klan, he had found that Confederates who had won U.S. Army release from being considered prisoners of war disappeared with their horses, pistols, and ammunition and joined the Klan's forces. Such veterans as these were eager to reestablish white dominance over the now freed population as fast as possible. They feared that chapters of the Union League were planning a general African American insurrection.[17]

Following an earlier surrender to white supremacy under Johnson, Republican Reconstruction began auspiciously. Shortly after taking the office of president in 1869, Ulysses S. Grant prompted congressional readmission into the Union of Virginia, Mississippi, Georgia, and Texas but stipulated that all citizens should have voting rights. He attached his name to a law guaranteeing equal rights to the residents, white and black, of Washington, D.C., and enforced laws with the Department of Justice. His attorney general, Amos Akerman, saw no reason to be overly conciliatory toward white Southerners. In 1871, under the Enforcement Acts, the administration faithfully pursued vigilantes like Klansmen in nine counties of South Carolina. Some federal troops occupied major Southern centers, though that number was far too small to be as effective as the need for aggressive intervention required.[18]

"Legally, the changes wrought by emancipation and the war amendments were colossal," writes historian Willie Lee Rose. Suddenly, slaves had become masters and mistresses of their own lives—a reversal of roles seldom if ever found in history. Southerners had thought blacks, Rose writes, too dangerous to hold the vote.[19] Indeed, the sudden conferment of rights was almost a miracle. Unfortunately, nineteenth-century laws and public attitudes did not foresee that the new citizens would need vastly more help than the times, money, and will could then provide. Only in the fourth generation after Reconstruction would there be the substantial social, legal, political, and attitudinal changes longed for by African Americans.

Political assassinations and murders, lynchings, beatings of both white and black Republican state and local officials, and lesser forms of intimidation made true two-party democracy nearly impossible in the former slave states. Between 1865 and 1872, whites slaughtered several hundred freed people. Lynchers claimed that their timely actions prevented black insurrectionary plots, but this explanation was so implausible it was soon abandoned. In reality, the federal conferment of suffrage for adult black men furnished reason enough for some of the most brutal attacks. Who in the South with white skin would tolerate such effrontery as blacks going to the polls? Nonetheless, some contests on local, state, and national offices did result in the election of freedmen.[20] It was a long, gory campaign; the blood chills and the heart almost loses faith in American ideals of fair play and democracy when thinking of the riots and deaths in towns throughout the South, especially in Memphis and New Orleans. The blacks' only offense was the attempt to exercise the right to vote.[21]

The sporadic violence against freed people was a way for white people to terrorize blacks into acquiescence by brutally killing those who intentionally or accidentally stepped over some invisible and shifting line of permissible behavior. The brutality was not generated because blacks outnumbered whites. Such regions of the Black Belt with high population densities saw relatively low rates of lynching. In such places, black people were more likely to know at least a few whites as neighbors or employers. They were also able to turn to black friends and allies should they be pursued by lynch mobs.[22]

Lynchings tended to flourish where whites were surrounded by what they called "strange niggers," blacks with no white to vouch for them, blacks with no reputation in the neighborhood, blacks without other blacks to aid them. Lynching seemed both more necessary and more feasible in places such as the Gulf Plain of Alabama and Georgia, including the Black Belt from the Mississippi River to the eastern coast. In those places, most blacks and whites did not know one another, much less share ties of several generations. The black populations often moved from one year to the next in search of jobs at lumber camps and large plantations and farms.[23]

Faced with a persistent Southern insurgency through both the Johnson and Grant administrations, the Civil War victors soon wearied of the expenses and complications of creating a biracial party system under a Republican policy of "nation-building." By 1876, the North welcomed an end to the democratic experiment. As the historian Nina Silber observes, we must "understand the crucial historical transformation in which, as some have said, 'the North won the war, but the South won the peace.'" Indeed, given the pressing business of making money and settling western lands, Northerners did not long dwell on the glories and miseries of the recent war. It was best, many seemed to feel, to forget the experience. Instead, a different view arose. "The past is dead," pronounced the *Trenton State Gazette.* "Let us live in the present and act the part of men."[24]

The effort to transform the South into a replica of the victors' culture and politics would become self-defeating. Minimal armed enforcement was insufficient against white violence designed to intimidate and humiliate black voters. But the country turned away from reform and even began to agree with Southern spokesmen that African Americans were unworthy of further concern. The abolitionist dream of a nation completely freed from the influence and mentality of the old "slavocracy" vanished from Lincoln's party and from the nation as a whole.

Wendell Phillips, the veteran abolitionist, had long entertained hopes that Republicans would not backslide from giving blacks voting rights and maintaining a close eye on events. It was not to be. Phillips reacted strongly when the Republicans won the presidency over Democrat Samuel Tilden in the disputed election of 1876. Republican Party leaders promised the Democrats that the first order of business after the inauguration of Rutherford B. Hayes would be to remove federal troops from the former slave states. Phillips, the embittered veteran New England reformer, warned that the results would be "starvation and blood" as a matter of Southern policy in ousting black officials, suppressing the vote, and leaving matters to white leaders eager for office and the return of white domination. What will occur, he wisely predicted, would be "a 'sold south'—the slave power under a new name," which would control the nation. But the Northern public cared little about further intervention southward. Phillips was almost the lone voice speaking against this act of betrayal and dishonor. Even as he fulfilled his pledge about the troops, Hayes did make a small gesture. In 1877, he appointed Frederick Douglass a U.S. marshal. Douglass also went on to receive further offices under the Republican banner. That kept one fiery speaker for the race very quiet. Other veterans of the antislavery cause had died, like Lewis Tappan of New York in

1870, or were old and feeble by this period.[25] Who would listen to old men anyhow?

This Northern effort, however flawed and understaffed, was to be the first of many failed attempts undertaken by American policymakers throughout succeeding years to impose egalitarian principles. Few succeeded. It was left to the blacks themselves to make their own way. Black women were especially active in this regard. Not until recent times have historians rediscovered the recollections and autobiographies of slave women. Harriet Jacobs was a most astute observer of her surroundings with whites as well as her own people. She and other women narrators described the inhuman treatment so many had endured under white ownership. Their male colleagues had not stressed the plight of masters' rape of black women slaves. It was too salacious for the polite, Yankee evangelicals who attended their lectures or read their books. Women were less constrained in the books they wrote on the subject of slavery and its humiliations. More than one hundred book-length narratives were written by women before the end of the Civil War. Thousands of freed women of color spent their closing years seeking family members lost during the war. Like the Confederate women engaged in "Lost-Cause" memorialization, black women formed associations to commemorate the men who had fought for freedom in the war.[26]

Meanwhile, to counteract their deep sense of humiliation out of the great loss, white Southerners developed the legend of the "Lost Cause." The memorialization of the glorious Rebel dead stoked the flames of bitterness about black freedom and Yankee domination for years to come. Damning myths took new life in the aftermath of black emancipation. It was widely believed that freedmen and -women carried contagious diseases. Years before, Dr. Benjamin Rush of the Philadelphia Hospital surmised that darker skin color arose because blacks were all afflicted with leprosy. Proslavery writers had reiterated similar theories.[27]

In the prerevolutionary backcountry, including the western portions of the Carolinas, Georgia, Mississippi, and into Texas, where some settlers went to escape doubtful pasts, it was occasionally difficult to figure who was white and who was black among the free population. They were far too busy to care: They were clearing land, raising cabins, and building roads. In "civilized" places, however, it mattered tremendously. The fluidity of southwestern society gradually hardened, and whiteness became a paramount necessity for advancement.[28]

Christopher Morris brilliantly teases out the muddled history of the family of Gideon Gibson in Mississippi. They were suspected of being not completely white, but their rise from poverty, illiteracy, and lower-class manners to wealth, literacy, and even piety, in one case, transformed their standing into acceptability. The family gradually covered their shame by fashioning legends about their distinguished origins. Morris concludes, "The strange career of Gideon Gibson is a story of the South, not only the South, mind you, but especially there, where what was black and what was white could never be known for sure but had to be to known for sure. The South was built on knowledge of white supremacy. Memory knows better."[29]

Still more humiliating than public doubts about one's fitness to belong in white society was the claim of black rape of white women, which was a significant fear among freedmen. Such alleged rapes justified burnings and hangings, even in the eyes of otherwise gentlemanly members of the Southern intelligentsia. Yet, these burnings and hangings were no less horrible than the contemporary stoning of women for alleged sexual misbehavior in some Islamic communities.

The Virginia-reared journalist Thomas Nelson Page applauded what he saw as the gallant impulse that drove Southern males to employ mob torture and murder as the means to retaliate for a white woman's loss of honor. Like other Southern leaders, Tom Watson as a young lawyer in Georgia was convinced that emancipation had been a colossal and perilous mistake. Freedom gave the lustful black male, he argued, access to alcohol and white women, and allowed such men to engage in brawls with whites, commit theft, and otherwise disrupt society. What if black boys began to run about nude? Could they be stopped? Still worse, shameless white girls might find these young black bucks attractive, bed with them, and wind up pregnant. The South would become a brothel devoted to mongrelization, Tom Watson predicted.[30] Such attitudes prepared the way for heightened white violence against vulnerable African Americans.

One factor in the heightening of white violence was not just fear of black competition in the white world but something far deeper—the persistent idea of vengeance for the overthrow of the old regime. The late, eminent historian C. Vann Woodward demonstrated that humiliation played a major role in this period of Southern life.[31] That sense of unbearable loss helps to explain, though not to justify, how newly freed African Americans became so harshly victimized.

According to one scholar, "In the end, Reconstruction did not fail; it was defeated." Union General George A. Custer, for instance, reported to a congressional committee that the assassination of blacks in Texas had risen to "weekly if not daily" tragedies.[32] Over two-thirds of such crimes against freed people were the work of small bands of guerilla vigilantes, former Rebel veterans.

The Joint Congressional Reconstruction Committee, established in 1865, was assigned by Congress to draw up what was deemed necessary for returning the South to the Union and protecting freedmen's newly acquired rights. In the face of the turmoil that whites were creating in the postbellum period, the committee reached the obvious conclusion that only additional military force could suppress the slaughter and mayhem. Riots, mob executions, and assassinations wrecked the Republican-organized legislative bodies. In Louisiana, for example, the state legislature overwhelmingly threw out Lincoln's 1864 liberal constitution, which included black representation, and reinstalled the Confederate constitution of 1861. James M. Wells, the provisional governor, however, issued a call for a new constitutional convention to meet in New Orleans in 1870. It was to be headed by a black member of the 1864 convention. Fearing for his life, Wells then conveniently disappeared from the scene. The New Orleans mayor, who led a mob of terrorists under the name of the Southern Cross, organized citizens and the police to stop the proceedings. They surrounded the meeting hall where 150 delegates had convened. A black clergyman urged the infuriated whites not to fire on them as they were all unarmed. He begged that they simply be arrested if need be. "We don't want any prisoners," came the reply. "You have all got to die!" In that engagement almost 50 lost their lives. The number of injured came to 170.[33]

South Carolina, the source of the initial disunion effort in the name of the revolutionary fathers, had another revolution on 4 July 1876, a centennial celebration as it were. A black militia outfit was marching in Hamburg, South Carolina. A pair of white men picked a quarrel with the unit's captain. Not long afterward, former Confederate general Matthew C. Butler ordered the black troops to disband and their leader to apologize to the whites for his so-called impudence. The captain refused. A fierce skirmish broke out between Butler's force and the black militiamen. At least thirty-five African Americans lost their lives. Some were killed after being captured. White South Carolinians agreed that Butler's men were fully justified in sustaining white honor and preserving white power. It was a second Fourth of July Declaration of Independence, gloated the Charleston *News and Courier*. General Butler's band had rescued the state "just as surely as the white Colonists were relieved by their own efforts, from British tyranny, so shall the white citizens of South Carolina be relieved, in one way or another, from the rapine and rascality of a so-called Republicanism."[34]

Along with even more horrendous riots and massacres in New Orleans, Memphis, and elsewhere, these deliberate though uncoordinated atrocities were successful in overthrowing the hated biracial experiment. The U.S. Army, functioning whenever local and state enforcement was weak or collaborating with the marauders, had been used sporadically and often half-heartedly to quell domestic racial riots and lawlessness. After the disputed election in 1876, Republican Rutherford B. Hayes promised the Democrats to withdraw the federal troops from the South entirely.[35]

Dispirited by the constant news of white insurgency against freed people, Northerners wondered if further military activity was worthwhile. In 1878, only a year after Hayes's surrender of the South to the victorious ex-Rebels, Congress passed the Posse Comitatus Act. It barred federal military interference in the states, a further betrayal of a national obligation to assure republican forms of government for all citizens throughout the nation. It left the freed people with no federal protection whatsoever.[36]

In the years after the Reconstruction effort failed, there followed an era of systematic black disfranchisement. Vagrancy laws were passed to hold black labor to the land, and an apartheid public policy assured white dominance and a persistent shaming of the under-race. Leaders of the African American community sometimes harken back nostalgically to the Reconstruction period as if it were, Woodward comments, a time of jubilee and freedom. To be sure, for a few years after 1865, freedmen could vote and a considerable number held office. Land ownership was not out of the question. African Americans mingled with whites on street cars and trains and in restaurants and hotels. A few here and there were able to attend schools with whites. But it was empathically not a "Golden Age," Woodward continues, "for anybody. There is too much irony mixed with tragedy."[37]

Yet, despite the oppressive circumstances, black resilience was remarkable. Psychologically, they were more stable than many whites. The suicide rate in African American communities was relatively low, compared with white figures. Suicide was far more common when blacks were in bonds. Likewise, freedmen in the South were less likely to commit murder than whites. Between 1872 and 1887, however, the homicide rate among African

Americans rose dramatically. Blacks killed other blacks at the same rate as whites were killing fellow whites, though whites killed more overall. African Americans felt keenly their loss of political power and the humiliations and terror that lynchings imposed on the whole community. New Orleans was easily the murder capital of the Deep South. There, blacks murdered one another at three times the pace of whites, a rate that soared to 30 per 100,000.[38]

Among whites, at the same time, veterans were not free from the traumas caused by the horrors of battle and military upheavals. Historian David Silkenat finds that in North Carolina, the role of postwar depression and suicide were primarily the result of war experiences. Post-traumatic stress disorder was not a known illness until the Vietnam War. Yet, little doubt remains that the disorder affected both former Union and Rebel soldiers in other states besides North Carolina. Medical and asylum records in the South leave much to be desired, but alcoholism and suicidal thoughts were not easily overcome. Constant artillery bombardments, sniper fire, rat-infested trenches, inadequate clothing, and worn-out footwear—these and other miseries, but especially the sudden fatality of a mate, could cause reactions of horror and dread. The onset of depression and actual self-inflicted death sometimes came years after the war. The celebration of the Lost Cause in parades, with bands playing jolly tunes, might relieve some feelings of aloneness but not always.[39] Such troubles added to the sense of despair that so many whites experienced in the postwar years—and that meant trouble for blacks. They were blamed for the tormented state of the whites' country.

In the meantime, the determination to overthrow Reconstruction became part of the Lost-Cause movement. This effort was intended to emphasize the glory of the secession effort and justify the repression of black power and hopes. The fires of the Confederate spirit were only partially extinguished. Gone was the dedication to slavery, and few wished it back from the grave. To advocate its return would have been foolish and counterproductive when white Southerners yearned for Northern capital investments to build the "New South." But that did not diminish Southern loyalists' continuing contempt for blacks and their aspirations. White hatred of the Yankee monster still flourished. Moreover, there was no repudiation of the Cavalier past. The South had done no wrong and promoted no injustice, so Southerners argued.[40]

The heroes of the Southern struggle stood in carved stone on their pedestals, facing North, muskets in hand, as they presided over county

courthouse squares. Insular in their outlook—as they always had been—
the Confederate enthusiasts expected the Northern people to acknowledge
the valor and daring of the Rebel officers and men. An expert on the Lost
Cause, Gaines M. Foster, observes that during the 1870s, "a coalition of organizations headquartered in Virginia began what amounted to a Confederate revitalization movement." General Jubal A. Early and his colleagues
"brooded over defeat, railed against the North, and offered the image of
the Confederacy as an antidote to postwar change." Early's organization
failed. But a later organization, the United Confederate Veterans, was
instantly popular and swiftly enrolled almost 100,000 supporters. In his
postwar memoir, Early bitterly fulminated, "We lost nearly everything but
honor, and that should be religiously guarded." What new outrages could
be expected from the Northern victors who would never offer fair dealings
and respect? Early believed the North was delivering to its conquered foes
"even more vindictive hatred than during the war, when we had arms in
our hands."[41]

Southern ladies were not to be outdone. Their society, The Sons and
Daughters of the Confederacy, was responsible for the erection of those
uniformed statues in the centers of Southern towns. Despite the still-active
nostalgia for the glorious past, Southern memorializers were hard put to
fund commemorations to the South's "noble sons." The Panic of 1873, the
collapse of small banks, and the rise of unemployment affected fundrais-
ing severely. But when the economy improved nationwide in the 1880s,
as historian David W. Blight points out, the veneration of the Confederate
cause stoutly revived. In the 1890s, the United Daughters of the Confederacy (UDC) was able to organize over four hundred chapters with seventeen thousand total members. This effort was a way for Southern whites to
match the Northern genealogical craze.[42]

One of the most popular organizations in the late 1890s was the Daughters of the American Revolution (DAR), which Congress chartered in 1896.
In this group, descendants of Revolutionary War heroes from the North
and South were honored by women who had descended from veterans of
that war. Both the UDC and the DAR were means to celebrate the longev-
ity, power, and social standing of ancestral glorification, a veneration of an
Anglo-Saxon heritage. In both sections of the country, then, honor found a
comfortable site in the minds of the rich and, in the white South, formerly
rich members of an American elite. Moreover, for Northern members, honoring the dead, recent or antique, was a white Protestant response to the

influx of immigrants from both Western and Eastern Europe. In the South, its purpose was to honor the white skin and dishonor the black.

At the same time, white Southerners wrapped the cloak of honor around their former slaveholding. That was hardly unexpected. No people steeped in a centuries-old tradition or custom will easily express remorse for deeds or habits that their forefathers had sanctioned. (The German reaction to defeat operated similarly after World War II.) In Columbus, Mississippi, the Presbyterian clergyman James Lyon, writes Gaines Foster, told his congregation that they "may have to lament before God, either for neglect of duty toward our servants, or for actual wrong while the relation lasted." That was a standard conviction of antebellum Christian slave owners and their wives. Lyon added that he saw no need for Southerners "to bow the head in humiliation before men, or to admit that the memory of many of our dear kindred is to be covered with shame, because, like Abraham, Isaac, and Jacob, they had bond-servants born in their own houses, or bought with their money." Such an interpretation of divine wisdom was commonly heard in many post–Civil War Southern pulpits. Northerners sometimes explained that God had punished the South for its sin of bondage. That judgment only elicited confusion and vigorous denial from Southerners. Instead, they retorted that Yankees would one day feel the fire of God's wrath for waging war against a peace-loving South.[43]

Other denials of Southern culpability were also popular in the wake of military defeat and continued in histories written in the early twentieth century. Walter L. Fleming, a leading Southern historian and officer in the Sons of Confederate Veterans, serves as a typical example of the conservative interpretation of Reconstruction. Along with the so-called necessity of mob actions against black offenders, Fleming accepted as essential the disfranchisement of African Americans. He and other scholarly professionals claimed that their votes were bought and sold by Carpetbaggers.[44]

Fleming wrote that black soldiers' occupying Southern states were "everywhere considered offensive by the native whites." He elaborated, "The Negro soldier, impudent by reason of his new freedom, his new uniform, and his new gun, was more than Southern temper could tranquilly bear, and race conflicts were frequent." Impudence had not been tolerated in the good old days of slavery. That epithet sprang into new life in the years following the war and well into the twentieth century.[45] Fleming was in favor of the Ku Klux Klan and the necessity, as he saw it, for black lynching. The Klan, he maintained, "frightened the negroes and bad whites into better conduct, and it encouraged the conservatives and aided them to regain control of society, for without the operations of the Klan the black districts would never have come again under white control." He did, however, admit that occasionally the methods used were too violent and weakened respect for established law.[46]

Given his bias, Fleming naturally understated the role of antifreedmen violence. In 1865, blacks had won a degree of freedom. They had actually mobilized their own military forces, called the Union League, as a response to roaming white Rebel veterans who began to terrorize freed people. In 1867, Northern chapters began planting branches in the defeated South to educate freedmen in their new rights, serve as labor arbitrators, and undertake other helpful activities for black farmers especially.[47] But such chapters became targets for white retaliation.

After 1888, violence against black voters grew far worse. Over seven hundred blacks and some whites were lynched between 1889 and 1893. The alleged crimes cited as justification included theft, murder, attempted murder, and rape (about 20 percent of the incidents). The point, however, was to humiliate African Americans and to drive them from the political arena. The practice continued well into the twentieth century. John Lee, mentioned in this chapter's epigraph, for instance, was executed by irregular justice and burnt in El Paso, Texas, in 1916.[48]

With business interests in the forefront of the effort, the still locally powerful white elite easily recruited farmers and laborers to join in the antisuffrage movement. In some instances, in what were called "fusionist" efforts, some lesser offices were assigned to black candidates on the Democratic slates to entice African American voters to abandon the Republican Party. But that policy proved ineffective. It was deemed insufficient for eradicating the African American vote. White Southern progressives claimed that African Americans would sell their votes to the highest bidder.

In Mississippi, the disfranchisement movement did not immediately win the support of all Democratic leaders. Governor Robert Lowry vetoed the bill to convene a convention to rewrite the state's constitution to lessen black influence. The expense was one factor, but the governor also believed it was unnecessary. Whites controlled nearly all public offices by 1890. But the Populists, mostly farmers, sought complete denial of all African American suffrage.[49]

The new white-dominated regimes throughout the South found little need for stable governance and inaugurated belt-tightening of the severest sort—chiefly at freed people's expense. The result of these measures meant the loss of nearly half the New Orleans policemen, most of whom were withdrawn from black districts. The African American members of the force were the first fired, and there were heavy cuts in public education. Unemployment undermined the black community's viability. These residents were the earliest to encounter the hazards of modern urban life in the South, according to historian Randolph Roth.[50]

The last blow to Reconstruction republicanism occurred in Wilmington, North Carolina, in 1898. The events there were preceded in 1896 by the U.S. Supreme Court decision in *Plessy v. Ferguson* that permitted Jim Crow full license by declaring the legitimacy of "separate but equal" treatment of African Americans. In Wilmington, whites overthrew the lawful government of the city in what could be called a coup d'état. Whites expelled the legally elected officials from the city and went on a rampage, killing and beating black residents. Neither the state governor, Daniel Lindsay Russell, nor President William McKinley responded to the crisis.[51]

Wilmington had grown in population during and after the war. In 1865, slaves from outlying areas went there to find food because of Union destruction of farms, crops, and cattle. Many blacks remained and prospered thereafter, forming a solid middle class. By 1898, African Americans comprised the majority of voters and had established a decent government under a biracial Republican Party banner. A leader of the black community, Alexander Manly, headed the only black newspaper in the state. His editorials in the Wilmington *Daily Record* stoutly defended his people against the lies and misrepresentations of the white supremacist Democrats under the direction of Alfred Moore Waddell.

Manly vigorously denounced lynching in an August 1898 editorial. The piece was a reply to a Wilmington *Messenger* article that claimed lynching was the sole answer to black lust for white women. Once again, raising the issue of women's honor was a way to assert white male dominance, to signal the subordinate place of women in the honor scheme, and to humiliate blacks. However justified Manly's position was, his denunciation of lynching added to the arsenal of white supremacist propaganda. This unrelenting determination to maintain the honor of white males at the expense of another race and gender was the deplorable legacy that the nineteenth-century South bequeathed to the next century.[52]

Lynchings grew worse during the closing years of the nineteenth century and the early part of the twentieth century. The purpose was to intimidate the black population into complete acquiescence. It is tragic but curious that this method enjoyed such widespread white appeal in an alleg-edly evangelical land. As theological professor James H. Cone eloquently laments the era, "African Americans did not doubt that their lives were filled with trouble: how could one be black in America during the lynch-ing era and not know about the existential agony that trouble created for black people? . . . Trouble followed them everywhere, like a shadow they could not shake." Cone points out that the cross that all Christians vener-ate was the most torturous mode of execution known to man, but in a sense "the lynching tree" was equally horrific. Sometimes the ceremony was prolonged to further humiliate and punish the black offender. White women and children were eager spectators as their men strung up blacks. The crime was often attributed to the alleged but unproven rape of a white woman, usually a fabrication. As W. E. B. Du Bois pointed out, "The white South feared more than Negro dishonesty, ignorance, and incompetency." What worried white Southerners most was "Negro honesty, knowledge, and efficiency." The white Christians' interpretation of their faith found nothing wrong with lynching and other crimes against blacks. In contrast, the Christian spirit sustained the African American community.[53]

The subject of lynching is vast and the historical literature so exten-sive that two examples will suffice. The first case concerns two victims, a husband and wife. They were subjected to hideous torture and death by a mob of forty armed whites in Okemah, Oklahoma, on 25 May 1911. Laura Nelson; her husband, Lawrence; and their fifteen-year-old son were seized after Lawrence killed a deputy sheriff who sought to arrest him for stealing a cow. He had pled guilty and was sent to state prison but was returned to the less safe jail in Okemah. Protecting her son, who had actually stolen the cow, Laura claimed she had fired the shot that killed the lawman and was arrested. An armed gang arrived and kidnapped them from the jail. Laura was raped. Then both were hanged from a local bridge. Hundreds witnessed the execution. Scores of Kodak cameras recorded the event, and some photographs were sold as postcards. The father of the folk singer Woody Guthrie attended the lynching.[54]

The second example concerns the gruesome fate of Jesse Washington. He was a seventeen-year-old black youth, born in 1897 in a small, rural town in Texas. His crime was the murder of his employer's wife, Lucy Fryer, near Waco. He admitted his guilt in the spring of 1916 and was convicted by the court. Inevitably, he was sentenced to death, but the Waco townspeople had a swifter punishment in mind. After all, he had murdered a white woman, the most serious offense a black could then commit. Within a few minutes after the sentence was announced, a horde of onlookers jumped over the court railing, seized the frightened defendant, and pushed officials aside. Beaten first with sticks, shovels, and bricks, Washington had all his clothes stripped off.

Screaming from the torture and humiliation, he found himself in front of the City Hall where a great bonfire was set ablaze under a tall tree. Fifteen thousand Texans were estimated to be present for the grim occasion—men, women, and children. Among the spectators were the Waco police chief and mayor, cheering the participants. Before meeting the flames, Washington received a coating of coal oil. The mob raised him under the tree and slowly lowered him into the inferno. After his agonizing death, some townsmen cut fingers off from the corpse as souvenirs. The final hideous insult was to hang the cadaver from a pole.[55]

The fate of Jesse Washington temporarily aroused national indignation, but the mood quickly evaporated. Although most lynchings occurred in the South and Southwest, the practice did include other parts of the country. In fact, twenty-six states, including Illinois and North Dakota, had at least one lynching on record by 1918.[56] When the issue arose in the Supreme Court, the justices appeared to be more concerned with preserving the law of segregation than they were with protecting blacks from such horrors.[57] Southern politicians prevented any action in Congress. A bill did pass the House but was tabled in the Senate. The two incidents of murder described above were merely a small fraction of the 4,743 people so treated between 1882 and 1968. Over 3,446 of these victims were black and three-quarters of them were in the South.[58] This was the legacy of white supremacy and the revenge for the South's humiliation in 1865.

6

AMERICA AS WORLD POWER, 1898–1918

HONOR, RACE, AND HUMILIATION

> Think
> Neither fear nor courage saves us. Unnatural vices
> Are fathered by our heroism. Virtues
> Are forced upon us by our imprudent crimes.
>
> —T. S. ELIOT, "GERONTION"

> *Maudite soit la guerre* — Accursed be war.
>
> —FRENCH WAR MEMORIAL AT GENTIOUX-PIGEROLLES

Given the tragic and costly Southern humiliation in the collapse of the Confederacy, one might expect Southern whites to have opposed further adventures in a European war, particularly under the Union flag. But the nation had fought Spain in 1898, "a splendid little war," and that may have helped allay some of the conservative Southern fears of entering a costly and centralizing war. Thus, military honor maintained a steady influence, especially on Southerners, through the Cuban intervention, the occupation of the Philippines, and the First World War. Each of these engagements presented a different set of issues. In each, there were moments of severe distress, even inexcusable violations of justice.

Consciousness of honor and what was required of it may have been expressed less often than in the Civil War by military and civilian alike. Nonetheless, the code still persisted among the general populace into the early twentieth century. Southern Populists, however, protested military adventures for fear of unexpected consequences affecting white control of politics. On this question honor still obtained, but how it should be advanced took different forms.

The Cuban situation raised questions in the South especially. Northern jingoists demanded an end to Spanish colonial rule, or misrule, of the island. Some Populists in the former slave states, however, were concerned that a liberated Cuba might export its excess labor to America and increase the so-called dangers that dark-skinned people would bring with them.

Moreover, Southerners raised their usual complaints about the further strengthening of a federal bureaucracy, an increase in federal taxes, and a possible return of Union troops to protect and encourage black voting.[1] All this would violate the white South's sense of honor and the age-old rules of white supremacy. There was especially strong opposition to Northern imperial dreams among some Southern congressmen. They feared Wall Street manipulations abroad would solely benefit the corporations and bankers of Manhattan.

"National bankers will profit by this war. The new bonds give them the basis for new banks, and their power is prolonged," wrote Tom Watson of Georgia, a leading Populist who became very racist after his defeat in 1896 for president, in his Populist journal. "What are we going to get out of this war as a nation? Endless trouble, complications, expense. Republics cannot go into the conquering business and remain republics. Militarism leads to military domination, military despotism. Imperialism smooths the way for the emperor." Indeed, Watson had a point when he observed that Spain was no worse than Great Britain, Belgium, France, the Netherlands, or other imperial powers in their oppression of their subjects.[2]

On the other hand, some wealthy Southerners came to the conclusion that the acquisition of colonial territory might enhance the prospects of industrialization and growing export interests in cotton textiles. Senator Roger Q. Mills of Texas linked forces with Joseph Wheeler of Alabama and ex-minister to Spain Hannis Taylor to promote opportunities in foreign trade. In 1898, one Georgia cotton factory owner announced, "We must have the people of the whole wide earth for our customers. It is commercial conquest upon which we should be bent."[3]

The prospect of seizing Cuba arose from the insurrection there in 1868. Southerners applauded the rebels' seeking freedom from Spanish imperialism. But racism created some ambivalence about the situation. Whites dreaded an influx of yet more dark-skinned people, having just reduced others to powerlessness. The Wilmington *Morning Star* warned North Carolinians that their state might anticipate an "incorporation of several millions of sable citizens into the 'grand brotherhood of the Union.'" There were Southern men with Northern ideas, such as Senator John Tyler Morgan and Congressman Hilary Abner Herbert, both of Alabama. They sought to expand markets, and build shipyards and other commercial ventures.[4] Yet fear of the federal government's intrusion into Southern race relations and higher tax rates kept most Southern politicians loyal to older alliances. That seemed more important than the pleasures and excitement of another war, still the standard honor code of old.

As Grover Cleveland's secretary of the navy, Herbert swiftly found the means to expand naval armaments and launch new warships. As it turned out, Admiral George Dewey would have a fleet equipped to rout the Spanish navy when the Spanish-American War began. That occurred after the sinking of the USS *Maine* in Havana harbor on 18 February 1898, an event in which 266 sailors died. A Spanish board of inquiry came to the conclusion that the explosion that destroyed the ship was due to combustion in the coal bunker located near the ship's munitions stores. Other inquiries, the last in 1998, conjectured that a submarine mine sank the battleship. The truth may never be fully known.[5]

In any event, the long simmering mistrust between the United States and the corrupt and brutal colonial rule of Spain forced President William J. McKinley to resort to war. The president, the last one to have fought in the Civil War, knew what military action might mean in terms of lives lost and money squandered, no matter the size or capability of the enemy. In his inaugural address on 4 March 1897, he stated his position: "War should never be entered upon until every agency of peace has failed; peace is preferable to war in almost every contingency."[6] It was an ideal that he hoped would mean no preemptive strike against Spain. Under political pressure, however, he had to abandon this policy as a fever to unshackle the suffering Cuban civilians grew worse, especially among Yankees. Vainly, McKinley strove for a peaceful resolution with the Spanish monarchy, but in its pride, Spain rejected all proposals. Thought to be weak and indecisive, McKinley lost public respect, a state of affairs that must have vexed him considerably. Once again, most Americans, including Southerners, found warfare the only solution.

Finally, on 11 April 1898, McKinley handed the issue to Congress. He did not ask for a declaration of war, but Congress voted for it anyhow on 20 April. After considerable debate on the joint resolution for war, the two houses denied in the so-called Teller Amendment any intention to annex Cuba. Senator Henry M. Teller of Colorado composed the text, which announced "That the people of the Island of Cuba are, of right ought to be, free and independent."[7] The amendment helped to allay Southern worries about an influx of dark-skinned voters into the Deep South.

Southern opinion grew ever more positive as war approached. Responding with the customary stress on Southern honor, Congressman (later Senator) Joseph Weldon Bailey of Texas reminded fellow Southern legislators that the Cuban people were undergoing trials similar to those the South had recently experienced in Reconstruction. He demanded vengeance for the sinking of the *Maine* while he claimed to have "no sympathy for those rash, intemperate spirits who would provoke war simply for the sake of fighting." The analogy with American Reconstruction was, of course, false. As the historian Joseph Fry points out, "These southerners had no genuine empathy for nonwhites, either within the United States or out or abroad."[8]

Senator John Sharp Williams of Mississippi worried that the nation was running the danger of moral collapse: When "Chivalry is dead; manhood itself is sapped." For Southerners, that dread was united with the opportunity to criticize Yankees for the gross commercialism of East Coast culture. The sentiment contrasted with the suspicion of Wall Street conspiracies by Tom Watson and Benjamin R. Tillman, a rabid racist and governor of South Carolina. War would cleanse the nation of money-grubbing and demonstrate the cowardice of the financial moguls who plotted to keep Southern entrepreneurs in thrall. According to Senator Wilkinson Call of Florida, disaster would come from letting "this god of business" sap "the manhood and courage of our people." Such had been the warnings of secessionists in the 1850s. Now the latent hostility toward the Yankee conquerors and so-called Carpetbaggers flared up for this conflict at the turn of the century.[9]

Meanwhile, ordinary Southerners were caught up in war fever and saw this as a time for rejoining the Union and hoping for a welcoming Yankee hand, which was indeed forthcoming. The North no longer had much interest in the plight of African Americans. Congressman Bailey of Texas declared that the war against Spain might "forever efface from the memory of our countrymen those dreadful times of civil strife." Former Rebel General John B. Gordon of Georgia, who headed the United Confederate Veterans, predicted that the "too long delayed brotherhood and unity of the American People" would now face the common foreign foe as one undivided nation.[10]

Southern love of military action in the name of "national honor," as they now willingly called it, had not atrophied after 1865. In the actual fighting, ex-Confederate military leaders played less of a role than many would have liked. An exception was Joseph Wheeler, a former Rebel general. McKinley appointed Wheeler, Robert E. Lee's nephew, a major general in charge of volunteers, heading the cavalry division. When confronting Spanish forces in the Battle of Las Guasimas, the first engagement of the short war, "Fighting Joe" Wheeler got overly excited. The old gentleman was famously heard to shout, "We've got the Yankees on the run."[11]

Under Wheeler's command were Theodore Roosevelt's "Rough Riders," many of them horsemen from the South and West. The cavalry unit made national headlines for bravery after its famous charge at San Juan Hill. Roosevelt himself overcame Republican corruption scandals to be elected governor of New York on the basis of his bold dash and heroic display of manhood in the Cuban expedition. Known for his liberality toward African Americans and Jews, Roosevelt as president, however, perceived military honor in a way that overrode his concern for justice and equity in an episode in Brownsville, Texas.

In August 1906, black troops of the 25th Infantry Regiment, upon their arrival in Brownsville, had been harassed and insulted by locals. In one fracas, a white bartender lost his life and a policeman was wounded. The townspeople were convinced that the soldiers had murdered the bartender and demanded revenge. The troops' commanders explained that the soldiers had been asleep in their barracks and did not commit the crime.[12]

Someone had planted false, incriminating evidence. The U.S. Army inspector general investigated and accepted the locals' version. As a result, Roosevelt ordered 167 soldiers dishonorably discharged. It was a devastating blow to black military morale. Booker T. Washington urged the president to reconsider the issue, but he peremptorily refused. Not until the 1970s was there a new inspection of the evidence that revealed the earlier travesty of justice. On Richard Nixon's orders, pardons were issued posthumously, and Dorrie Willis, the only survivor, was honored in Washington.[13]

In the Spanish-American War, Teddy Roosevelt was delighted to have his Rough Riders at San Juan Hill flanked by black troops. As Roosevelt led his men up the hill, the Spanish fired at them from all sides. The black reinforcements were a distance away but moved swiftly to join the battle. Despite some losses, according to a New York reporter, they began "firing as they marched." Their aim, he continued, "was splendid, their coolness was superb, and their courage aroused the admiration of their comrades." According to one Rough Rider, "If it had not been for the Negro cavalry the Rough Riders would have been exterminated." Five African Americans earned the Medal of Honor. Another twenty-five received Certificates of Merit.[14]

Despite a successful conquest of Cuba, Southerners had reasons to worry. Those on the racist left—Benjamin R. Tillman of South Carolina and Tom Watson of Georgia, for example—continued their carping on familiar themes. Although Tillman managed to get over five million dollars in contracts for Charleston's seaport, he sneered about McKinley's war enthusiasm. He accused McKinley of collaborating with his bond-holding friends. Watson saw the poor white man's Populism as a victim of the fight with Spain. "The blare of the bugle drowned out the voice of the Reformer," he bewailed in his newspaper.[15] The new war bonds, issued to pay for the war, gave the wealthy cliques up North the means to establish profitable banks to the detriment of Southern interests.

Although Southern young men were enlisting daily, others, not necessarily Populists, had their doubts. Some remembered the effects of war from the disaster of 1861–65. The burden, others believed, would fall on the South more than on any other part of the nation. Industries just getting started would be stifled, taxes would rise, men would die from war wounds or yellow fever. Moreover, honor seemed a relic of the past for some whites. One wrote that he could not think of anything "more galling and humiliating than a gentleman serving under such conditions" as those he faced in a Houston militia unit. While others in Alabama relished the dances, parades, uniforms, admiring ladies, and banquets, they had little desire to liberate Cubans from their miseries.[16]

Unlike the reluctance of young white Southerners to fight in Cuba, African Americans again relished the opportunity to demonstrate their military prowess and sense of honor. Members of the entire black community gained heart from reports of the heroism of their compatriots in arms. The historian Willard B. Gatewood Jr. notes that an outpouring of material in books and the thriving black presses celebrated the valor of black troops. The hope was that the attention to this new American empire in Puerto Rico, the Philippines, and Cuba would lead to a renewed national interest in the problems and aspirations of black citizens at home. That was not to occur, at least not on the scale that the times required. Nonetheless, it is significant that war once again offered blacks a chance to renew their sense of dignity and self-identity.[17]

There was a sad irony in this expectation of better things to come: The only way, it seems, that black manhood would be even partially recognized in the white world was in fighting a war over other dark-skinned people. Nonetheless, while it was naive to anticipate white gratitude, it was an opportunity for young African Americans to show bravery equal to that of their forebears in the Civil War.

Four black regiments of the regular army, the 24th and 25th Infantry and the 9th and 10th Cavalry, had been established just after the Civil War ended. The War Department sent this contingent into Cuba before any other regiments due to an unrecognized racism: The department thought blacks would weather the tropical climate and fevers of that region better than whites. Happy to serve, however, the troops assumed that it was an honor to be the primary force.

The behavior of the white people of Tampa, Florida, from where the troops were to depart for the Cuban enterprise, dashed the black troops' hopes for better treatment by whites. The soldiers were subjected to demeaning experiences. Citizens and the local newspaper warned that there would be no breach in the segregation customs and laws, regardless of the blue uniforms. Of course, black soldiers resented this Southern white attitude. It was a relief to step aboard the ships taking them to Cuba.[18]

Their treatment in Florida may, however, have spurred their battle bravery. They acquitted themselves with high distinction at Las Guasimas, El Caney, and San Juan Hill. According to Gatewood, the African American troops "took their places alongside Crispus Attucks, Peter Salem, and others in the echelon of Negro American military heroes." In many black households, plaques depicting the 10th Cavalry's charge at San Juan occupied places of prominence. Scores of poems extolled the military exploits of the black troops in Cuba. Of these, perhaps the most popular was a lengthy hymn of praise entitled "The Charge of the Nigger Ninth."[19]

Naturally, black troops expected more than a casual pat on the back, but Russell Alexander Alger, McKinley's secretary of war, did nothing to honor these fearless veterans. Not one was recommended for promotion into the officer ranks of the regular army. One soldier wrote, "Colored men are always forgotten in war when our arms meet with success, but are speedily remembered when defeat perches above our door."[20] An anonymous writer in the 10th Cavalry unit complained bitterly. He explained that "our non-commissioned officers and privates have not been recognized as they should be." Some, he admitted, won places in volunteer regiments. Yet, he continued, "Would it not be more of an honor if they had the appointment in their own regiment? Is this prejudice to be continued? If they are worthy to step to the front and take command and lead through the greatest danger and yet are not worthy to hold a commission in their own regiments?" He suspected that the answer would come that bravery alone was not sufficient. Blacks were not educated "well enough to hold that position and have not had that military experience." They supposedly had to serve only under white officers. "Mr. Editor, it has been proven beyond a doubt that they were wrong. Where were our white officers on July 1st and 2nd; about one half were left behind in safety and made their appearance after the battle?"[21] Given the rank discrimination against them at the hands of the military and civilian populations, the soldiers showed remarkable forbearance, even when outrageously provoked.[22] Moreover, the racism displayed against the black regiments, and the politicians' warnings of postwar calamities in managing these mixed-race colonies, were most discouraging to the African American community.

✚ ✚ ✚

If, despite the Teller Amendment, Cuba presented continuing racial troubles for Southern whites, the Philippines, the new American colony, presented an even worse set of circumstances. The United States had acquired this colony as part of its victorious campaign against Spain. Hilary Herbert of Alabama, secretary of the navy under Grover Cleveland, warned that ignorant and uncivilized Filipinos could not possibly govern themselves and certainly could not rule Americans. The demagogue Tillman imagined fellow South Carolinians to be lying awake at night fearful of nightmarish thoughts. "Malays, Negritos, Japanese, Chinese, [and] mongrels of Spanish blood" would flock to America in the millions.[23]

Such views coincided, however, with Northern imperialist designs that included denigrating the character and integrity of the Filipino nationalists. Ironically, Northern ideas of honor were now being pronounced, it would seem, with a Southern accent. Americans would build a new, utopian society out of the supposedly unpromising materials of the Asian land. Congressman William H. Douglas, Republican from New York, explained that Americans would "show to the Filipino Man the necessity of taking on their shoulders a more active part in the domestic circle and support of the family." It was assumed that they lacked such basic abilities and only knew how to fight in uncivilized ways. Douglas's approach was similar to that of another congressman, James Albert Norton of South Carolina. He predicted that the United States would "vitally effect a change of character and conditions of the Filipino people for their good." President McKinley assured the nation that "benevolent assimilation" would characterize American control of the levers of power.[24] Such absurd dreams of transforming other peoples' society was not to end with the suppression of the

Philippine nationalist struggle under the famous guerilla leader, Emilio Aguinaldo.

The African American troops, particularly the 10th Cavalry, were divided in 1900. Some were assigned to remain in Cuba until 1902 doing garrison duty. Because they encountered far less hatred and humiliation in Havana than they had suffered in Tampa, it was, one soldier declared, "the finest" duty that they "had ever had." The rest of the cavalry unit were shipped to the Philippines.

The U.S. troops already there greeted them with insults. One soldier shouted, "What are you coons doing here?" Several members of the 25th Regiment, another all African American unit, retorted, "We have come to take up the White Man's Burden." Back home, the black press pointed to the hypocrisy of this adventure in imperial policy. The Indianapolis *Recorder* noted the lack of respect for the Filipinos, whose color, apparently, determined their political inadequacies. How could a nation, the editor queried, that would not protect the property, lives, and rights of the dark-skinned folk in America claim to bring American justice and sound governance to the Philippines? At first, the Filipinos were themselves overwhelmed and even fearful of these strange-looking soldiers. Over time, the Filipinos came to appreciate them in contrast to the mistrust the white troops engendered. The black troops were taller and huskier than the natives, but they looked similar, at least comparatively speaking.[25]

Not surprisingly, the reaction of these brave soldiers varied considerably. Some began to treat the natives with the kind of contempt and disrespect they knew all too well from their own American experiences. Those who had been humiliated might visit the same sort of treatment on others that they had experienced. Others, though, according to Gatewood, rejected white, Anglo-Saxon prejudices and mocked the notion of a "white man's burden." They sympathized with the rebels against the Americans' fellow countrymen. That was a dangerous line to take under military discipline, however, and the vast majority probably kept their opinions to themselves.[26]

Despite the continued hostility of white officers and men, black troops were proud of their participation, even during the antiguerilla phase of the Philippines enterprise. A member of the all-black 48th Infantry wrote a black newspaper about his feelings of resentment and his sense of honor. He praised his fellow soldiers for their "brilliant work," especially those led by black officers. He acknowledged that some white officers were sending out circulars applauding the black volunteers. It was quite appropriate "to tell the world that somebody is doing noble work." Unfortunately, he continued, too many white officers "are deadly opposed to Negro men wearing the bars. It matters not how soon the war will end (of course after the war is over the commissions will be taken from the noble blacks as was done after the close of the Spanish-American War)." He explained that "the Negro captains and lieutenants of the 48th are by their bravery and daring vindicating the race and stamping the lie to those rumors that the Negro makes poor officers and for Negroes to accomplish anything in battle must be commanded by white officers. The men of our regiments are proud of our black officers and will follow them where ever they lead."[27] The racist tensions in the army were not to be solved for many years to come.

If racism applied in the army to the treatment of black soldiers, so too were the native Filipinos subjected to humiliation. Honor disappeared entirely in the American attitude toward Emilio Aguinaldo. He had headed the insurrection against Spain with American assistance and served as provisional president, but was pushed aside when the United States decided to make the islands a colony. The Philippine leader remained defiant. Admiral George Dewey, who had transported Aguinaldo from his Hong Kong exile to Manila in May 1898, warned that Aguinaldo was "a defiant personality." Dewey himself had his early doubts about what should be done with the insurgency. "From my observation of Aguinaldo and his advisers I decided that it would be unwise to co-operate with him or his adherents in an official manner," Dewey declared condescendingly. "In short, my policy was to avoid any entangling alliance with the insurgents, while I appreciated that, pending the arrival of our troops, they might be of service." Dewey volunteered, though, a shrewd but prejudiced assessment of the rebellious Filipinos: "In my opinion, these people are far superior in their intelligence and more capable of self-government than the natives of Cuba."[28]

When the Spanish commander surrendered the colonial capital after Dewey's stunning victory over the Spanish navy, there was enough honor to gratify both the American and Spanish sailors, who had fought valiantly but were outgunned. But none was left for the insurgents, who were denied entry into Manila proper. The realization that they were not considered worthy allies was a hard reality to accept. Thus, U.S. policy was duplicitous from the start. Admiral Dewey predicted shrewdly, however, that it would require a huge American army to crush the anticolonial rebellion.

Faced with a devious power, Aguinaldo had every reason to be infuriated. He wrote a letter that the U.S. consul general Rounsevelle Wildman

had published in the New York *Journal:* "'Why should America expect me
to outline my policy, present and future, and fight blindly for her interests
when America will not be frank with me?' Tell me this: Am I fighting for
annexation, protection, or independence? It is for America to say, not me."
In an interview with President McKinley in Washington, Aguinaldo announced Philippine independence but was met by the president with stony
silence.[29] By the Treaty of Paris of 10 December 1898, Spain surrendered
to the United States the Philippines as well as Puerto Rico, the Marianas,
and Guam.[30] The United States would send 300,000 soldiers to the Asian
country to suppress the resulting rebellion.

American duplicity and dishonorable conduct did not exist in the
diplomatic sphere alone. From the very beginning, both sides committed
outrageous atrocities. The Americans, though, deserve greater condemnation since they had unjustly decided on a "nation-building mission" in the
customary imperial fashion. On 13 November 1898, Emilio Aguinaldo announced that his forces would engage in guerilla warfare. The insurgents
were generally illiterate, although the Moro people, an ethnic minority, had
mastered Arabic and studied the Koran. They had a keen sense of "humor;
honor, dignity, pride, self-respect, courage."[31] But literacy mattered far less
than fighting capacity.

Within a few months, five hundred U.S. troops had lost their lives. Am-
bushes and quick raids brought insurgent victories at a number of places.
As the list of the American dead and wounded mounted, McKinley even
thought of withdrawal. Instead, he began the alternative: total war, no
doubt to uphold national honor and wipe away any sign of cowardice or
military weakness before the international community.

Early guerilla successes led the adjutant general, Major General Henry
C. Corbin, to declare "that the time has arrived when more aggressive
operations would be in order." Secretary of War Elihu Root agreed: The
army was obliged to employ "methods which have proved successful in
our Indian campaigns in the West." To prepare for the new measures, on
20 December 1900, Major General Arthur MacArthur placed the islands
under martial law. Aguinaldo's rebellion had collapsed at the close of 1899.
In response, army garrisons were put in various parts of the islands. Still,
sabotage flared up. As a result, in 1900, thousands of Filipinos were forced
into concentration camps. Conditions in the camps were unspeakable.[32]

Still worse, the Americans adopted techniques of torture that Spain
had developed. The most disgraceful means of extracting information was

the "water cure." Now called water boarding, the practice was the invention of the Spanish Inquisition about 1620, possibly earlier. The Roman
Catholic church had prohibited the drawing of blood to identify heretics
and dissenters. The near drowning of the victim became its substitute. The
interrogators would close the nostrils with pincers and pour great amounts
of putrid water, sometimes bile or urine, down the victim's throat until the
stomach was about to burst. The sufferer would then be pommeled and
kicked in the gut. Evan Wyatt, a private in the 8th Infantry U.S. Volunteers,
explained his reaction to witnessing its application: "The spectacle was
so horrible I walked away." The method could be lethal. American forces
justified its use on the grounds that it could help to uncover the location of
enemy units, spies, and false friends. This occasion would not be the last
time that the practice was carried out in American hands. Nor was it the
only time that U.S. officials claimed innocence of any wrongdoing.[33]

Other kinds of atrocities were common. On occasion, soldiers' letters
boasted of how the war was being fought. They could report on villages
burned to the ground; men, women, and children killed; tortures inflicted.
"On Thursday, March 29th [1900]," wrote one trooper gleefully, "eighteen
of my company killed seventy-five nigger bolomen and ten of the nigger
gunners." Prisoners might not be allowed to live: "When we find one who
is not dead, we have bayonets."[34]

Other horrors included what was called "the telephone." The torturer
would clap his hands on the ears of the victim, creating a vacuum that might
burst the eardrums. Another was the "wet submarine." A prisoner would
be forced to put his head in a foul toilet bowl. If that failed to satisfy, one
could use the tried and true whip or apply electricity to the genitals. These
activities were designed not only to gain information and punish but also
to humiliate and demonstrate who was in charge. Even worse was the tactic
of "salvaging," by which security and military authorities euphemistically
meant clandestine executions. These would be conducted without trial or
show of evidence. The often mutilated body would be left in a conspicuous
place so that Filipinos could ponder a fate they might have to face.[35]

News of such tactics received national press coverage, but, of course,
Washington denied all charges. Secretary of War Elihu Root claimed that
the enemy, not the Americans, fought dishonorably. And it was true, as
Root suggested, that the insurgents assassinated friends of the United
States, killed U.S. troops while carrying flags of truce, tortured to death
American prisoners, buried some alive, and mutilated the bodies of the

dead. Americans had to respond, he asserted. He also admitted that American "bad apples," to borrow a more recent term, might sometimes have gone too far. But, after all, war is war.[36] (Unfortunately, the heritage the Americans left behind when the Philippines gained their independence in 1945 did not mean the end of the use of torture there. In 1975, Amnesty International urged the Philippine government to prohibit such practices as "'Russian roulette,' electric shock, the application of what the prisoners describe as 'truth serum' and all other forms of brutal treatment."[37])

Southerners were not all applauding the war and how it was conducted. Senator James H. Berry of Arkansas believed that the government was guilty of shame and gross hypocrisy. He stated, "If the doctrine that 'all just powers of government are derived from the consent of the governed' was true in 1861, it is true in 1898." He was more sympathetic, however, than Senator John W. Daniel of Virginia. Daniel expressed concern that the army was occupying a "witch's cauldron," inhabited by a "mess of Asian potage." Despite his sympathy for the Asian colonials, Berry did worry that the Filipinos might obtain equality as American citizens.[38] More prominent were the Northern anti-imperialists who formed a league to protest the annexation of the Philippines. They included Charles Francis Adams Jr., the railroad regulator; Jane Addams, the famous reformer; Ambrose Bierce, a well-known writer; John Dewey, the philosopher and educator; William Dean Howells, the author and editor; and Oswald Garrison Villard, son of the abolitionist William Lloyd Garrison; and others.[39]

At least one Southern senator made better sense than most. Senator Edward W. Carmack of Tennessee denounced what he called the rape of the Philippines.[40] Important figures were appalled about the conquest of the Philippines. Moorfield Storey, Carl Schurz, and such journals as the *Nation* opposed the drive for colonial domination. Mark Twain's dismay about the annexation of the Philippines appeared in several of his newspaper articles. Compassionate toward the natives whose nations were then being exploited—the Philippines by the Americans, India and Burma by the British—Twain was still somewhat resigned to the opportunity for capitalistic exploitation that such colonies provided. He foresaw that these ventures could well lead into a world war. Such a catastrophe would mean the spread of brutality, death, and wasted resources. It could be argued that Twain's *A Connecticut Yankee in King Arthur's Court* was an anti-imperialist fiction to challenge Rudyard Kipling's 1899 "The White Man's Burden."[41]

⊹⊹⊹

Mark Twain's sober observations introduce the next important American engagement in war, honor, race, and humiliation. In this case, it is important to note the causes of the conflict that became the so-called Great War. As early as 1887, Friedrich Engels predicted a catastrophic European war. In a German pamphlet, he wrote, "Eight to ten million soldiers will swallow each other up and in doing so eat all Europe more bare than any swarm of locusts." It would be far more destructive than the Thirty Years' War. The result would be "famine, sickness, want, brutalizing the army and the mass of the population." Countries and whole industries would turn bankrupt, and the old political systems would crumble. "Crowns will roll by dozens in the gutter and no one be found to pick them up."[42] His prescient forebodings accurately characterized the war that began in 1914.

Indeed, like the ancient biblical messengers of God, the famous Communist was very much a modern prophet of doom. But explaining why the war was fought has baffled historians for years, and no one has yet found the exact answer.[43] But one factor is pertinent to the themes of this text. The English political scientist Avner Offer provides a persuasive case that the kings and leading statesmen before 1914 were deeply concerned with issues of manliness, honor, and the seeming necessity of never appearing indecisive or weak before the world. Like Wilhelm I, his grandfather, German Emperor Wilhelm II was a nearly obsessive devotee of the code. In 1900, he ordered the disciplining of a naval officer. The offender had failed to demand satisfaction after being insulted. The kaiser publicized the matter for the enlightenment of his armed forces officers.[44]

At age eighteen, the young prince was installed in an order of knighthood and admitted into the Most Noble Company of the Black Eagle. He had to swear to "to maintain the honour of the Royal House, and guard the Royal privileges."[45] Always touchy about a perceived lack of respect, Wilhelm took far too seriously some of the honors nobles traditionally gave one another as signs of preeminence. To flatter King George V, his cousin, and win a sign of regard, he conferred on George's brother Albert an admiral's rank in the German navy. Albert's imperious, sharp-tongued mother, Alexandra of Denmark, made him refuse. But George himself accepted a colonelcy in the Prussian dragoon regiment. "So my Georgie," she wrote him, "has become a real live filthy blue-coated Pickelhaube German soldier!!!" She was disgusted, but at least he would be no admiral.[46]

The kaiser also faithfully denigrated anything in a man that suggested effeminacy. Homosexuals, hidden or openly gay, were publicly denounced and rendered socially unacceptable. A scandal arose when one of Wilhelm's closest advisors, Count Philipp zu Eulenburg, was exposed for belonging to an intimate group of homosexuals. Wilhelm had ignored the court gossip about Eulenburg for many years. Once the story was in the newspapers, however, the kaiser had to respond. He ruled that the miscreant would be banished from the court and that none of its members was ever to speak to Eulenburg again.[47]

The ideals of masculinity, honor, and sexual conformity dominated the German mentalité more than in any other European nation. According to one historian, "The repression of the feminine was pushed to an extreme unknown anywhere else in Europe."[48] Wilhelm gushed over German dueling clubs, which he considered "the best education which a young man can get for his future life." In the logic of the duel, intention counted far more than outcome. Yet, the participants in these encounters were very much in earnest. The pistols employed were often equipped with rifled barrels to increase accuracy. Needless to say, the Prussian officer corps highly prized such personal combat. Kevin McAleer, an expert on German duels, suggests that "the determined snobbery of German duelists may have derived from some sneaking sense of inferiority, especially vis-à-vis the English Gentleman." For whatever reason, German duels were the deadliest in all of Europe. Sabers did little more than draw blood, but pistol duels, the style that military men of honor preferred, were fought not so much to kill the opponent but to present an attitude of contempt for danger.[49]

In Germany, the middle and lower classes as well as the aristocracy believed that the British and American nations were enamored solely with business transactions and profits and had no regard for principles of honor. The Prussian general Friedrich Adolf Julius von Bernhirdi, a member of the general staff, claimed that German ideals would always prevail over the low morals of "commerce and money-making." (The same sort of sentiment was a common thought in the Old South.) Heinrich von Treitschke, a Prussian historian, saw in the duel a model of the international position Germany should adopt: "If the flag of the state is insulted, it is the duty of the State to demand satisfaction, and if satisfaction is not forthcoming, to declare war, however trivial the occasion may appear, for the State must strain every nerve to preserve for itself the respect which it enjoys in the state system."[50]

With this emotional and highly charged background, it is hardly a wonder that the German military hoped to win supremacy by means of war.
Eulenburg, the kaiser's closest advisor, had been a strong supporter of German expansion but skeptical about a plan of Admiral Alfred von Tirpitz for
the building of expensive dreadnoughts and battleships to equal the Royal
Navy's. Eulenburg thought it unnecessary because Germany was "neither
an island nor a boot, but a beautiful green field on the Continent in which
the sheep, guarded by the military sheepdogs, get fat while the oxen engage
in politics." After Eulenburg's constraining presence was gone, the kaiser
looked to the military for advice. Throughout the 1890s, Admiral von Tirpitz had been transforming the navy into a genuine rival against the British on the high seas. Germany's decision to challenge English hegemony
inevitably meant a deep antagonism between the two monarchies. Wilhelm
had long been an admirer of the Royal Navy but grew determined to challenge its dominance. How could a proud nation submit to an inferior status and yet retain its honor? Some people unsuccessfully urged Germany
to relinquish this effort. Charles, Baron Hardinge of Penshurst, a British
diplomat, approached the emperor on the topic. Wilhelm's response was
unsatisfactory. Hardinge pled for a "slower rate" of ship building, fearing
that soon Germany would have as many dreadnoughts as the Royal Navy.
The kaiser stood his ground, declaring "That [issue of disarming] is a question affecting national honour and dignity. We should prefer to fight!" The
English baron flushed with anger.[51] Germany's decision would eventually
draw the United States into the conflict when Tirpitz's navy proved no
match for the British and turned to submarine warfare against all shipping
headed for England.

Anglo-German competition was not the only factor leading to the
coming conflict. Germany and her ally, Austria-Hungary, both feared the
rearming and expansion of the Russian army. Tsar Nicholas II refused negotiations about reducing his forces. He felt honor-bound to defend Serbia
after Austria drew up an ultimatum to punish Serbia for the assassination
of Prince Frans Ferdinand at Sarajevo. The heads of the European nations
knew that the material for a great conflagration was in place by August
1914. All that was needed was a match. The Serbian nationalist Gavrilo
Princip, the assassin, provided it on 28 June at Sarajevo.

Yet, curiously, the German generals, while eager for war, also predicted
that this would be a devastating conflict. Their nation might even be soundly
defeated. One Austrian military leader, Franz Conrad von Hötzendorf, also

had doubts about the outcome. But these leaders saw an obligation to fight whatever the ultimate result. In a letter dated 28 July 1914, Helmuth Johann Ludwig von Moltke, deputy chief of the general staff, was convinced that the coming war "will annihilate the civilization of almost the whole of Europe for decades to come." Nevertheless, he concluded that the war would be worth fighting—in the name of German honor.[52]

Meanwhile, in the United States, for the first time since James K. Polk, an elected Southerner occupied the Oval Office. Woodrow Wilson, raved a Georgia journalist, was a man *of southern blood, of southern bone and of southern grit.*[53] Wilson was Southern by birth, but he had spent most of his career in the North at Johns Hopkins University, Princeton University, and then as the popular governor of New Jersey. Nonetheless, he carried primaries in Texas and the Carolinas. His position on a lower tariff benefited the cotton interests, and he was hostile toward Wall Street bankers, a position that most of the white South shared. Once Wilson won the election, aided by a Republican Party divided between support of William Howard Taft and Theodore Roosevelt, he filled his cabinet and ambassadorships with Southerners. (An exception was the aging midwesterner William Jennings Bryan as secretary of state.) Even the old Southern Bourbon bosses fell into line behind the president. They were thirsting for patronage after sixteen years in the political cold.[54]

The outbreak of war in August 1914 came as no surprise, but it was shocking nonetheless. Colonel Edward M. House of Texas, an unofficial but influential advisor to Wilson, had reported the saber-rattling that he had witnessed in Europe. Wilson was determined to keep America neutral—at least as long as possible. The Germans announced a blockade of Great Britain, even though the sinking of an American vessel would risk the United States' entry into the war. A German submarine sank the RMS *Lusitania* in May 1915. The British liner sank in less than twenty minutes, killing 1,198 passengers and crewmen, many Americans, though 700 survived. Wilson urged calm and self-control, although he admitted that the "honor and self-respect of the nation" was at risk.[55]

Germany had little respect for American military power. German opinion showed only contempt for the United States and belittled the possibility of American fighting competence. It was a nation of shopkeepers, the German High Command believed. Albert Einstein in Berlin wrote a friend of this German attitude, "I am convinced that we are dealing with a kind of epidemic of the mind. I cannot otherwise comprehend how men who are thoroughly decent in their personal conduct can adopt such utterly anti-thetical views on general affairs. It can be compared with developments at the time of the martyrs, the Crusades, and the witch burnings."[56]

The war was going badly for the allies. French mutinies erupted through-out 1917 despite executions of rebels and deserters. Such occurrences were triggered by the heavy losses the French army had endured: Over 50,000 died during the Somme campaign of 1916 alone. The French people were devastated. As the epitaph at the beginning of this chapter indicates, they had no desire for a second war, having lost ignominiously in 1870. On the other hand, Germany collectively ascribed to the inscription: "Not one too many died for the Fatherland." A desire to restore French honor fueled revenge against the Germans. These problems of morale impeded success, even though Germany was close to complete exhaustion. As early as 1916, some Germans were starving. And over 120,000 Germans died in 1916, as a result of the British blockade of German ports, which had begun in 1915.[57]

Antiwar sentiment also grew in Britain. The Somme campaign, a 25-mile frontal assault, had decimated whole corps of troops. German trenches were dug in enough to withstand ferocious bombardment. When the Brit-ish advanced, machine guns and mortars wiped them out. On the very first day of the British assault, 60,000 were killed or severely wounded. A total of 419,654 British Commonwealth troops died over the course of the battle. The British battalions had met tanks for the first time, along with mortars, artillery, and machine guns. Most British soldiers were volunteers who were serving as units representing one town or another. Thus, whole villages and localities might have had all of their young men wiped out merely to gain six miles of German territory. Bravery and self-sacrifice were at their height. The general public in the Allied nations were, on the whole, less skeptical about the nature of war than were the intelligentsia and poets of the period. Nonetheless, the waste and impact of heavy losses weighed down many a mother, wife, and child.[58]

Under these horrific circumstances, the possibility that the Americans might ride to the rescue lifted Allied spirits. To be sure, at home, opinion was not unanimous about Wilson's decision to enter the war. Some South-ern leaders, though dismayed by the sinking of the *Lusitania*, nonetheless worried that entering the war would extend the central government's power, lead to increased taxation, and hinder Southern exports. The presi-dent, however, stood for an idea of national honor that won over the greater number of Southern leaders. He would not permit any German effort to attack merchant ships with Americans aboard, whether the ships were armed for defense or unarmed.[59] Irascible and truculent Senator Carter Glass of Virginia denounced those fellow Southerners who opposed the president. Glass insisted that no patriot should submit to an "abject relinquishment of cherished National rights." Glass continued, "There are some men, but precious few who seem to be willing to haul down the American flag and circumscribe the rights of American citizens on the high seas." In his mind and that of many others, regional honor and national honor were one and the same.[60]

Glass was undoubtedly referring to the brilliant demagogue Tom Watson, among others. Watson was best known for his unrelenting campaign in 1915 against Leo Frank, a Jewish Atlanta manufacturer falsely accused of rape. Watson's blasts of invective against Wall Street industrialists and bankers, and his hatred of Frank, resulted in Frank's lynching after he was taken from his prison cell. In the following year, Watson turned his anger to Wilson's entry into war. Watson claimed that the South would suffer economically. Contempt for the centralizing tendencies of the federal government and resentment of any infringement on local self-governance dominated his rhetoric.

The Spanish-American War, Watson believed, had been the work of greedy bankers. Then, in 1917, he was once again convinced that the bankers were conspiring through the recently passed conscription law to make "slaves" of law-abiding citizens. In parts of rural Georgia, armed men proposed to fight against federal agents to preserve their liberty and dignity. Senator James Vardaman of Mississippi also opposed the entry of the United States into the war. Like Watson, he argued that the war measure was the conspiratorial work of industrialists who were willing to sacrifice the livelihoods of Southern farmers to advance their money-making schemes.[61] But Southerners, by and large, followed the president's lead.

Wilson saw no alternative to war: National honor was in peril and peace no longer seemed possible. German submarines began their indiscriminate torpedoing of American shipping in February 1917. When the German High Command refused to halt its assaults, Congress voted on 4 April for war, 373 to 50, and issued a formal declaration two days later. In the fall of 1917 into the winter of 1918, Wilson gave speech after speech across the country defending the decision. In December 1917, he addressed Congress: "The masters of Germany have shown us the ugly face." The combination of deception in negotiations and countless intrigues exhibited to the world, he continued, demonstrated the perfidy of the Germans. They operated "without conscience or honor or capacity for covenanted peace." That power had to be "crushed, and if it be not utterly brought to an end, at least shut out from the friendly intercourse of the nations." In speech after speech, Wilson referred to the necessity of upholding the principles of national honor: "The purposes of the Central Powers strike straight at the very heart of everything we believe in; their methods of warfare outrage every principle of humanity and of knightly honor; their intrigue has corrupted the very thought and spirit of many of our people; their sinister and secret diplomacy has sought to take our very territory away from us and disrupt the Union of the States. Our safety would be at an end, our honor forever sullied and brought into contempt were we to fail."[62]

Once the United States entered the war, the nation rallied behind its Southern-born president. The peacetime U.S. force had only a meager 126,000 regulars. Some African Americans served but at a level not indicative of their prior record for valor. In forming the new armed forces, much would depend on West Point graduates, the institution that Thomas Jefferson had founded. The school provided three points to advance its purpose: a sense of belonging, a fund of technical and military knowledge, and self-governance in which cadets would police, try, and judge violators of the school's code of honor. This last policy had its imperfections, like other forms of justice. Nonetheless, the principles of the school's honor code were compatible with the ideals of valor, loyalty, self-sacrifice, and deference to higher authority.[63]

The war required a huge increase in officers and enlistees. Zealous to prove their valor and pride of race, African Americans signed up in greater numbers than whites. Soon after the nation went to war, blacks filled their quota of volunteers. Still, a draft was required because the total number of white volunteers was too small. Selective Service boards sprang up in every community, but discrimination occurred throughout the draft process. Republican governors appointed cronies to serve as draft judges, and Democrats oddly gained fewer exemptions than fellow Republicans. At a Georgia camp, Slavs and Italians were assigned to their own separate units, but at least they were provided with officers speaking their languages. When the process was criticized, the draft boards replied that this form of organization was done to win a war, not to create an integrated national front.[64]

Before the outbreak of hostilities, the black community had been worried that the Virginian in the White House would continue to uphold Jim

Crow, despite his deceptive friendship toward blacks in the prepresidential period. Not long after assuming his duties, Wilson had imposed a policy of resegregation in the federal government to divide black and white federal workers. William Edward Trotter, editor of the Boston *Guardian*, confronted Wilson on the matter. The black journalist noted that some of his people had voted to elect Wilson and now felt betrayed. He asked the president, "Have you a 'new freedom' for white Americans and a new slavery for Afro-American fellow citizens?" Wilson took offense and replied that keeping black and white workers apart was to prevent friction between the races. He urged Trotter and his followers not to raise these issues as it would take generations to resolve the situation. Trotter shot back that the black federal employees were "humiliated and indisposed" in consequence of that misguided, racist policy.[65]

For African Americans, racial prejudice was all too evident in the draft process. Draft boards in the South told black draftees to turn down a corner of their applications so that they could be easily identified. In Fulton County, Georgia, the board had to be replaced because the members exempted 526 of 815 whites but only 6 of 202 blacks.[66]

Rather than send white boys into action, Southern draft boards sought to fill their quotas with young African Americans. The result was that 13 per cent of inductees were men of color, a higher percentage than white inductees. While trying to sort out how to handle the mobilization, the War Department then had to confront a race riot in Houston, Texas. Regular black soldiers, long in service in the 24th Infantry, 3rd Battalion, erupted on 23 August 1917. The soldiers fiercely resented the enforcement of the city's segregation statutes. In the melee, seventeen whites died. The white South reacted in utter horror and demanded prompt retribution. The centuries-old fears of slave and black insurrection seemed fulfilled. The kind of justice that Senator John Sharp Williams of Mississippi and other irate Southern politicians demanded was soon meted out. The battalion was disbanded, over a hundred men were sent to New Mexico to stand trial, and thirteen were quickly hanged before any appeal over the courts-martial could be registered. Members of the black community were irate. They recalled Teddy Roosevelt's hasty and sad dismissal of black pleas for reconsideration in the Brownsville, Texas, affair.[67]

Despite maltreatment by the public, and official indifference, outright hostility, and isolation, 350,000 African Americans served with the American Expeditionary Force on the Western Front. Only one of every five of these soldiers in France, however, met enemy fire. Whites, by contrast, participated at a ratio of two of three. A staff report in 1918 declared, "the colored drafted men cannot be used for combatant troops." Instead, they should be assigned to manual labor. Many worked as stevedores, cooks, waiters, cleaners, and other menial jobs such as ones they might have held at home.[68]

Yet, the army, in contrast to the Marine Corps and Coast Guard, which excluded them entirely, did train and use African Americans. They could be located in infantry, medical corps, cavalry, signal, engineer, and artillery units. The navy only employed them in noncombat positions, for instance, as orderlies and galley workers. Before the end of the war, the number of black officers serving in the army totaled 639. Most units, however, had white officers, including some Southern planters who presumably were assigned to command black troops because they allegedly knew how to manage them.[69]

One such figure was William Alexander Percy of Greenville, Mississippi. A poet and later famous memoirist, Percy kept both the black officers he liked and those he disliked at arm's length by a "meticulous politeness" and turned down invitations to mess with them. His lack of regular contact with common soldiers meant that he, like most Southern whites, did not change his opinions about racial inferiority. To be sure, he was kinder than most of his class. Nonetheless, he learned too little from his wartime experience. Such deep-seated attitudes were scarcely unusual in the former slave states.[70] Some sort of miscommunication at headquarters led several battalions of black troops to panic in the absence of clear leadership. Yet, the rest of the regiment performed with outstanding success, particularly in the last battle in the Argonne sector before the Armistice. French military leaders were more impressed by the black troops' record than white Americans.[71]

Honor, though often denied members of the black race, could not be totally extinguished. An African American corporal, Freddie Stowers of Sandy Springs, South Carolina, earned a Medal of Honor. He was the first African American so celebrated for his courage and self-sacrifice in World War I. But the ceremony occurred in April 1991, long after his death in battle. In the citation at the White House, President George H. W. Bush announced that on 28 September 1918, just six weeks before the end of the fighting, Germans pretended to surrender. When the Americans exposed themselves, lulled by the false declaration, the enemy opened fire with machine guns and mortars. Stowers did not retreat even though half his comrades perished. Instead, he and the survivors rushed the Germans and overpowered them in the trenches. Struck twice but still moving forward, Stowers died of his wounds on the field. The 369th Infantry Regiment, dubbed the "Harlem Hellfighters," served at the front for six months, which was a longer span than any other American unit. A total of 171 members of that regiment were given the Legion of Merit.[72]

The black press initially complained that war would detract from protests against lynching, disfranchisement, and other crucial problems in their communities.[73] Once the war began, however, journalists realized that Northern industries would require fresh workers. The "Great Migration" from the segregationist South gained strength. The Chicago *Defender*, one of the largest circulating black papers, applauded the African American invasion into the North. Over a half million men and women of color fled to better employment between 1915 and 1925.[74]

The great black leader W. E. B. Du Bois hailed the returning black compatriots but declared the time had come to demand equality of treatment and the rights that veterans, indeed all blacks, deserved: "By the God of Heaven, we are cowards and jackasses if now that that war is over, we do not marshal every ounce of our brain and brawn to fight a sterner, longer, more unbending battle against the forces of hell in our own land."[75]

Needless to say, Southern whites also hailed their heroes. Sergeant Alvin C. York of Pall Mall, Tennessee, near Murfreesboro, was the second most decorated soldier during the war. (Lt. Samuel Parker won even more honors.) York joined the U.S. Army and was in the ranks of the 328th Infantry Regiment, 82nd Infantry Division, at Camp Gordon, Georgia. He received the Medal of Honor along with two French medals, one Italian, and a number of American ones. He managed to capture singlehandedly 132 German soldiers. Although a devout Christian with pacifist leanings, he was an excellent marksman and killed six Germans who were rushing him while firing their guns. York's fame helped to reestablish the notion of honor for warrior virtues.[76] In the battle, he recalled, "There were over thirty of them in continuous action, and all I could do was touch the Germans off just as fast as I could. I was sharpshooting."[77]

In 1940, York finally permitted a motion picture to be filmed about his military exploits. Howard Hawks convinced the reluctant hero to sign a $150,000 contract. Gary Cooper played York, and the picture garnered 11 Oscar nominations. Coming out in 1941, it also won applause from Franklin

Roosevelt because, he hoped, its screenings across the country might help to advance a closer relationship with Great Britain and quiet the highly critical anti-Roosevelt isolationists.[78]

Another representative of honor in war was George Patton of the newly formed Tank Corps. At the very beginning of the Meuse-Argonne campaign, Patton took his tankers to the front lines while rallying the infantry they were protecting. Patton was badly wounded and had to be hospitalized. Nonetheless, his bravery was rewarded with promotion to a colonelcy. Later he won a Distinguished Service Cross for valor along with a Distinguished Service Medal for "high military attainments, zeal, and marked adaptability in a form of warfare comparatively new to the American Army." A dedicated man of Virginia honor, he chafed at his hospital confinement, which caused him to miss so much action in the field. Patton later expressed his feelings to General Pershing: "War is the only place where a man really lives."[79] He carried that approach into the second great fight against Germany, too.

The American participation in the war was relatively short. Yet, it was a decisive factor in the Allied victory. More than a million Americans were engaged in the Meuse-Argonne offensive, a battle that raged for nearly seven weeks where losses were high. The war was the first in which machine guns mowed down advancing forces as if they were grass ready for cutting. A total of 26,000 American soldiers died on that front. Honor played a role in the fighting and the motivations of all participants from Europe and America. Disillusionment, however, over time would also be part of the reaction to the death and destruction.

Honor played a role in the fighting and the motivations in all participations, but the social bonds of hierarchy, noblesse oblige, and other accouterments of the code were diminished. Black intellectuals considered the war a humiliation, with white-skinned people trampling on the rights of dark-skinned people in the colonies that were taken over after the war.[80]

National honor fell victim to a revulsion against war. Americans were introduced to the ugliness and gross inhumanity of warfare: poison gas, zeppelins' bombing civilians, machine guns, and the indiscriminate torpedoing of submarines. Unavoidable indignities were personally even more immediate in the lives of the "doughboys." Paul Fussell writes of the "unchivalric experiences as soldiers' passively trembling under artillery shelling hour after hour or soiling their trousers for weeks with acute dysentery . . . or milking down their penises monthly before the eyes of bored and contemptuous medical officers alert for unreported gonorrheal discharges." Fussell thus explains why honor died along with the disappearance of monarchies all over Europe.[81]

The "War to Save Democracy" had become a war to grab and hold weaker countries as the French and English sliced up the Middle East and reaffirmed their control of the prewar imperial system. Americans saw no value in creating a new and equitable world but went about making money with little respect for law or moral integrity. The cynicism of the period was evident not just in the palaces of Europe but in the boardrooms of corporations. The Great Depression and collapse of the American economy caused a further loss of interest in world affairs.

The result of the war was the lessening of the honor principles in the public mind in the United States, England, and France. But, tragically, the ideals of military power with honor as its justification was soon to arise again with the fascist regime of Hitler and the weakening of civilian governance in the Weimar Republic. America would also rediscover honor's values in the struggle of World War II.

7

HONOR, RACE, AND HUMILIATION IN WORLD WAR II AND KOREA

A sweet thing is war to those who have not tried it.

—PINDAR

In dealing with World War II and Korea, the issue of national honor figures less prominently than in other American engagements. In the era of the wars against fascism and Communism, the question was self-defense against brutal aggressors. The enemy in Korea was thought to be Stalin's Russia and the regime of Mao Zedong and Zhou Enlai in China. The overwhelming and pointless losses in men, materiel, and morale in the Great War had led to a diminution in thoughts of honor. The horrors of World War I had driven a stake through the heart of honor, except, unfortunately, in the vengeful spirit of Nazi Germany. But Japanese and then German operations against the United States abruptly altered that perception that honor no longer mattered. This was also true of the Korean engagement under the authority of the United Nations. These wars were not preemptive but were forced on the nation.

The jingoism that rallied the public for the First Great War and the usual rhetorical flourishes about preserving national honor were not needed for World War II. Instead, the United States responded to the actual threat of a prolonged and bitter struggle against Nazi and Japanese dictatorships and their plans to dominate the world. The old warrior ethic was quiescent in the Western nations prior to the war, but acts of dishonor by Americans during the course of the war require exploration. Continued racism and ethnic prejudices during World War II marred American claims to totally clean hands. Only in Korea was there a more enlightened policy regarding African American servicemen.

Although more or less abandoned elsewhere, honor was very much alive in Nazi Germany. *Blut und Ehre*—"Blood and honor"—was the motto of the *Schutzstaffel*, or SS, under Heinrich Himmler and his aide, Reinhard Tristan Eugen Heydrich. Another slogan was *Meine Ehre heißt Treue*—"My honor is my loyalty." The elaborate Waffen SS (the armed unit of the SS) ceremonies to instill total obedience unto death were borrowed from the brotherhood of the Knights Templar.[1] The SS and the whole anti-Semitic thrust of the Nazis placed honor as a redoubt against Germany's humiliation in World War I. The practice of dueling was laid aside as a gentleman's ritual after the Great War. Adolf Hitler did not revive it in part because his strength lay in the middle and lower ranks of society. (It did continue among the upper classes in Italy, however.) But military prowess and the mysticism of Aryan superiority became part of the new and belligerent language of the Third Reich.

Honor was very much a motivating factor in Hitler's mind. In *Mein Kampf* (1925 and 1926), he wrote, "Where is the border that separates duty towards the community from the obligations of personal honor? Must not every real leader refuse to be degraded in such a way to the level of a political profiteer?" Hitler rhapsodized on the idea of national honor. "The honor of the nation; something that, despite all opinions to the contrary," he continued, "is still present today or rather ought to be present." Nations that lacked that virtue would end up as slaves, and deservedly so: "But he who wants to be a cowardly slave must not and cannot have any honor, as thus honor would become subject to general disdain within the shortest time. It was for the struggle for its human existence that the German people fought, and to support this struggle was the purpose of the war propaganda; the aim had to be to help it to victory."[2]

Hitler's initial success in the invasions of Poland and France was quite astonishing. Yet, some historians claim that his supposed misunderstanding of military strategy led to a disastrous blunder. In the French theater, he withheld a tank assault on the beaches at Dunkirk and the British Expeditionary Army escaped back to England. Some historians have suggested he restrained his forces because of a sense of shared Nordic honor with the British, but that analysis is misleading. The German army had limited tank numbers at this stage, and they were needed to deal with the remaining French defenses.[3]

No army could surpass the fighting qualities of the German army, the Wehrmacht. "*Soldantentum*" signified the German fighters' "spiritual vocation," something far less pronounced in the American and British ways of life. The Wehrmacht was, writes military historian Max Hastings, "one of the most effective armies the world has ever seen." Fortunately for the sake of world civilization, however, the battlefield victories came to nothing.

Hastings explains that the army's prowess was undermined by "the stunning incompetence with which the German war machine was conducted."[4] An equal obstacle to German victory was the Nazi goal of Jewish removal and extermination, which became an ugly replacement for the tradition of honor. Slavs, gypsies, homosexuals, the disabled, and the mentally vulnerable were also victims of this inhuman eugenics movement. On that foundation was supposed to arise a "master race." But it wasted manpower; personnel who could have been in the fighting ranks were instead administering death camps, constructing gas chambers, and committing other atrocities. In the meantime, the crudest of men were in charge of this social policy, even as the army proved its mettle. Among the most despicable were Himmler, Hermann Göring, Dr. Paul Joseph Goebbels, and Reinhard Tristan Eugen Heydrich, "the man with the iron heart," as Hitler called him. Heydrich and others had Hitler's full license to imprison and murder millions while claiming the unrestrained loyalty of the German people.[5]

Like their German ally and its ambition to conquer all of Europe, the Japanese thrust for world recognition and domination in the Pacific also rested on the idea of national honor through the veneration of the Japanese emperor. To that end, the Japanese induced Hitler to join in the war against America. On 11 December 1941, four days after the Pearl Harbor attack, the two nations signed, along with Italy, a pact to make no separate peace with any of the Allies. The treaty no doubt enhanced Japanese prestige and made the emperor even more popular at home.[6]

The honor code that dominated Japanese culture was linked with worship of the head of state as a semideity. "Japan," writes economist Paul Herbig, "is a highly honorable society, in which individuals are deeply bound by obligations of gratitude, loyalty, and deference. The honor and discipline of Japanese life are based on highly personal loyalties—to the feudal lord, to the honor of the family," and, it might be added, to military readiness. The "warrior ethic"—the famous Samurai tradition—was intense. Torii Mototada (1539–1600), a feudal lord and vassal to a higher nobleman in the sixteenth century, wrote a last testament to his son. He knew that his forces would soon be overwhelmed in bloody defeat: "It is not the Way of the Warrior to be shamed and avoid death even under circumstances that are not particularly important. It goes without saying that to sacrifice one's life for the sake of his master is an unchanging principle. . . . That I should be able to go ahead of all the other warriors of this country and lay down my life for the sake of my master's benevolence is an honor to my family and has been my most fervent desire for many years."[7] That idea of duty continued among the Japanese in the centuries that followed.

In that nation, the concept of *bushido* governed the mentality of both officers and common personnel. The term refers to what translates as "the Way of the Warrior-Knight." It requires unswerving duty to follow all commands. In a real sense, it was analogous to medieval ideals of Spartan simplicity, fidelity, mastery of arms, and honor even to the point of self-sacrifice and death. For instance, in 1945, when the war against America proved hopeless and the Americans were proceeding closer to the mainland, Japanese Vice Admiral Onishi Takijiro came up with the idea of piloting old war planes into enemy ships. These suicide missions were not dissimilar to suicide bombers used in more recent Asian terrorist strategies. Leaders of both Japan and Al-Qaeda promised those who undertook these missions that they would gain eternal renown for their valor and dedication. Tragically, it worked to Japanese advantage. Scores of American ships were struck, and the USS *St. Lo* was sent to the bottom.[8]

The Japanese motivations for such self-destructive acts were part of their "dread of humiliation." A "yearning for renown" and a compulsion for revenge when challenged or insulted animated the spirit of the Samurai. This warrior tradition stretched back thousands of years. The great pressure of preserving honor drove the Japanese need to achieve, as St. Francis Xavier, the Jesuit Catholic missionary to the Japanese in the sixteenth century, shrewdly observed. "There is no nation," he wrote, "in the world which fears death less." He considered that "no people" were "more punctilious about their honour than the Japanese, for they will not put up with a single insult or even a word spoken in anger." They were, the Jesuit thought, "much braver and more warlike than the people of China, Korea, Ternate and all of the other nations around the Philippines."[9] An insular people, the Japanese were customarily suspicious of strangers and possible enemies. These factors all played into the military ethos of the 1930s, even though Japan was no longer feudal but industrial in its economy.

The actual way Japanese soldiers fought in the Second World War revealed the power of honor. At Okinawa, rather than surrender, the overwhelmed forces chose to die until the last bullet was available. Japanese resistance continued on that island until 21 June 1945. Many soldiers hid themselves in caves in the hill country. A Japanese governor of the island, Masahide Ota, and another leader committed *seppuku*, ritual suicide, in their command headquarters on Hill 89 in the closing hours of the battle.

Another leader, Colonel Hiromichi Yahara, was one of the few command-ers to warn his leaders that counterattacks would simply kill thousands of soldiers and ultimately fail. He believed that they should be used solely for defense. Higher-ups ignored the advice. They laughed at him and stated that, as Samurai, it would violate their honor to do as he suggested. The result, even they later admitted, had been a foolish waste of manpower. In-deed, Japanese casualties were nearly 100,000. Americans suffered 62,000 casualties and 25,000 or more dead.[10] The ferocity of the siege made it the most lethal of all the campaigns in the Pacific, even more than the numbers killed at Iwo Jima shortly before.

The Okinawa civilians were persuaded or compelled to commit *sep-puku* in the name of lost honor. An unknown number of common soldiers undertook a modification of the *seppuku* ritual using hand grenades. It is thought that there were thousands of troops in the caves whose entrances the American military engineers sealed off with soldiers and civilians in-side. The tradition of death instead of surrender, captivity, and internal-ized humiliation was central to Japan's military code: Loyalty and honor meant more than life itself. As mentioned earlier, the basis for the *kami-kaze* attacks—flying human bombs aimed at American ships—lay within this tradition. Over 70 hits sank or crippled their targets, though only 14 percent of the pilots actually succeeded. That sentiment of indifference to life also applied in the treatment of prisoners of war. They were considered human garbage because they had permitted themselves to be captured. Just before the atomic bombs were dropped in August 1945, fifteen airmen in Japanese hands were decapitated. Prisoners throughout the empire were given meager rations; nutritional diseases were commonplace.[11]

Ironically, this deep-seated Japanese sense of desperation and honor prompted the Americans to use the atomic bombs at Hiroshima and Naga-saki. The American government believed that the use of that tragic means would end the war without the heavy U.S. casualties that a final defense of the homeland, only 350 miles from Okinawa, would require.[12]

Although one might question if dropping the bomb was an act of honor, its use made strategic sense, not only for the United States, whose troops would have died by the hundreds of thousands in an invasion of the main-land, but also for the Japanese. This act was so devastating that Japanese forces saw that it would be no dishonor to surrender with grace. Two days beforehand, 720,000 leaflets were dropped on the two cities urging people to leave at once or be destroyed. Not one civilian left town. Had the creation of the bomb occurred even faster, how many more lives would have been spared in Germany as well as among the Allied forces?

In contrast to these totalitarian allies, Benito Mussolini, Hitler's subordinate partner, was opportunistic, theatrical, disorganized, and blustering; the notion of honor simply was not a significant factor in his thinking. He was also no ideologue. Fascism, however, did unite a geographically divided nation, and that became the basis for what ideology there was in Italy. Mussolini's charismatic personality and displays of power appealed to the Italian lower middle classes. As the historian David D. Roberts writes, "The very thought of fascism brings forth forbidding images: the squat figure of Mussolini, jaw protruding, fists on hips, leading his country to humiliation and disaster as Hitler's very junior partner."[13]

The American sense of national honor revived in 1941 after years of isolationism. War revitalized the economy and also the sense of national military purpose. Soldiers in this war belonged to the generation that knew of fierce combat largely through such grandiose epics as D. W. Griffith's *The Birth of a Nation*. The film had thrilling shots of masses of soldiers storming ahead with cannons and muskets blazing away. It was romantic and far from the reality of battle. Young men embraced the romance of war, though pacifists and intellectuals held back. At the beginning of the Great War, English war poet Rupert Brooke had expressed the exhilaration of the new glory-seeking British soldiers. He portrayed his generation "as swimmers into cleanness leaping, / Glad from a world grown old and cold and weary." Such, too, were the dreams of the enlistees in America. Young men of the South whose grandfathers had fought in the Civil War were far more likely than Northerners at this time to approve a war against foreign enemies. These Southern young men and their seniors were incensed that Woodrow Wilson's plans to join the League of Nations had failed. It worried them that, once again, the South, with less of an industrial and financial base, would lose national influence with the Republicans' continuing isolationism.[14] When Hitler invaded Poland, 77 percent of Southerners favored an alliance with England and France.[15]

An ethnic component also influenced opinions. More Southerners boasted a British background than other parts of the nation. Once the United States became partners with Great Britain, Prime Minister Winston Churchill was as much an inspiring hero as President Franklin D. Roosevelt. Lend Lease, Bundles for Britain, and other pro-Allied ventures were immensely popular in the Southern states. Some Southern men joined the armed services even before Pearl Harbor. Much of this energy was derived from a continuing disdain for Yankees, whose politicians, like Senator Gerald P. Nye, a Republican from North Dakota, carried their anti-Wilsonian crusade into foreign relations as late as the close of the 1930s.[16]

In the North, general public sentiment took the British and French governments' side in opposing Hitler's and Mussolini's threats of war. After the German invasion of Poland, and Great Britain's and France's declarations of war against Germany in 1939, that attitude in America did not change, though a desire to stay out of the war remained a powerful force. Throughout the late 1930s, other factors fed into the isolationist impulse. Charles A. Lindbergh, the famous flyer, led the America First movement, which promoted American neutrality. Few Southerners joined that cause. In the North, continued isolationism was also fed by the pacifists, many of them seminarians and clergy. In addition, in eastern Pennsylvania and along the East Coast, including New York and New Jersey, the German-speaking communities and far right fanatics produced the American Bundist movement, which paraded with Nazi banners and ranks of uniformed young men shouting "Heil Hitler!" They marched down East 86th Street in New York City and Main Street in Harrisburg, Pennsylvania. I remember as a child in Harrisburg hearing about the Nazi parade. There was little if any popularity for this group in the South. A further deterrent was American anti-Semitism. The Bundists sought a boycott of Jewish stores, but that cause failed.[17]

Once the war began in December 1941, Southern politicians and their constituents sought and obtained huge increases in war-related jobs. Southern congressmen successfully lobbied for the placement of over half of the new army training camps in the South, at a cost of four billion dollars to the federal government. Mississippi and Alabama coastal shipyards flourished. Millions of African Americans and Appalachian whites flocked to Northern cities for war work. Women, too, took the place of men who had gone off to war, establishing new identities as skillful workers and not just as homemakers and caregivers.

That particular situation created a ruckus. Civilians were very skeptical about women's taking up war work. Massachusetts congresswoman Edith Rogers's great achievement, however, was successfully to guide through Congress the 1942 bill that created the Women's Army Auxiliary Corps. Military honor would no longer be the exclusive property of men. GIs (a sardonic term for soldiers, standing for "Government Issue") were unhappy.

Perhaps frightened about losing their old jobs to female replacements, they spread rumors against those women who were no longer confined to household duties. Women were thought to be invading a male preserve, a state of affairs that allegedly diminished manhood. On the other hand, General Douglas MacArthur praised the WACs (Women's Army Corps, as it became in 1943) as "my best soldiers." He argued that they worked harder, grumbled less, and were more disciplined than their male compatriots.[18]

Roosevelt and the propagandists boasted of the success of immigrants who overcame great economic difficulties to achieve full status as Americans. But that did not include some ethnic minorities, especially African Americans. Richard Wright in his *Twelve Million Black Voices* challenged this hypocrisy. "Wright," argues historian Dan Shiffman, "outlined a gap that needed to be closed: not a gap that separated older stock Americans from the newer immigrants, but one that economically and politically separated blacks from whites. These divisions could not simply be smoothed over with patriotic rhetoric."[19]

Indeed, Wright struck on an undeniable fact. Along with the sense of dislocation created by the inclusion of women in war activities was the emergence of African Americans as a force to be reckoned with. They were again visible in uniform, and that was not a welcome sight in the Deep South especially. Felix Hall, an African American private, was lynched on the camp grounds of Fort Benning, Georgia, in April 1941.[20] At a Mobile, Alabama, shipyard, whites rioted when a dozen black workers were promoted to welder status. Army troops had to be summoned to suppress the conflict.[21]

Given the longstanding segregated character of the military, the same old prejudices were no different from prior wars, though in each of those wars, black soldiers showed they could more than pull their share of the fighting load. "Yeah," crudely remarked one GI in 1942, "there were a few Niggers around, but they weren't fighting. They drove trucks; that's about all they were good enough to do."[22]

Aviation was a dream for many black young men in the prewar period, but few could receive the necessary training. Judge William H. Hastie, civilian aide on Negro affairs to the secretary of war, began new programs for black aspirants to learn to fly, not only for combat but for weather reconnaissance, since there were so few available experts in that field. The Army Air Corps commanders were reluctant to cooperate. In reaction to the slow progress, Hastie resigned his position under Secretary of War Henry L. Stimson.[23]

The regular army was not willing to provide equal treatment to African Americans either. Harry Johns of the 999th Field Artillery served under General George Patton in North Africa and Italy and was one of a million African Americans who fought in World War II, largely in segregated units. He recalled, "These men and women discharged their duties with great pride in the face of blatant discrimination and humiliation."[24] Not one black soldier, however, won the Medal of Honor. Twenty-four-year-old Captain Harold Montgomery had served in the heavy weapons unit of the all African American 92nd "Buffalo Soldiers" Infantry Division. The unit gained that nickname from the Civil War period, when it adopted a buffalo mascot and fought Native Americans. In World War II, these African American soldiers enlisted for duty to fight in the Western theater. The Indian enemy respected these fighters in a way that whites did not. In the Italian campaign so many years later, the company weathered the formidable German defenses along the western coast of Italy.

The Italian villagers, now liberated, greeted him with cheers and wide smiles. Montgomery and his fellow GIs were their saviors. The cheering throngs handed them flowers and bottles of wine. In ugly contrast, the veterans' reception in the army's accounting office in Washington was quite different. There, a plaque on the wall listed the names of all those in service—save the ones who were black. When Montgomery's boss informed Montgomery that he would not receive the same pay raise as other veterans, he quit on the spot.[25]

With no regard for the morale of the black troops, the authorities inflicted a number of other humiliations. During USO (United Service Organizations) concerts, black soldiers had to sit behind German prisoners of war. Those black soldiers who fought in Germany were ordered off the streets of occupied cities, streets that they had fought hard to seize. James Strawder had joined the army when Dwight D. Eisenhower called for African American volunteers to take the places of fallen white troops during the dreadful Battle of the Bulge. Poor aerial reconnaissance and Allied overconfidence made this German offensive in the Ardennes forest a turning point. Hitler had hoped the surprise counteroffensive would split the British and American forces, and the Allies would agree to peace on Germany's terms. Thanks in part to the black response to the crisis, the

Allies overcame the Wehrmacht, which was thereafter much depleted in manpower and supplies.[26]

As soon as Germany surrendered, the surviving volunteers had to return to all-black units while their former white comrades boarded ships for America. Strawder and some two hundred others of his color refused to work under such blatant discrimination. Their commander threatened them with court-martial trials and possible execution for insubordination and disobedience. So, the men entered the stockade and dared the white hierarchy to proceed with the punishment. "I had already risked death [in battle], I didn't give a john," proudly recalled Strawder at the age of eighty-three.[27] The command was rescinded, probably due to fear of a national outcry.

The situation for Japanese Americans was hardly more uplifting. The decision to incarcerate California and Hawaiian Japanese, many of them second-generation Americans, showed how deeply ethnic and color prejudice had permeated the national psyche. The "Japs," as they were derisively called, were deemed "un-American." Even before the war, these immigrants were told to "speak, dress, and think American." After that fateful Sunday in December 1941, whites in Hawaii and California set Japanese flags and books, along with any correspondence with kin in Japan, afire.[28] The internment camps were not only inadequate, but the experience was degrading, as it was meant to be. The justification, of course, was the fear of spies' hiding in the midst of the innocent. But the way of Samurai was not practiced by these ambitious, hard-working people.

The story of the lives of the Japanese camp inmates is wrenching to recount. Consider the narrative of Donald Nakahata, a twelve year old in San Francisco. His father, a journalist and community leader, felt he had to hasten to San Jose to help the Japanese community there just as the war began. His son walked with him to the Southern Pacific train and never saw him again. The senior Nakahata was arrested practically upon his arrival. "Dad was gone, and we just heard from him a little," remembered his son. "We have a few letters from him." The father's health deteriorated rapidly, and he suffered several strokes at Fort Sill, Oklahoma, and Camp Livingston, Louisiana. Donald believes he may have died in another internment camp in Bismarck, North Dakota. He cannot be sure.[29]

In Hawaii, some Japanese were initially elated by the attack, shouting "Banzai! Banzai!" and rejoicing at the destruction of the U.S. fleet as an overdue retaliation for past insults. Other Japanese, though—the vast

majority—felt shame and loss of face. The treacherous assault was wholly
dishonorable in their eyes. They had taken pride in the ancient heritage of
"feudal honor and honesty." Their parents and seniors had preached these
principles repeatedly, in the hope that the younger generation would retain
something of their Japanese culture. Now they all despaired, undone by "an
uncaring native country whose aggression placed them in such danger,"
according to historian Franklin Odo.[30]

It is hardly a wonder that the Japanese in Hawaii feared the police and
sudden arrest. There were also ethnic tensions on the Pacific islands held
by the United States. Filipinos, Koreans, Chinese, and others on these islands resented Japanese economic success in Hawaii and elsewhere. The
Japanese empire's despoiling of their homelands also caused much hatred
against Japanese Americans. Surprisingly, whites were more sympathetic
to the plight of Japanese Americans than perhaps others of Pacific origins. Japanese schoolchildren were not, as a rule, harassed too severely. At
the same time, the Japanese were considered ineligible for naturalization,
particularly as they came to be stereotyped as potentially untrustworthy
aliens.[31]

Japanese Americans were eager to prove their loyalty and their bravery
to the rest of the nation. Luckily, they had a champion in Kendell Fielder,
head of army intelligence. He begged General George Marshall to permit
the formation of what became the 100th Battalion in June 1942. Later,
Fielder succeeded in establishing the 442nd Regimental Combat Team.
Others in the War Department loudly criticized the policy of using Japanese Americans as soldiers, but he held his ground. The 442nd vindicated
his trust. They fought heroically throughout the Italian campaign and then
in southern France and Germany.[32] They did so despite the fact that many
of their relatives were in internment camps. Their fierce determination to
do their best earned them the greatest number of awards of any unit in U.S.
military history, including twenty-one Medals of Honor.[33]

This contest differed from those in the past in regards to the operations of the war. By the Second World War, generals had realized, after
the slaughter of men in the First, that armies could not march in ranks
against machine guns, heavy artillery, and mortars. "What I thought this
war would be is all turned around," mused soldier John Babcock. Instead
of men moving in waves out of trenches, they now were dispersed and
formed small groups that advanced warily. Historian Christopher Hamner
cites one exception. In 1944, nearly one thousand Germans, "numerically

strong, well disciplined, backed by plenty of artillery, brave and willing to die," marched across the field. The Americans fired a barrage of mortars, automatic weapons, and artillery as the Germans approached. All but a handful died in a matter of ten minutes. Here was honor epitomized, but on this occasion, more blood was spilled and less honor achieved.[34]

The notion that soldiers should form comradely bonds was no longer possible in exactly the way it had been in the Great War. Men were now separated from each other, not buddies rubbing shoulders in trenches. Interdependence did develop but along different lines. Soldiers in the field had more autonomy but also had mutual obligations to act swiftly to aid GIs some distance away. The camouflaged uniforms that replaced more visible clothing increased the chances of "friendly fire," as did a greater reliance on long-range artillery and air power. Thus, tragic errors occurred in which inaccurate firing of artillery killed fellow soldiers. Airmen also could be mistaken in their choice of targets, causing chaos and death on the ground.[35]

Despite the problems, the old honor code still found a place. A drill sergeant told his trainees, "What's going to drive you, aches or no aches, . . . is the knowledge that if you don't hold up your end you'll be marked as a sissy and a quitter, a softy and a gold-brick, by the other men of your own outfit." Masculine honor, writes Hamner, would remain a steadfast goal. He also quotes a GI in the 106th Division who hoped to get out of the infantry. But a session with a sympathetic physician made the GI reverse himself: "I think I felt guilty about leaving the men I had trained with for the last four months." He had come to love his squad mates and could not bear the thought of letting them down. It was vitally important to be a member of the team.[36]

The distribution of medals for valor was a source of inspiration and pride to those in the same unit. It signified that higher-ups actually took notice and were grateful for the sacrifices made. These factors kept alive the spirit of honorable conduct.

The end of army segregation was long overdue. There were few black regular army personnel in the 1930s. Only one GI in forty was African American. Those few did not receive adequate battle training. Black units with black officers were rare. In the late 1930s, there were just a little over four thousand army troops of color with five black officers, three of them chaplains.[37]

When the draft was introduced in 1940, nothing changed. Selective Service Director General Lewis B. Hershey opposed the segregation policy, but he had no authority to override the army's discrimination. Roosevelt was battling for reelection, however, and the black vote, for once, was crucial. The president had Henry L. Stimson, his secretary of war, establish black air force pilots and the formation of black combat units. The heroic airmen from Tuskegee have lately been celebrated, albeit belatedly. Contrary to some early accounts, the bomber units did lose planes, but their record indicates that these airmen were as brave and skillful as any in the army air force.[38] In March 1944, Roosevelt urged passage of a measure that would permit blacks in service to vote. Southern leaders objected, insisting that states should decide separately who should be given that privilege, and blocked Roosevelt's plan. Still, however timidly, the government was attempting to loosen the Southern insistence on white honor alone.[39]

By and large, black heroism, along with their voting rights, was largely ignored. Historian Robert Edgerton relates a tragic story. During the attack on Pearl Harbor, Dorie Miller, a black galley sailor on the USS *West Virginia*, singlehandedly fought a fire and moved the wounded captain of the battleship to a safer location. Miller had never fired a machine gun before, but he manned one and shot down two enemy planes. According to Edgerton, "As he did so, his usually impassive face bore the deadly smile of a berserk Viking." Yet, even though Miller won a Navy Cross for bravery, he was not reassigned but continued waiting on officers' tables. He was lost at sea when a torpedo sunk the escort carrier USS *Liscome Bay*.[40]

The Americans and British had decidedly better commanders than their enemies did. General George C. Marshall was named chief of staff despite Roosevelt's initial dislike of him. Marshall was, according to General Omar Bradley, "the most impressive man I ever knew, one of the greatest military minds the world has ever produced." Marshall was a gentleman with high moral principles. He was aloof and cultivated neither favorites nor friends, though he was solicitous of his subordinates' well-being, both officers and foot soldiers. His attributes included a willingness to make quick decisions, to see the larger picture, and, in every respect, to locate the "honorable" path. He once wrote to students in a friend's class: "The most important factor of all is character, which involves integrity, unselfish and devoted purpose, a sturdiness of bearing when everything goes wrong and all are critical, and a willingness to sacrifice self in the interest of the common good."[41]

In the ranks on the Western Front, there were many heroes. One was infantryman Staff Sergeant Lucian Adams, who exemplified the highest example of courage under fire. Near St. Die, France, on 28 October 1944, this Texan was maneuvering through a dense forest when German machine guns opened up and three in his company were killed. Adams was undeterred. While his mates held back, he ran forward, his rifle blazing. He dodged grenades and machine-gun bursts and managed to wipe out three German machine-gun nests in his advance. Adams personally killed nine Germans and made it possible to open vulnerable supply lines. He won the Medal of Honor for his exploits. Bernard Bell, a technical sergeant from West Virginia, showed similar valor. "By his intrepidity and bold, aggressive leadership," reads his Medal of Honor citation, Bell "enabled his eight-man squad to drive back approximately 150 of the enemy, killing at least 87 and capturing 42. Personally, he killed more than 20 and captured 33 prisoners."[42]

In the ranks of general officers, none stood out more vividly for the principle of honor and initiative than George S. Patton. He represented in the starkest terms two aspects of honor—gallant innovation and antipathy to the apparent cowardliness of others. His tank corps leadership was legendary. Patton was particularly effective in the invasion of Sicily. Churchill and Roosevelt in January 1943 decided to take this action, hoping it would compel the Wehrmacht to withdraw troops from the Russian front. Patton seized Palermo on the west coast of the island on 22 July. That loss exposed fifty thousand Italian troops to capture. Further actions secured Sicily and prepared the way for the invasion of the Italian boot.[43]

Patton's heroics and drive, however, came at a price. During the Sicilian operation, American soldiers massacred seventy-three Italian prisoners. General Omar Bradley ordered two participants to stand a general court-martial trial for premeditated murder. The soldiers' defense had the ring of truth: They claimed Patton had ordered the men not to take any surrendering prisoners. One of the witnesses recalled that Patton had explained in his speech, "The more prisoners we took, the more we'd have to feed, and not to fool with prisoners." So essential was Patton's leadership that Bradley quashed the trial, which would have exposed Patton's violation of international law.[44]

No less dishonorable was Patton's widely publicized confrontation with Private Charles H. Kuhl in a military hospital ward. The bedridden soldier felt guilty because he had been admitted for shellshock or post-traumatic stress disorder. When Patton asked him why he was there, Kuhl answered miserably, "I guess I can't take it." One soldier who was present reported

that Patton "slapped his face with a glove, raised him to his feet by the collar of his shirt, and pushed him out of the Receiving Tent with a final 'kick
in the rear.'" On recovery, Kuhl was very gracious; he guessed that both
of them were suffering from combat fatigue. Still worse, though, Patton
informed all under his command that he would not tolerate that sort of
escape from combat: "Such men are cowards, and bring discredit on the
Army and disgrace to their comrades."[45]

At another hospital, Patton repeated this ugly scenario. He discovered
a hapless patient, Private Paul G. Bennett, who claimed to have shattered
nerves. Patton turned purple with rage: "Your nerves. Hell, you are just a
goddamned coward, you yellow son of a bitch. Shut up that goddamned
crying. I won't have these brave men here who have been shot seeing a
yellow bastard sitting here crying." He pulled out his gun and threatened
to shoot Bennett on the spot. After similar threats, Patton returned the
pistol to his holster but then struck the soldier twice on the head with his
fist. A medical officer in charge of Bennett reported the assault to General
Eisenhower. Eisenhower's concern was not so much Patton's behavior. It
was worthy of a court-martial, but the larger implications for winning the
war was uppermost in Eisenhower's mind. He told his staff: "If this thing
ever gets out, they'll be howling for Patton's scalp, and that will be the end
of George's service in this war. I simply cannot let that happen. Patton is
indispensable to the war effort—one of the guarantors of our victory." The
press heeded Eisenhower's plea to keep the story out of their columns until
months later. He did, however, order Patton to apologize to the recipients
of his anger.[46]

In 1945, Patton himself had to enter a hospital as a patient at Walter
Reed Army Hospital in Washington. With doctors and nurses hovering
around the great hero, he bitterly declared, "You sons of bitches want to see
me slap another soldier, don't you?" He walked through a lengthy ward and
was touched by the sight of the injured. He pulled out a big handkerchief
and, uncharacteristically, burst into tears. "By God," he grieved, "if I'd been
a better general, most of you wouldn't be here."[47] Even the toughest men of
honor may have a softer side.

In contrast to Patton's remorse, black soldiers returning from the war
came out of the experience with a greater sense of confidence and self-
respect. Yet, some paid dearly for their newly expressed dignity and refusal
to tip the hat, as it were, to any white. The reappearance of blacks in uniform enraged members of the Ku Klux Klan. Sergeant Isaac Woodard, age

twenty-seven, in the Marine Corps was discharged at Camp Gordon, Augusta, Georgia. For sitting where he liked, he got pulled from a public bus while he still wore his trim uniform. The police beat him severely, punched out an eye and blinded the other eye as well. In Alabama, a uniformed young black soldier pulled down a Jim Crow sign in a trolley. Incensed, the conductor drew out a handgun and shot the soldier several times. As he staggered off the streetcar, a policemen pulled out his gun and shot the man in the head, not out of mercy for his agony but out of sheer hatred. In Louisiana, for refusing to hand over some war souvenir, a black soldier was castrated and blow-torched, and his body dismembered.[48]

In Monroe, Georgia, two black men (one a veteran who did not show proper deference and the other accused of flirting with a white woman) and their wives were surrounded by a lynch mob of over thirty. They tied the victims to trees and then fired at close range into their faces. One of the men was also castrated. One of the women had her spine severed by the force of sixty bullets entering her body. The other woman was seven months pregnant. Outrageously, newly released files in 2007 reveal that the FBI investigated suspicions that the three-term governor of Georgia, Eugene Talmadge, sanctioned the murders to sway rural white voters during a tough election campaign. No one was ever arrested. In general, however, white extremists were not as prevalent; Southern politicians and their legions of voters intended a nonviolent domestic war in support of segregation and discrimination.[49]

Wartime propaganda insisted that the Allies were fighting to save democracy and crush totalitarianism and ethnic prejudice. Indeed, the National Association for the Advancement of Colored People (NAACP) membership rolls increased dramatically. Throughout the war years, especially in the late 1940s, the organization grew to 600,000 or more members. Its work was to serve as an advocate in the federal and state courts and to lobby legislators to pass antilynching measures and end state segregation laws. One of the organization's most frustrating efforts was attempting to break the color barrier in labor unions. Herbert Hill, who headed the struggle, did his best, but real change did not come until 1977. That victory was largely owing to a weakening of union membership in hard times. The manpower crisis forced open doors for African Americans.[50]

In the meantime, honor-bound whites of the South grew increasingly alarmed about blacks' aggressiveness. Earlier Supreme Court rulings on civil rights had not aroused much reaction in ardent defenders of segregation. But the *Brown v. Board of Education* decision in 1954 set off a panicked response. Was this not a direct overturning of ancient white custom and the elevation of blacks to equal status? The possible results made many shrink in terror. They imagined lust-driven black school boys raping the sweet young white things sitting next to them in classrooms. The old myths about lawless, power-mad blacks were once again trotted out.

A white Citizens Council sprang up in Mississippi, founded by Robert Patterson, a war veteran and large plantation manager in LeFlore County in the Delta region. He swore that "I, for one, . . . would gladly lay down my life to prevent mongrelization. . . . There is no greater cause." Soon there were approximately 60,000 Citizens Council members throughout the Deep South. This was more an upper-class or business-class organization. Unlike the Klan, there was no hooded paraphernalia or mumbo-jumbo. Rather, the group has been called a Rotary Club with a racist agenda.[51]

Honor figured in the literature and speeches of white men as if time since 1860 had stood still. Men had to prove their manliness, and what better way to do so in troubled times than to resurrect the past? A Greensboro, North Carolina, citizen claimed, "It is difficult to see how a man can retain his 'own self-respect' unless he also maintains his pride in his race." Tom Brady of Mississippi authored *Black Monday,* a diatribe against the high court for the 1954 *Brown* decision. The justices simply did not know blacks the way Southern whites did, Brady argued. He extolled the virtues of the antebellum ladies, "the loveliest and purest of God's creatures." Any black boy who besmirched a white woman would justifiably meet with "trouble."[52] Meanwhile, Senator Strom Thurmond of South Carolina thundered, "The court has flung a challenge of integration directly into the South's face." The justices were demanding Southern "surrender" again. The use of the language of the duel was appropriate for another age, perhaps.[53]

"Segregationists," writes historian Steve Estes, "hoped that a combination of honor and shame would galvanize the white community consensus against integration." He noted, however, that the stress by male, anticourt Southerners on their masculinity provided little or nothing for women to do, eager though some were to participate. Some organizers expressed the view that this was an all-male cause, and women should submit gracefully.[54]

Teenager Emmett Till, visiting from Chicago shortly after *Black Monday*'s publication, was murdered by two whites near the Delta town of Brookhaven, Mississippi. That event seemed to fulfill Brady's warning. The trial of the two men was naturally a fiasco, even though the pair readily

boasted of their complicity in this honor killing. They and their compatriots believed they were protecting white female integrity. Not surprisingly,
this brutality did not generate any remorse by the Citizens Council, though
some claiming gentlemanly status found it regrettable.[55]

Many lynchings made few headlines, but the outrage over the Till murder was not confined to the Northern black press and radio. It touched a
central nerve for many Americans, even some Southern journalists. In a
sense, Till did more in his death to advance the cause of freedom than he
could ever have guessed. The civil rights movement, which was in part
the result of the rediscovery of black male honor and self-reliance in war,
followed after VJ Day. Despite the intense exertions of Southern whites,
the movement progressed with the Freedom Riders, Rosa Parks, and the
voting efforts of black and white volunteers in Mississippi. While the elo-
quence of the black clergy was essential to the success of the movement, an
overlooked element was the role of the African American military. Indeed,
it could be said that the inspired leadership of Martin Luther King Jr., Ba-
yard Rustin, Medgar Evers, Rev. Fred Shuttlesworth, Andrew Young, and so
many other courageous black leaders benefited from the African American
veterans' experience.

Honor played a limited role in the stalemated U.S. war against North Korea
and its Chinese Communist allies. The army of Kim Il Sun, dictator of the
impoverished North Korean nation, invaded and conquered most of South
Korea in June 1950, only five years after the end of the Second World War.
President Harry Truman succeeded in having the United Nations' Security
Council authorize a military response. This war was forced on the nation;
no other choice but to fight was possible if the UN was to retain any credibility and the United States was to continue to be seen as a defender of
international law. Honor and humiliation had little to do with the eventual
recovery of most of South Korea, nor did they figure in the propaganda
about the invasion of South Korea and the American response. In Tokyo,
General Douglas MacArthur, a Medal of Honor recipient, had managed the
Japanese transition from military dictatorship to democracy. His next success was the brilliant seizing of the South Korean port of Inchon. Tragically,
however, MacArthur pressed his all-consuming pride and sense of superiority too far when he ordered the Allied forces, including those of Great
Britain and other nations, to proceed all the way to the Chinese border.

He had a mistaken view of the Red Chinese, shared by others from Harry Truman to the most junior member of the Pentagon staff: that the Communist Chinese were incapable of winning any engagement with American forces.

When the American 7th Fleet steamed into the Formosa Strait, China's leaders believed an imminent assault to retake all of China was in the offing. Writing to UN Secretary General Trygve Lie, Chinese Foreign Minister Zhou Enlai declared that this move was to prepare for the invasion of the mainland. Mao Zedong urged a violent crushing of "any provocation by the American imperialists."[56] Dean Acheson and others assumed that the Americans had the superior forces and thought China's reaction was mere bluff. Honor and a sense of superiority of arms were the basis for this misreading. The U.S. government made the decision to send the U.S. Army across the 38th Parallel and move further into North Korea. According to the historian Chen Jian, Chinese Communists believed it was their duty to expose the "imperialist nature" of American policy, to strike at the "arrogance" of American attitudes toward China: "The imperialists reckon that eventually we will beg alms from them in order to live." "Beating American arrogance" became a central propaganda theme in China when Truman came to South Korea's defense.[57] The new Chinese Communist regime felt threatened and poured over the border, pushing the Allies back until a stalemate and truce were reached.

Although he acted with dignity and even forbearance, MacArthur must have felt deeply humiliated when he found himself dismissed from the Korean campaign. Truman, along with his UN-sanctioned allies, was ready to reach peace through negotiation. But MacArthur had demurred. According to historian William Manchester, "He was a great thundering paradox of a man, noble and ignoble, inspiring and outrageous, arrogant and shy, the best of men and the worst of men, the most protean, most ridiculous, and most sublime." On 24 March 1951, MacArthur, hoping for an invasion and victory over all of China, publicly urged the United Nations to authorize the seizing of the enemy's coastal areas and interior bases. He argued that this advance would bring the Red Army in Korea to a point of "imminent military collapse."[58] He was defying the president, and that insubordination could not be tolerated. MacArthur's sense of failure was devastating, even though his right-leaning political supporters defended him vociferously. Such an abasement seldom has received as much publicity and controversy as MacArthur's loss of face.

Although misguidedly led by their commanders into further dangers, U.S. soldiers did not lack courage in the Korean engagement. In the lower ranks, one Medal of Honor recipient was Donn Porter of Baltimore, a member of my 1949 class at St. James School, near Hagerstown, Maryland. A cut-up in school, he was very popular and a football star. Porter enlisted and was sent to the front lines after training in 1952. Moving forward under heavy artillery and mortar fire, two enemy platoons attacked his combat post, destroyed all radio communications, and killed two of his three-man crew. Despite these losses, Porter retaliated by maintaining his position; he "poured deadly accurate fire" into the ranks of advancing Chinese "volunteers," exterminating fifteen of them and forcing the rest to flee. They soon returned for revenge and stormed his position. Bayonet in hand, Porter moved toward the enemy and killed another six. On his way back to his outpost, he lost his life from an artillery shell. In the words of his Medal of Honor citation, "Sgt. Porter's incredible display of valor, gallant self-sacrifice, and consummate devotion to duty reflect the highest credit upon himself and uphold the noble traditions of the military service."[59]

In the higher ranks, the invaluable leadership of General Matthew Ridgway rectified the errors of his predecessor, MacArthur. After MacArthur was relieved of command by Truman in April 1951, Ridgway was promoted to full general and took command of all United Nations forces in Korea. Ridgway earned the nickname "Old Iron Tits" because he wore hand grenades attached at chest level. One of his first acts was to restore morale in the ranks, a highly effective effort. One means to that end was to rotate out those division commanders who had been in action for six months. He would then install new commanders, all of whom were ordered to visit the front lines for longer stretches than they spent relaxing at command posts. Ridgway's increased use of artillery barrages gave the Chinese heavy losses. For stabilizing the Korean situation and for his many other accomplishments, Ronald Reagan awarded Ridgway the Presidential Medal of Freedom on 12 May 1986. The president exclaimed, "Heroes come when they are needed; great men step forward when courage is in short supply."[60]

Korea was the first war in which black soldiers came into their own. They could be found in all branches of the military. Moreover, they participated in all of the major battles including those that MacArthur had commanded to confront the Chinese invasion. In June 1950, close to 100,000 African Americans were involved in the conflict. Before it ended with the armistice in 1953, at least 600,000 had served. Among those in the ranks was Corporal Charles Rangel of Harlem, then eighteen when he enlisted in 1948. He won a Bronze Star and a Purple Heart for his valor fighting on the Chinese border. One of the reasons for his enlistment was the availability of a college education under the GI Bill. By that means, thousands of enterprising young African Americans advanced themselves and their careers. Rangel has since sat in the House of Representatives and been frequently reelected.[61]

From 1951 to 1953, hundreds of thousands of blacks were not merely assigned as truck drivers or dishwashers. Some held command positions. Most notable was black Lieutenant Colonel Samuel Pierce Jr., who successfully led three infantry companies that recaptured Yech'on. This was the first victory of the war, and it received national publicity and celebration. Captain Charles Bussey, who commanded an accompanying engineer company, earned a Silver Star. He had halted a North Korean advance on the flank and his unit killed over 250 enemy troops. His abilities and courage set a worthy example of what black soldiers could do.[62] Although progress toward desegregation was slow in peacetime, war hastened the process. The Pentagon and the Truman and Eisenhower administrations realized that black servicemen were underutilized. At last, the principles of self-respect and honor found official recognition.

8

HONOR AND SHAME IN VIETNAM AND IRAQ

All men dream, but not equally. Those who dream by night in the dusty recesses of their minds wake in the day to find that it was vanity: but the dreamers of the day are dangerous men, for they may act their dream with open eyes, to make it possible.

—T. E. LAWRENCE, *The Seven Pillars of Wisdom*

It has always been my view that terrorism is not spawned by the poverty of money; it is spawned by the poverty of dignity. Humiliation is the most underestimated force in international relations and in human relations. It is when people or nations are humiliated that they really lash out and engage in extreme violence.

—THOMAS L. FRIEDMAN, *The World Is Flat: A Brief History of the Twenty-First Century*

Unlike their two predecessors, the Vietnam and Iraq wars were preemptive. They need not have been fought. In both cases, the nation was more or less tricked into believing that world civilization would topple if Ho Chi Minh of North Vietnam and Saddam Hussein of Iraq were victorious. Leaders conjured up the peril that Communist Vietnam would seize control of Southeast Asia and even threaten Australia. Saddam was supposedly well on the way to gaining a nuclear device and other weapons of mass destruction. Neither story was true. Entry into these conflicts violated the codes of military honor taught at West Point and the Naval Academy.

Americans of the Vietnam generation differed from their older brothers who fought in Korea. In that Asian country, defeating a Communist power seemed fully justified. Thirteen allied nations supported this worthy cause with troops in the rice paddies and on the barren hills of Korea. The American troops in Vietnam, like the veterans of Korea, were draftees. But as the Vietnam War progressed, the grunts in the ranks grew more and more disillusioned, not only by the seemingly pointless engagement but also by the increasingly infuriated protests against the war in the homeland.

British veterans of World War I had repudiated the old-fashioned, gentlemanly aim of achieving patriotic glory through warfare. The poet Wilfred Owen denounced "The Old Lie: Dulce et decorum est / Pro patria mori." In his 2003 poem, Gary Jacobson, a wounded infantryman in Vietnam, echoed similarly disillusioned sentiments when he wrote, "It Don't Mean Nuthin'": "Turning stone-faced from fears to walk away / As though something's stolen part of their soul / Left no way sorrow's grief to console / Led too far astray in hell's battles darkning gray / Forever boyhood humanity to betray . . . / Staggering memories stored way down deep on the pile / Hidden from the light of day . . . for awhile! / 'But It Don't Mean Nuthin'.'"[1]

Poetically, Jacobson's writings may be less inspired than Owen's war poems. Yet Jacobson expressed a common feeling. Long gone was the exhilaration that the English poet Rupert Brooke had experienced before death from sepsis in 1915: "War knows no power. Safe shall be my going, / Secretly armed against all death's endeavour; / Safe though all safety's lost; safe where men fall; / And if these poor limbs die, safest of all." Brooke was young, untried, and immersed in the lore of romantic warfare.[2]

At the head of the U.S. government during Vietnam was President Lyndon Johnson, a Southerner steeped in the ideals of his region. Like T. E. Lawrence's statement in the epigraph, Johnson was a dreamer by day: the fantasies to gain immortality through action in wartime, to rescue a foreign nation from itself and Communism, and to plant American democracy in the Far East. Next to Jefferson Davis, no American leader was as dedicated to the principles of the honor code as Johnson. From an early age, Sam Johnson's son had been drilled never to forget his honor and always to fight back. The old man was a strict taskmaster, and Lyndon grew up afraid of him. Lyndon once told a story of how, at age fifteen, he had wrecked his father's car. He was so scared of his formidable parent that he fled by bus to a neighboring uncle's house. He felt like he "was going to the guillotine," he later confessed. Everyone in town knew about the unfortunate decision. When his father called Lyndon to the phone, Sam gave him instructions. Sam had turned in the wreck and bought a new automobile. He claimed he was too busy to retrieve it from the dealer. Lyndon was to pick up the new car and to drive it around the courthouse square at least twice. That way, the onlookers would know that Sam Johnson did not raise a coward who fled from his father's wrath.[3]

Throughout the Vietnam War, Lyndon Johnson was determined to sustain his popularity by showing strength, determination, and a manly outlook. His intense self-regard drove him obsessively to exercise power as a means to receive the gratitude of the public, which alone could ratify his claim to honor. Instead, as the war went on, the collapse of his national reputation drove him to despair and shame. To be thrown from the cliff of honor into the morass of ridicule and derision was an experience not to be repeated. According to biographer Doris Kearns Goodwin, "With each year in office, Johnson lost one supporter in ten." The mass of street and campus protests against the draft and against a distant, bloody, unwinnable war weakened his presidency. It could not recover. In response, Johnson halted the bombing in Vietnam and took himself out of the 1968 presidential race. By the time he made those decisions, only 26 percent of those polled were still loyal to him.[4]

To be sure, honor did not cause the Vietnam War, or, at least, was far less of a cause than it had been for nineteenth-century American wars. Nonetheless, did Johnson's engagement in Southeast Asia meet the criteria of "rational" motives to pursue a "just war"? According to a Gallup poll in 2004, nearly 62 percent of those polled concluded that the Vietnam War was not a "just war."[5] Donald Kagan, the Yale historian, notes that we in the West recognize only the so-called rational categories for war: territorial expansion, national security against perceived enemies, and overt demonstrations of power. But, he says, the role of honor that we might deem irrational often provokes the outbreak of violence. "Nations also react strongly to the fear of dishonor, to assaults on their dignity that are the result of passion and hatred, not calculation." By these standards, North Vietnam scarcely posed a threat, immediate or distant, to the security of the United States. On the other hand, Dean Rusk, while undersecretary of state for Far Eastern affairs in 1951, had articulated the "domino theory." Rusk was born in Cherokee County, Georgia, and was educated in Atlanta and at Davidson College in North Carolina. As he saw it, the Communist thrust in Indochina had to be countered by preemptive action. Otherwise, Burma, Thailand, Indonesia, India, and other nations would fall to the influence of the Soviets. As secretary of state under John F. Kennedy and Johnson, Rusk remained true to his early convictions. By 1962, he believed the spread of Communism would reach as far as Australia and even Africa unless checked in Vietnam.[6]

In advice to President Dwight D. Eisenhower in 1954, Admiral Arthur Radford, head of the Joint Chiefs of Staff, however, had concluded that "Indochina is devoid of decisive military objectives." For America to get involved would "be a serious diversion of limited U.S. capabilities."[7] Ten years later, Senator Richard Russell of Georgia was equally skeptical. He counseled Johnson that the North Vietnamese posed no threat to vital national interests. Following the Gulf of Tonkin incident, however, Russell joined the patriotic chorus for war, no doubt after learning about its popularity in his home state. The *casus belli* was based on a fiction. The North Vietnamese navy did not fire first on the U.S. destroyer *Maddox* on 4 August 1964, as the administration claimed.[8] But the charge had its intended effect in arousing the public. Johnson announced that these actions endangered America's national honor and threatened the United States with the loss of the "respect of other nations." Likewise, Senator John Cornelius Stennis of Mississippi initially doubted the need to assume a cause that France, the previous foreign power in Vietnam, had abandoned. Once the commitment to war was made irreversible, though, he rejoiced that Johnson's Great Society programs would have to be "relegated to the rear" in order to destroy the Viet Cong and gain "peace with honor." That phrase echoed around the Oval Office thereafter. Johnson was aware that the Southern conservatives "hate this stuff, they don't want to help the poor and the Negroes. . . . But the war, oh, they'll like the war."[9]

Unaware of the centuries of mistrust between China and the Vietnamese, the Johnson administration assumed that the small Southeast Asian country was merely a puppet of international Communism, governed not in Hanoi but in Beijing and Moscow. Such a distortion of reality was bound to be disastrous. Behind the scenes, Johnson expressed his chief worry. A hasty escalation of the war that Stennis and others were promoting on behalf of the Pentagon could well initiate World War III with China and Russia. Johnson was wrongly convinced that the Communist powers would unite to spark a general conflagration. For that reason, he adopted an incremental approach, embracing the delusion that each increase in commitment of men and materiel would bring victory.[10]

At the same time, Johnson's public pronouncements were thoroughly drenched in the rhetoric of honor. Two writers about the legendary Alamo concluded their work by remarking, "For Johnson, the soldiers in Vietnam were descendants of the Alamo, and he, at least in spirit, was William Barret Travis." In the psychology of honor, concern for reputation always plays an important role; Johnson's case was no exception. As a young serviceman in World War II, he had somehow managed to receive official recognition for bravery in the Pacific theater. A journalist later wrote that Johnson's medal was "one of the least deserved but most often displayed Silver Star in American military history." In retirement, speaking of his former senatorial colleagues, Johnson told Doris Kearns Goodwin, "You've got to understand the beliefs and values common to all of them as politicians, the desire for fame and the thirst for honor, and then you've got to understand the emotion most controlling that particular Senator when he thinks about this particular issue." He was actually describing himself.[11]

Personal honor can become a matter of sheer hubris. While maintaining that national "credibility" punctuated the pronouncements of other politicians, this president relied on the terminology of his native state. With his Texan bravado, Johnson put the matter succinctly almost exactly a century after Robert E. Lee's surrender at Appomattox: "If America's commitment is dishonored in South Vietnam, it is dishonored in forty other alliances or more." And at another time, he noted, regardless of consequences, "*We do what we must.*" By his perspective, honor has its own logic. Practical political considerations and the fear of Republican charges of Democratic cowardliness created in the president's mind the imperative to cast prudence aside. "We love peace. We hate war. But our course," Johnson announced in 1965, "is charted always by the compass of honor."[12] In the White House Rose Garden, he told members of the National Electric Cooperative Association, "Our national honor is at stake in Southeast Asia and we are going to protect it." A week later, he dispatched hundreds of thousands of American soldiers to meet that goal.[13] We are engaged in Vietnam, Johnson declared on another occasion, "because we have a promise to keep. . . . To dishonor that pledge, to abandon this small and brave nation to its enemies, and to the terror that must follow, would be an unforgivable wrong. . . . We will not be defeated. We will not grow tired. We will not withdraw."[14]

Johnson was no prophet. The nation eventually did grow tired and did withdraw, but it took time. Throughout the latter days of fighting, Johnson and his defense team debated how to end the war quickly. In 1968, with the country in political turmoil, Assistant Secretary of Defense Paul Warnke urged the president to press the South Vietnamese government to agree to negotiations as fast as possible. Warnke voiced the opinion that victory was not possible against a persistent North Vietnam and guerilla forces in the South. He, along with Henry Cabot Lodge Jr., worried that the public would no longer support a long and costly war. Protests were constantly mounting. But like other leaders past and present since Woodrow Wilson, Warnke and Lodge eventually came to believe the myth that "nation building" could finally win the day. Warnke advised Secretary of Defense Clark Clifford, "we have to scale down military activities to the point where our costs, particularly their human costs, are at a level that the American people will be willing to sustain for the long haul." That was a further delusion. But at last realities began to shape reactions. Instead of shipping thousands more troops into this conflict, Warnke suggested that the American government should announce "our intention to withdraw some 50,000 troops as early as September." Another advisor, Townsend Hoopes, undersecretary of the Air Force, was blunter. He simply told the truth: The Americans could not defeat the enemy. To think otherwise was a "dangerous illusion."[15]

For a ruler to distinguish between the cause of national honor and the desire for personal vindication may require uncommon wisdom, a quality Johnson lacked. He was sincere about his faith in the ancient virtue. Yet the distinction between the good of the country and the wielding of personal power eluded him. Years later, he told Doris Kearns Goodwin that in his fear of rejection during the Vietnam conflict, he often dreamed that "I could hear the voices of thousands of people. They were all shouting at me and running toward me: 'Coward! Traitor! Weakling!' They kept coming closer." He also explained that Harry Truman and Dean Acheson "lost their effectiveness" when China went Communist. Their problems, though, were "chickenshit compared with what might happen if we lost Vietnam." He predicted that he would be called "a coward. An unmanly man, a man without a spine."[16] The greatest dread that a man of honor faces is public repudiation and its psychological accompaniment, humiliation.

In 1968, when Clark Clifford asked a task force of Pentagon authorities if the enemy showed any signs of diminished will, he got an emphatic "no."[17] Ho Chi Minh intended to wear down the enemy's will to fight by prolonging the war beyond its apparent utility. "You will kill ten of our men, but we kill one of yours," Ho once declared, "and in the end it is you who will tire."[18] When bombing North Vietnam produced no results, Johnson persisted despite his own doubts. He told his cabinet on 22 August 1968: "We want peace now worse than anyone in the world—but with honor, without retreat."[19] To admit loss was no more in Johnson's character than it had been in Jefferson Davis's.

In the fighting, honor played a role in inspiring the white lower ranks, especially at the start. The Georgia General Assembly spent thousands of dollars to provide troops with the state flag, which included within it the old Confederate flag, an emblem of heroism from a different war. The army, however, prohibited display of the banner after the 1968 tragedy of Martin Luther King Jr.'s assassination.[20]

In the upper ranks, both the symbols and practice of the honor ethic were in short supply. For the sake of promotion, commanders lied about body counts; atrocities committed by U.S., South Korean, and ARVN (Army of the Republic of Vietnam) troops; the incompetence of the abysmally corrupt South Vietnamese army; and increasing problems of morale. General Paul Harkins, commander of the U.S. troops in Vietnam prior to General William C. Westmoreland, falsified intelligence reports about the number of guerillas killed and greatly distorted the realities of the war. Historian Douglas Kinnard describes another major problem, which was officially presented in a 1970 report to General Westmoreland. The general learned that the "lack of professional skills on the part of middle and senior grade officers" was a serious obstacle in the war effort.[21]

Despite this handicap, initiative gradually shifted from civilians to the military, with its heroic traditions. Journalist David Halberstam explains that the officer cadre had a "stronger hold on patriotic-*machismo* arguments (in decision making they proposed the manhood positions, their opponents the softer, or sissy, positions)." Thus, Westmoreland, a ramrod-straight West Pointer from a Spartanburg, South Carolina, textile mill–owning family, insisted that he needed massive reinforcements. By and large, he got them. The more that Allied troops were sent to the theater, from Great Britain, New Zealand, Australia as well as the United States, however, the more resentment and disaffection grew in the native population, and the greater the sense of meaninglessness in the demoralized Allied ranks. French General Charles de Gaulle had warned George Ball, a presidential advisor to Lyndon Johnson, as early as 1964 that the more the United States invested in the conflict, "the more the population would turn against it." Nonetheless, Johnson escalated the conflict because, as a political psychologist framed it, "his honour and dignity were too intimately tied to avoiding the appearance of failure or cowardice."[22]

Nearly sixty thousand Americans and three million Vietnamese were casualties in this inessential struggle. American combat troops suffered physical casualties at a rate of 16 percent while 12.6 percent needed psychiatric treatment for post-traumatic stress disorder or "battle fatigue." Save for on the Southern side a hundred years earlier, Americans had never before chosen defeat over continuing to defend the concept of national honor and "nation building." Eric T. Dean points out that the soldiers of the Civil War and both World Wars endured much greater misery than the American veterans in Vietnam. The latter GIs were well-fed, well-housed, well-clothed, and blessed with much better medical care than at any other time in national history. Dean does not, however, mention that Civil War servicemen at least understood their enemies' language.[23] Also, Civil War soldiers found slaves and sometimes Unionist whites willing to assist. The soldiers in the Asian war and, later, in Iraq were equipped with neither language skills nor trustworthy native friends. In Vietnam, that intelligence limitation created great anxiety and imperiled morale.

Nonetheless, as in all their wars, American boots on the ground appeared somewhat misleadingly to exemplify the very best of military honor—valor, initiative, discriminant killing to spare civilians. The army was fully integrated, but white resentments still were in the air. The relations of richer whites and poorer African Americans in this "mean, dirty war" also served as a segregating factor. Racial differences appeared especially after Martin Luther King Jr.'s assassination in 1968. Confederate flags floated in front of some tents until black troops complained.

But there were, too, recorded memories of close friendships with white soldiers. A television documentary showed a reunion of an African American pilot and a white Air Force veteran. Both captured, they had shared a prison cell, and the white pilot had managed to have his companion's daily whippings ended and nursed the black pilot after his beatings. Once again, black troops demonstrated their capacity as excellent soldiers. Twenty won Medals of Honor. In 1967, President Johnson conferred on U.S. Army Specialist Five Lawrence Joel the highest award the nation gives. He had, his Medal of Honor citation reads, a "very special kind of courage—the unarmed heroism of compassion and service to others." As a medic in 1965, he saved many troops under a fierce ambush. Against orders, he refused to leave any behind; though wounded twice, he defied Viet Cong gunfire and ministered to the troops still on the ground.[24]

One white hero will serve to stand for hundreds of others who were equally brave. Peter Lemon was among the 204 Medal of Honor winners in this war, most awarded posthumously. He survived and has three children, who will be shaped in part by his courage, modesty, and wisdom. Over six feet tall, with broad shoulders, he was nineteen when he went into combat. Struck by shrapnel from a mortar assault, he witnessed the slaughter of his nearest and closest comrade during an attack by four hundred Viet Cong in Tay Minh province that lasted three hours. Lemon and eighteen members of his platoon withstood two waves of determined guerillas. He fought furiously and was again wounded, yet kept going. The third assault was far worse than the first two. "I said to myself," he recalled, "You're not going to make it through this one." Not giving up, he found a machine gun and, though fully exposed in his position, kept on firing. He and his teammates held the outpost, but he and most of the others took weeks to recover in the hospital. Despite his inspiring experience, Lemon felt unworthy of the Medal of Honor. He thought his mates were far worthier, particularly those who died in the battle.[25] Similar acts of self-sacrifice and courage did not always win appropriate medals for valor in this unpopular war—a war for imperial grandeur and little more.

In the aftermath, veterans returning home found two negative reactions to their arrival. Opponents of the war cursed them for fighting it. Others heaped blame on their heads because they had not won. One civilian called them "baby killers and drug addicts." Nor did officials in Washington and throughout the country help them in finding jobs; they were mainly treated with indifference. But some soldiers rose above these handicaps. As the same documentary demonstrates, the war had its heroes, its moments of inspiration. Bob Mountain, from Millen, Georgia, lost a leg from a mortar assault. Nonetheless, he managed to train himself as a world-champion sprinter. "That kind of courage can only increase the feeling of shame that viewers" of this documentary "may be left with," a television reviewer noted. In the years since the Asian fighting, the nation has come to realize that there should be respect for the fallen as well as for those who survived. Unfortunately, the other lessons of Vietnam—how it all began and why it was an unholy muddle—were swiftly forgotten.[26]

In contrast to the American use of its own soldiers in Vietnam, during the British takeover of Iraq in the 1920s, the imperialists chiefly sent units from colonial India to crush the Arab rebellion against the British regime. The exclusive use of troops from a colonial subsidiary had not been possible either in the post–Civil War Republican Reconstruction or in Vietnam— or in Iraq under the Americans in the 2000s. The Iraqi population in the 1920s was only three million, which permitted a ratio of one Indian soldier for every twenty-three civilians. The ratio of Union soldiers to the number of civilians was far worse in the Civil War. A small number of troops in each state was practically limited to the state capitals. Enforcement had therefore been generally ineffective. But, until President Barack Obama withdrew American troops from Iraq in 2011, for the population of 25 million in Iraq, the scale was 174 Iraqis to every one coalition soldier.[27] With so small a group of army personnel, it is no wonder that insurgents opposed to the American invasion found comfort in the eventual American disillusionment with efforts to rebuild the occupied country by military coercion.

President George W. Bush and his colleagues worked hard to convince the public that Iraq represented a major threat, greater than that posed by the Islamic extremist group Al-Qaeda. The administration claimed that Iraq under Saddam Hussein possessed weapons of mass destruction, were building nuclear warheads, and had connections with Osama bin Laden's insurgents.

Even Secretary of State General Colin Powell was drawn in, probably against his better judgment. In early May 2004, Powell made a startling admission. On a Sunday television talk show, he confessed that Central Intelligence Agency (CIA) operatives had lied to or, more diplomatically, "misled" him about weapons of mass destruction in Iraq. He elaborated, saying that, in the words of a *New York Times* reporter, "he regrets citing evidence that Iraq had mobile biological laboratories in his presentation to the United Nations on February 5, 2003." This was supposedly the top reason for bringing down Saddam Hussein. Powell, a political general, had researched the relevant CIA documents but deflected the blame from the intelligence agency to the misleading sources the operatives had used. "Unfortunately, that multiple sourcing over time has turned out not to be accurate," Powell averred. In any event, this usually shrewd, perceptive general officer had been betrayed. His UN speech convinced millions of Americans that this would be a "just war." Honesty and truth-telling, usually part of the honor principles, were not present as they should have been. It turned out that the inventor of the story, an engineer linked to the Iraqi National Congress, an untrustworthy group of Iraqi exiles, had dreamed up the scenario. Why intelligence officers swallowed the story of Saddam's plots remains a mystery. But Powell, a man of integrity, has to live with the thousands dead and money lost in this unwholesome war. What could he say about that unfortunate situation? "'It turned out that the sourcing was inaccurate and wrong and in some cases, deliberately misleading,' Mr. Powell said in the interview, broadcast from Jordan. 'And for that, I am disappointed and I regret it.'" His remarks must not have been appreciated at the Pentagon or White House. Shortly afterward, Vice President Dick Cheney asserted that the administration still believed that the vehicles shown to Powell in the aerial photographs of a site in Iraq were part of a program of unconventional weapons, and added that Cheney "'would deem that conclusive evidence' that Mr. Hussein in fact had such programs."[28]

The occupation actually undermined the very idea of democratization in a land where primary loyalties are to family, clan, tribal leader, and mosque, not to a truly national entity. Moreover, unlike in postwar Japan and Germany, the populations of which had become disenchanted with totalitarian ideologies and were open to democratic philosophies, Iraqis still relied primarily on their fidelity to Islam, their tribes, and their sense of individual and collective honor. In post-Nazi Germany, for instance, local leaders—teachers, community leaders, clergymen, and newspaper and radio publicists—collaborated with an effective media campaign to adopt the occupiers' democratic ways. In contrast, according to post-Saddam opinion polls, the coalition forces when fully engaged in the country were "widely hated." In the words of Edward N. Luttwak, the Americans were considered "the worst of invaders, out to rob Muslim Iraqis not only of their territory and oil but also of their religion and family honor." Even the Kurds, who took part in the assault on Saddam and his army, with their history of autonomy, depend on the traditional sources of power in the mosque and tribe.[29]

The occupation's governance was bungled from the start. Ambassador Paul Bremer's initial act after replacing General Jay Garner, the first coalition commissioner, was his worst misstep. Bremer dismissed all members of Saddam Hussein's Baathist Party from the government. This policy meant that those people most expert in governance were excluded from their positions. In addition, Bremer disbanded Saddam's armed forces. Garner again protested: "Jerry, you can get rid of an army in a day, but it takes years to build one." The abolition of the Iraqi army and Baathist bureaucracy took place on 16 May 2003. Suddenly, 450,000 soldiers and officials from Saddam's bloated military and security forces lost status and income, with perhaps one million of their dependents left unsupported. The prospect of a violent backlash did not deter the new American ruler. The imposed regime was not a liberation force but, according to the Iraqis, a humiliating return of yet another imperialist foreign government.[30]

Paul Bremer's peremptory orders were based on the false premise that most Iraqis hated Saddam to such a degree that the Americans would be hailed as saviors. A diplomat without any experience in the Middle East, Bremer was bold but a hopeless and clueless strategist. Jay Garner had tried to remove only the top layers of the Baathists in military and civilian positions. Lower echelons could hold their jobs. Otherwise, the 24 million Iraqis would have no experienced administrators upon whom to rely.[31]

Saddam Hussein was a Sunni as was his Baath Party. It was a major force within Islam, but not in Iraq. The majority Shiites were constantly at odds with the Sunnis. The resulting scale of the conflict between the two was not immediately grasped by the Americans. The Pentagon and Bremer's government were afflicted with what David L. Philips, a former official in Baghdad, called "naivete, misjudgment and wishful thinking." It finally dawned on Bremer in May 2004 that the chaos in Baghdad and other centers could only be overcome with more troops. He requested a modest number—40,000 additional soldiers—but Secretary of Defense Donald Rumsfeld and the Pentagon were dedicated to the original plan of minimal forces. By this time, Moqtada al-Sadr, an Iraqi insurgent, had gained control of a large force that, though Shiite, turned against their American "liberators" and wreaked havoc. Al-Sadr's insurgency grew so severe in cutting American supply lines that Bremer had to think about food rationing in the Green Zone, a small area of the capital city of Baghdad controlled by U.S. forces. Thousands of Americans would have been affected. Only a year into the occupation, the world's greatest military power could not even supply food to its own people. Lieutenant General Ricardo Sanchez and Bremer both knew that the Iraq capital was in shambles and lawless, but they made no public or even private protest to higher authorities. Perhaps they were simply following orders in the traditional military style, but it showed an abysmal lack of courage and honor.[32]

As it was, the situation encouraged an emboldened insurgency to increase their suicide bombings and guerilla tactics. They, as well as the cashiered Iraqi army and bureaucratic personnel, had every reason to feel resentful of this "liberation." Some Baathist members of the police and army forces lost *sharaf*, a term in this context meaning honor as applied to Baathist loyalists. (Its original meaning was high birth or nobility of blood.) Although once honored, these well-trained professionals could no longer offer non-Baathist citizens a sense of security. A film clip that circulated showing the inspection of the captured Saddam's beard for lice was surely a deliberate effort to shame him. Even lightly touching another's beard signifies deep disgrace in Arab culture. That humiliation would also be seared in the memories of foreign Islamists, Sunnis, and Baathists who saw the incident.[33]

Many more Iraqis were stripped of *ihtiram*, that is, the element of deference and respect that the holding of coercive might demands and receives.
The disbanding of the agencies of the former government denied their leaders the weapons needed to protect their families, clans, and tribes. (Iraq
has over 150 tribes and approximately 2,000 clans.) The unemployment
rate was already high under Saddam, but it grew much higher after the
coalition conquest. The loss of economic power compounded the loss of
honor. The abrupt dismissal of Iraqis from their government positions left
an even greater power vacuum than the one in the Reconstruction South.[34]

On another level, Bremer had not only humiliated considerable numbers of men but also denied them the ability to shield their women from
the possibility of assault and rape. Protection of women's honor, *ird*, in-
flames Iraqi males to near obsession. In Middle Eastern cultures, women
are judged to be at the very center of male ownership rights. Whether
true or not, rumors that American soldiers would take Iraqi women into
their tanks and Humvees for lovemaking or rape were pervasive in Baghdad. Whoever the rapist may be, to dishonor a woman in that fashion is
to disgrace her and her kindred. In much of the region, relatives would be
required to kill the victim, no matter the extenuating circumstances, to
restore family honor.[35]

This type of blunder was not new in American history. During the Civil
War, as a nationalist Whig, Abraham Lincoln greatly overestimated the vi-
tality of Unionist sentiment as it had been expressed in the Constitutional
Unionist antisecession party of 1860. The Northern armies, he believed,
would liberate these silent loyalists from the toils of a rebellion they earlier
had disapproved. But having sworn allegiance to the Confederacy, former
Southern Whigs did not rally to the stars and stripes in the numbers needed
to sustain a postwar government. Likewise, during the Vietnam conflict,
Marine Corps General Lewis W. Walt and others promised to win the
"hearts and minds" of the South Vietnamese. It was supposedly a double
strategy—first, to confront the enemy aggressively using good intelligence,
and, second, to liberate ordinary peasants under Viet Cong control so that
they could be free to rally behind the anti-Communist effort. Such feck-
less plans for nation-building after the Civil War and during the Vietnam
conflict were doomed. The same lack of diligent preparation appeared in
the second Gulf War.[36]

Compounding the problem was the slimmed down U.S. Army in Iraq,
which would be vulnerable to attacks. Its limited size encouraged disrespect

for the occupiers. A large force would have had the opposite effect, but Rumsfeld, Undersecretary of Defense for Policy Douglas J. Feith, and others with little or no combat experience, showed contempt for those who were skeptical about the management of the occupation, such as U.S. Army chief General Eric Shinseki and his supporters. They urged a military presence of 350,000 or more soldiers to police the big cities and conduct antiguerilla operations. Rumsfeld denied the request. After the occupation, he even refused to call the upsurge of armed Sunnis against the imposed government and U.S. forces what it was—an "insurgency." In November 2005, he claimed to believe that these rebels were scarcely worth the elevated term "insurgent." He announced this "epiphany," as he called it. When the new chairman of the Joint Chiefs of Staff, Marine Corps General Peter Pace, used the forbidden word, Rumsfeld came up with a substitute: "Enemies of the legitimate Iraqi government." "How's that?" he asked. Insurgency implied that the United States was engaged in a second fiasco like Vietnam. The highest-ranking officials preferred analogies with fighting Hitler, Mussolini, and other enemies of democracy far better.[37]

The false analogy of Saddam Hussein's tin-pot dictatorship with Hitler's onslaught in Europe was ludicrous but firmly repeated in Pentagon and White House circles. Historian David Leverenz points out that "Liberating the Iraqis became almost analogous to liberating the Jews from Nazi concentration camps." It was hard for American leaders to see that a terrorist organization like Al-Qaeda was not state supported, at least not by a secularist Arab like Saddam Hussein. Earlier claims by Dick Cheney and others that Saddam and Osama bin Ladin were in alliance helped to justify the war as avenging the humiliating attack on 9/11. By 2006, it was quite clear that the whole scenario was phony. On 21 March 2006, President Bush pulled away from that rationale for the war. He declared that he had been misunderstood: "First . . . I don't think we ever said—at least I know I didn't say that there was a direct connection between September the 11th and Saddam Hussein."[38]

Aside from such mischaracterizations and full-blown arrogance, another source of confusion was the absence of experts in the country's languages. Rumsfeld and other Pentagon officials were suspicious of diplomats in the State Department who spoke Arabic. Presumably, they would be too soft on the enemy and show little spunk and manliness. A. Kevin Reinhart, an Arabic speaker sent to Iraq, explained in a January 2004 address at Vanderbilt University that in the entire time he was assisting in the development of political structures in Iraq, he had encountered only one other American who had any knowledge of Arabic. "The U.S. civilians," he said, "increasingly have almost no contact with any Iraqis aside from the handpicked elite. They live in a bunker—and this is seen as symbolically significant—in Saddam Hussein's palace and, literally, they never go out or if they go out, they go out in big convoys, in huge white SUVs that might as well have big targets painted on them." That distancing meant that Iraqis and Americans had too little knowledge of each other, their respective cultures, and their objectives. In addition, the American troops were increasingly overstressed, dealing with an insurgency, sometimes in temperatures as hot as 133 degrees, and with Iraqis clamoring for help or making complaints about the slowness of reconstruction and a host of other problems.[39]

The result was a deep sense of Iraqi mortification. That state of mind, however, was what Pentagon officials and the interrogators at the prisons at Abu Ghraib, Guantanamo, and elsewhere counted on: crushing not just enemy guerillas but the morale of all the people. Humiliation would encourage submissiveness—that was the expectation. No one would dare make that into publicly known official policy, but it lay beneath the surface.

In contrast to these gross errors of judgment and action, bravery and honor, as always, did appear on the sands and in the swamps of Iraq. For instance, Staff Sergeant Shannon Kay was in the rear of his Stryker armored infantry vehicle when a huge explosion ripped through the vehicle. "It was a huge physical force—the biggest I ever felt," said Kay, aged twenty-nine. "Some of the guys inside were kind of unconscious, so we dropped a ramp and dragged people out. It was just a natural reaction—any soldier would have done the same." With a full ambush underway, Kay, though wounded, showed unusual gallantry. He was bleeding from shrapnel wounds to his head, shoulder, and hand but refused medical treatment, instead assisting in quenching the flames around the stricken Stryker. According to the military report, "The fireball was enormous and the Kevlar blankets, tires and other components of the Stryker were on fire." The sergeant saved the lives of seven squad mates on a blood-soaked, debris-cluttered road in western Mosul, Iraq. For his swift reaction and courage, he earned a Silver Star. "Shannon is a natural leader. He has a strong sense of duty and honor," affirmed his mother. "He's always been a risk-taker and daredevil in sports—he was always the 'go-to' guy." Over 2,500 Americans lost their lives in this war. Shannon Kay's bravery was matched by hundreds of others, whether they survived or not.[40]

The upper ranks of the military also demonstrated boldness. Captain Ian Fishback of the 82nd Airborne Division publicly denounced the problems with detainee treatment. That failure in the upper command, he argued, led directly to atrocities not just in Iraq but elsewhere in U.S. prison camps. The lack of clear guidelines so disturbed Fishback that he urged the matter be investigated. His commanding officer, however, warned him to "remember the honor of the unit is at stake." While this disingenuous reply indicated that no action would ensue, the West Point–trained captain believed that the practices violated the military academy's honor code. He considered that set of rules as establishing the highest standard of conduct for everyone in the armed services.[41]

Another outspoken leader was Gulf War veteran General H. R. McMaster. In 1997, he published a devastating account of the Vietnam failure entitled *Dereliction of Duty,* originally written as a Ph.D. dissertation at the University of North Carolina at Chapel Hill. In it, he explained how Secretary of Defense Robert McNamara, President Lyndon Johnson, and the Joint Chiefs of Staff never had the brains or foresight to work out a practicable plan for defeating the Viet Cong and the North Vietnamese army. McMaster was passed over twice for promotion despite his clear military talents; he did not become a brigadier general until August 2009, at which time he was back in the United States. His task in Iraq had been to secure Tal Afar, a city of 250,000 near the Syrian border. The Sunni majority there harbored insurgents against the Shiite minority, terrorizing whole neighborhoods. McMaster changed the pattern by breaking with the tactical policy used hitherto. Previously, troops had moved around the countryside during the day but returned to base each night. The insurgents were thus left in command in the evenings, with the population too afraid of beheadings and other killings to report suspicions to the Americans. McMaster had the men occupy the city, and befriend and protect the town-dwellers. It was the first success in defeating the Sunni insurgents in Iraq.[42]

"When we came to Iraq," Colonel McMaster told *New Yorker* journalist George Packer, "we didn't understand the complexity—what it meant for a society to live under a brutal dictatorship, with ethnic and sectarian divisions. . . . When we first got here, we made a lot of mistakes. We were like a blind man, trying to do the right thing but breaking a lot of things." Later, McMaster further explained, "You gotta come in with your ears open. You can't come in and start talking. You have to really *listen* to people." The residents of Tal Afar started to cooperate, no longer threatened by the opposition forces.[43]

Despite the successes of the strategies of McMaster and his mentor, General David Petraeus, the abuse of prisoners at Abu Ghraib prison (formerly one of Saddam's prisons) outraged the Arab populace and increased sympathy for Al-Qaeda. The first public notice of U.S. troops' committing torture occurred following the killing of Manadel al-Jamadi. Photographs that shocked the world showed a grinning interrogator leaning over an ice-covered, battered corpse. Al-Jamadi had died within a few hours of his capture and incarceration at Abu Ghraib. He had been beaten and died in a strappado hanging, hung from his wrists with his hands tied behind his back. It was murder. The two CIA interrogators involved in the case have never been charged.[44]

The incidents at Abu Ghraib were the clearest example of how little respect or humanity some members of the military showed in dealing with the occupied nation. The tortures and humiliations of Iraqi prisoners were primarily the work of U.S. soldiers Lynndie England and her lover and superior, Charles Graner. The pair, apparently with the tacit or explicit consent of senior officers, photographed some salacious scenes. In one photo, England was watching a man forced to masturbate. In another, she and Graner observed a pyramid of naked prisoners. The publicizing of these atrocities inflamed the Arab world and nearly brought forced the resignation of the foolish and impatient Donald Rumsfeld as head of the Defense Department. But Bush refused to accept Rumsfeld's resignation. After Republican congressional losses in 2006, he did resign despite Vice President Cheney's continued support. After praising Rumsfeld for six years in office, President Bush blamed a bunch of so-called "bad apples," not the Pentagon, for the events at Abu Ghraib. No changes were undertaken to improve the treatment of prisoners. At least four deaths were attributed to the CIA, which apparently approved the techniques used at Abu Ghraib. But in March 2005, Porter J. Goss, director of the CIA, swore before a congressional committee, "We don't do torture." The press office of the agency published a statement: "All approved interrogation techniques, both past and present, are lawful and do not constitute torture. . . . C.I.A. policies on interrogation have always followed legal guidance from the Department of Justice. If an individual violates the policy, then he or she will be held accountable." Yet, Goss had approved the destruction of tapes about the treatment of prisoners.[45]

The photographs of Abu Ghraib prisoners were an effective recruiting device as well for the insurgents.[46] For instance, a Yemeni in Fallujah,

Iraq, before Fallujah's fall to U.S. forces told a reporter that the Abu Ghraib pictures had pushed this family man from driving a taxi in Sana to joining the ranks of the insurrectionists. Insurgency, writes Steven Metz, is "not won by killing insurgents, not won by seizing territory; it's won by altering the psychological factors that are most relevant."[47] There was truth in the comment. But still, the imposition of genuine order to overcome anarchy required a massive degree of force as well—if always under careful restraint. That was something a small, beleaguered number of coalition troops could not supply.

Graner and England received prison sentences of ten years and three years, respectively, in separate trials. General Janis Karpinski, who headed the Abu Ghraib contingent, was reprimanded for dereliction of duty and reduced in rank to colonel. She claimed that she was only following orders from above, but no heads higher than hers rolled.[48]

American cultural expansiveness, over which policymakers had no control, played into the hands of terrorists in Iraq as well as elsewhere in the Middle East. In his determination to purify Islam and the Arabic world from the corruptions of the Saudi royal family and the West, Osama bin Laden successfully combined two emotional forces—resentment of disgrace allegedly imposed by Americans and religious zealotry. He and other fanatics recalled centuries-old provocative incidents of defeat and betrayal to justify current hatreds. As in all honor societies, myths and memories of ancient wrongs figured into current politics and rationales for violence. Bin Laden warned, "If the Americans refuse to listen to our advice . . . then be aware that you will lose this Crusade Bush began, just like the other previous Crusades in which you were humiliated by the hands of the Mujahideen, fleeing to your home in great silence and disgrace."[49] He assumed that modern westerners still relish chivalrous victories over those medieval Saracens. But except for Hollywood films, most Americans would scarcely know anything about the feudal wars against Islam. Certainly, the installation of forty-eight substantial military bases throughout the Persian Gulf and Central Asian regions over the past twenty years, along with sizable diplomatic and troop support agencies, are bound to quicken Middle Eastern rancor, necessary though these undertakings may have been.

Two months before September 11th, an Arab viewer faxed Faisal al-Qassem, the television host in Qatar, these sentiments about Bin Laden:

"In light of the terrible Arab surrender and self-abasement to America and Israel, many of the Arabs unite around this man, who pacifies their rage and restores some of their trampled honor, their lost political, economic, and cultural honor." Under President Bill Clinton, the United States had withdrawn from Islamic Somalia, giving heart to the terrorists. "We found [the Americans] had no power worthy of mention," Bin Laden declared, and added, "America exited dragging its tails [sic] in failure, defeat, and ruin, caring for nothing."[50] Pax Americana has carried with it a fervent missionary zealotry to spread the idea of democracy worldwide. It was a fundamental tenet of Woodrow Wilson after World War I, and the Bush administration followed the same policy. In the past, however, the attempt to remake the world in the American image has been selective and short-lived.

+ + +

In conclusion, the United States entered these conflicts first to stem the tide of communism in Vietnam, and more recently in Iraq to eliminate an Arab dictator and his supposed nuclear and poison gas productions. Both efforts were based on false premises, and hundreds of thousands lost their lives. American casualties also were high in these misguided confrontations. The disaster of American struggles in Vietnam should have alerted the civilian and military leaders to their risks in the Second Gulf War. That divisive and unnecessary Far Eastern adventure was undertaken in an unfounded disrespect for communist North Vietnam. Honor can breed fantasies of easy victory. Vietnam was no removable pawn on the chessboard of international communism.

In Iraq, the deceptions employed has resulted in chaos in that country but also lost the trust that had been an aim in the process of nation building. Moreover, with Saddam's downfall, the Iranians had no serious rival and felt free to pursue their chief desire, nuclear capability. In the minds of successive administrative officials, fantasy overcame reality. Among the ethical violations arising from dreams of a democratic and peaceful Far and Middle East, honor gained nothing.

CONCLUSION

One idea has become clear. Once donned, the armored visage of national honor is not easily removed. American leaders do so, however, more frequently and readily than patriotic rhetoric suggests. The public speedily wearies of war leading to ambivalent consequences at best. For instance, the results in the Civil and Vietnam wars were eventual abandonment of both cause and allies—the Southern black community and the South Vietnamese anticommunists, respectively.[1] Iraqis, already suspicious of America's true intentions, will perhaps soon discover the same fate. A Gallup poll released in June 2005 revealed that 53 percent of Americans thought the invasion and occupation of Iraq was a mistake, a significant change from the 75 percent in favor of the war at the start.[2]

In a sense, however self-serving it appears, an American willingness to desert hopeless situations could make pragmatic, if brutal, sense—when costs in lives and treasure outweigh the dictates of honor.[3] Moreover, a degree of prudence suits a nation in which the benefits of freedom, individuality, and democratic practice are highly treasured. Who would have it otherwise? Americans prefer minimalist wars: quick, cheap engagements in which soldiers are not casually sacrificed. (The Barbary pirate engagement, the Spanish-American War in 1898, the various incursions into Latin America in the 1920s, the bloodless Panama and Granada takeovers, and the brief Gulf War of 1991 spring to mind.)

Disadvantages, however, can arise from hopes for a quick end. Lyndon Johnson's decision to use limited means in Vietnam serves as a case in point. He sought to save the country from a possible third World War. Tragically, he found that the political, economic, and human costs were much too high for whatever was the ultimate and always vaguely conceived goal. Likewise, George W. Bush sought a cheap, quick conflict with minimal troops, as if the objective were simply a shrewd political maneuver to display a posture of heroism. The son thought he would do better than his presidential father; he would destroy Saddam Hussein.

Of course, other factors besides showing off American might were involved in Iraq. But hidden beneath the ultra-conservative doctrines of "nation building" and policing the world lies the basic arrogance and vanity of power. The imperialism that Americans seem willing to accept imperils the nation and sets a course toward military domination, albeit run under civilian management.

Honor will always be useful as a national device for collective and military action. Probably at the present moment, to summon citizens to unsheathe swords to protect national honor would seem ludicrous to all but the most dedicated Civil War reenactors. Nonetheless, referring to the brave men under his command in the Gulf War, for instance, General Colin Powell described how army morale rested on one's comrades in arms being "clean . . . dedicated . . . motivated . . . selfless, patriotic, loyal . . . respectful, tolerant, and caring." He did not use the term "honor," but his list of attributes represents the military code at its best. A secular society finds nothing "sacred" about this essential path to battlefield survival. Still, Powell entitled his memoir *Sacred Honor*.[4]

In spite of Powell's endorsement, this nation no longer views honor as an indispensable factor in the affairs of state, as people thought it was during the Civil War. But in parts of the world today, the concept remains powerful, even commanding. Seeking to attain honor is an important stimulus for noble action on the battlefield, as well as in the seats of civilian power. Humanity is unlikely to forgo the honor imperative altogether. The American nation was and still is engaged in a war against Islamic extremism and ethnic and religious insurgencies in countries where honor and shame have the greatest intensity imaginable. The war in Afghanistan lies outside the range of this work. Nevertheless, it is appropriate to ask, is the American dream of remaking a foreign people being repeated there?

Regardless of that situation, a sad conclusion emerges. As early as 1966, at the height of the Vietnam crisis with its antiwar protests and street violence, the poet Robert Lowell voiced what he feared lay ahead. In a letter to the *Partisan Review* in 1966, he cannily prophesied, "I have a gloomy premonition . . . that we will soon look back on this troubled moment as a golden time of freedom and license to act and speculate. One feels the steely sinews of the tiger, an ascetic, 'moral' and authoritarian reign of piety and iron."[5] While still surprisingly diffident about the distant Asian wars, the American public discovered that Lowell's prediction was all too accurate. As a guiding principle in political relations, honor may well prove misleading and futile. At times, it becomes tragically so. This statement arouses among some an immediate and negative reaction. What about the essential qualities of military honor—are they to be forgotten or thrown away on the trash heap of useless traditions? No, never. The monuments for the dead heroes in Washington and throughout the land memorialize the defenders of liberty and of honor itself. Janus-faced, the ethic is a highly regarded imperative in wartime but often overlooked in the heat and turmoil of warfare. But it can be a dangerous and sometimes lawless force in the ordinary routines of civilians at large.

⁜ ⁜ ⁜

I hope this work will be only the first of many to explore the interrelationships of honor, race, and humiliation. Such an approach should identify the many versions of honor that have existed and still persist today. I present here those aspects that are the most salient to the theme of honor and male, military life, chiefly in the past. The work has covered a limited range, leaving much still to be explored by others.

The era of the twentieth century, for instance, should engage considerable attention. Likewise, regional variations may be discovered: Discussion of the North could be filled out more thoroughly than was done here. And perhaps people of the Midwest and West have developed their own ethical modes. In addition, class and social hierarchy matter. We are all recipients of our cultural heritage—the ways we have of speaking, thinking, praying, and doing life's demands from birth forward. These forces have a tremendous emotional and mental impact that could be linked to the themes this book engages. Both rebels against the social order and rigid conformists are equally affected by the larger patterns of the place and style of their surroundings. Cultural and environmental imperatives are so significant that historians would do well to link them to this trio of ideas. Above all, female honor, race, and humiliation deserve a full-scale exploration. It would present a much-needed perspective on the role women, white and black, have played with regard to these matters.

Nowadays, many schools and colleges present honor codes in one form or another. Thomas Jefferson's University of Virginia formally began the trend in 1842 when the faculty adopted an honor code for cheating offenses on examinations, but the history of such codes at Virginia stretches back to earlier years. The West Point code was developed by Douglas MacArthur in 1922, following that of Stanford University a year earlier. The Naval

Academy claims not to have a honor code but rather an "honor concept." That term means some cheaters may be expelled and dishonorably discharged, but others undergo a process of rehabilitation. Other institutions have similar documents, usually stating that students should never lie, cheat, or steal. As these pages have sought to demonstrate, the American military and diplomatic branches of government have long required loyalty, deference to authority, and steadfastness of purpose in all their transactions.

The history of honor in America is not a happy one. In this country, some aspects of honor have fortunately lost their heft. Revenge is no longer always thought to be a necessary response to humiliation and insult. Nor does honor accrue any longer to one race or another. Even so, racial divisions abide. The pathology of honor once demanded forceful imposition of humiliation on victims for insults or other shows of defiance. While that principle has lost some of its popularity, it still exists in the behavior of youthful street gangs in Los Angeles, Detroit, Baltimore, Boston, and other cities. Sometimes headlines announce honor killings by immigrant parents or relatives against a woman who was raped; refused marriage to an older, parent-selected man; or was thought by the family and community to be defiled by her sexual practices.

Elsewhere, especially in the Middle East and North Africa, the old traditions have recently taken a virulent upsurge. Honor killings and disfiguring with acid splashed in a woman's face are common and horrifying to modern minds. But the American record of lynchings and other actions to humiliate and intimidate blacks, which took place as late as the mid-twentieth century, highlight American shame.

Whether modern or more traditional—even in some cases what we consider to be primitive—some forms of honor will prevail. What kind, however, only the future will reveal.

NOTES

Introduction

1. Michael Paul Rogin, *Fathers and Children: Andrew Jackson and the Subjugation of the American Indian* (New York: Knopf, 1973), 147.

2. Google books Ngram Viewer, "honorable," http://books.google.com/ngrams/graph?content=honorable&year_start=1800&year_end=2000&corpus=0&s.

3. Kevin Sieff and Richard Leiby, "Afghan Troops Get a Lesson in American Cultural Ignorance," *Washington Post*, 28 September 2012, http://www.washingtonpost.com/world/asia_pacific/afghan-troops-get-a-lesson-in-american-cultural-ignorance/2012/09/28/6882621a-08d4-11e2-a10c-fa5a255a9258_story.html; "Iraqi Journalist Throws Shoes at Bush in Baghdad," CNN, 14 December 2008, http://articles.cnn.com/2008-12-14/world/bush.iraq_1_al-zaidi-iraqi-journalist-shoe?_s=pm: world; "Shoes Thrown at Bush on Iraq Trip," BBC News, 15 December 2008, http://news.bbc.co.uk/2/hi/7782422.stm.

4. Bertram Wyatt-Brown, *Southern Honor: Ethics and Behavior in the Old South* (New York: Oxford University Press, 1982), 51.

5. Kristin L. Hoganson, *Fighting for American Manhood: How Gender Politics Provoked the Spanish-American and Philippine-American Wars* (New Haven, Conn.: Yale University Press, 1998); Margaret S. Creighton, *The Colors of Courage: Gettysburg's Forgotten History: Immigrants, Women, and African Americans in the Civil War's Defining Battle* (New York: Basic Books, 2005); Nina Silber, *Gender and the Sectional Conflict* (Chapel Hill: University of North Carolina Press, 2008); Amy S. Greenberg, *Manifest Manhood and the Antebellum American Empire* (New York: Cambridge University Press, 2005); Stephen W. Berry II, *All That Makes a Man: Love and Ambition in the Civil War South* (New York: Oxford University Press, 2003).

6. Mary Boykin Chesnut, *Mary Chesnut's Diary*, ed. Catherine Clinton (New York: Penguin, 2011). Other works to consult include Elizabeth Fox-Genovese, *Within the Plantation Household: Black and White Women of the Old South* (Chapel Hill: University of North Carolina Press, 1988), and Catherine Clinton, *The Plantation Mistress: Woman's World in the Old South* (New York: Pantheon, 1982).

7. See Bertram Wyatt-Brown, *The Shaping of Southern Culture: Honor, Grace, and War, 1760s–1880s* (Chapel Hill: University of North Carolina Press, 2001), 253; United Daughters of the Confederacy, Missouri Division, *Reminiscences of the Women of Missouri during the Sixties* (n.p., 1913), 294–98.

8. One view of how men thought of women in the nineteenth century was revealed in the writings of Charles Darwin. Man, he argued, seeks "a higher eminence, in whatever he takes up, than woman can attain—whether requiring deep thought, reason, or imagination, or merely the use of the senses and hands." Anthony Gottlieb, "It Ain't Necessarily So," *The New Yorker*, 17 September 2012, 88.

9. Lope de Vega, *Los Comendadores de Córdoba*, quoted in Donald R. Larson, *The Honor Plays of Lope de Vega* (Cambridge, Mass.: Harvard University Press, 1977), 5.

10. Henry Adams, *John Randolph* (Boston: Houghton Mifflin, 1898), 293; Ritchie Devon Watson Jr., *Normans and Saxons: Southern Race Mythology and the Intellectual History of the American Civil War* (Baton Rouge: Louisiana State University Press, 2008), 14.

11. Paul Robinson, *Military Honour and the Conduct of War: From Ancient Greece to Iraq* (London: Routledge, 2006).

12. J. A. Pitt-Rivers, *The People of the Sierra* (Chicago: University of Chicago Press, 1971); Pitt-Rivers, *Mediterranean Countrymen: Essays in the Social Anthropology of the Mediterranean* (Paris: Mouton, 1963); J. G. Péristiany and J. A. Pitt-Rivers, *Honor and Grace in Anthropology* (New York: Cambridge University Press, 1992); J. G. Péristiany, ed., *Honour and Shame: The Values of Mediterranean Society* (Chicago: University of Chicago Press, 1966); Mary Douglas, *Purity and Danger: An Analysis of the Concepts of Pollution and Taboo* (New York: Routledge, 2002). Works on European honor include James Bowman, *Honor: A History* (New York: Encounter Books, 2006); Robert A. Nye, *Masculinity and Male Codes of Honor in Modern France* (New York: Oxford University Press, 1993); Kevin McAleer, *Dueling: The Cult of Honor in Fin-de-Siècle Germany* (Princeton, N.J.: Princeton University Press, 1994); James Kelly, *"That Damn'd Thing Called Honour": Duelling in Ireland, 1570–1860* (Cork: Cork University Press, 1995); and Kwame Anthony Appiah, *The Honor Code: How Moral Revolutions Happen* (New York: Norton, 2010).

13. Larry Welborn, "Brothers Convicted of Killing Teenager over 'Disrespect,'" 14 April 2011, http://www.streetgangs.com/news/041411_killing_over_disrespect#; Tracy E. Barnhart, "'Bloods' More Gang Knowledge," 15 October 2009, http://www.corrections.com/news/article/22428-bloods-more-gang-knowledge; Elijah Anderson, *Streetwise: Race, Class, and Change in an Urban Community* (Chicago: University of Chicago Press, 1990).

14. Douglas L. Cairns, ed., *Oxford Readings in Homer's Iliad* (New York: Oxford University Press, 2001), 336; Richard Holway, *Becoming Achilles: Child-Sacrifice, War, and Misrule in the Iliad and Beyond* (Lanham, Md.: Lexington Books, 2012); Kenneth John Atchity, *Homer's Iliad: The Shield of Memory* (Carbondale: Southern Illinois University Press, 1978), 276; M. I. Finley, *The World of Odysseus* (1954; reprint New York: New York Book Review, 2002), 117–20.

15. Evelin Lindner, *Making Enemies: Humiliation and International Conflict* (Westport, Conn.: Praeger, 2006), 23. Other useful works by Lindner include *Emotion and Conflict: How Human Rights Can Dignify Emotion and Help Us Wage Good Conflict* (Westport, Conn.: Praeger, 2009), and *Gender, Humiliation, and Global Security: Dignifying Relationships from Love, Sex, and Parenthood to World Affairs* (Santa Barbara, Calif.: Praeger, 2010).

16. William Ian Miller, *Humiliation and Other Essays on Honor, Social Discomfort, and Violence* (Ithaca, N.Y.: Cornell University Press, 1993), 131. See also E. P. Thompson, "Rough Music Reconsidered," *Folklore* 103 (1992): 3–26; Ning Zhang, "Prostitute Humiliation Dents Police Image," China Network Television, 27 July 2010; Donald C. Klein, "The Humiliation Dynamic: Viewing the Task of Prevention from a New Perspective," *Journal of Primary Prevention* 12, no. 2 (1991): 87–121; Helen B. Lewis, *Shame and Guilt in Neurosis* (New York: International Universities Press, 1971); Nora Femenia, "Healing Humiliation and the Need for Revenge," unpublished paper, presented at the PARC (Program on the Analysis and Resolution of Conflicts) Conference on "Cutting Edge Theories and Recent Developments in Conflict Resolution," Maxwell School, Syracuse University, 27 September 2007.

17. Douglas L. Cairns, *Aidos: The Psychology and Ethics of Honour and Shame in Ancient Greek Literature* (Oxford: Clarendon Press, 1993), 15; Gabriele Taylor, *Pride, Shame and Guilt: Emotions of Self-Assessment* (New York: Oxford University Press, 1985), 64–67.

18. Sandra Tan, "Teenager Struggled with Bullying before Taking His Life; Boy Talked of Suicide Multiple Times Online" *Buffalo News,* 20 September 2011, http://www .buffalonews.com/apps/pbcs.dll/article?AID=/20110920/CITYANDREGION/309209931; Leonard Pitts Jr., "For Gay Kids, 'It Will Get Better'—But Only If We Help," *Baltimore Sun,* 23 October 2011, http://articles.baltimoresun.com/2011-10-23/news/bs-ed -pitts-20111023_1_gay-life-fight-bigotry-troubled-kids.

19. Eugene Genovese, *Roll, Jordan Roll: The World the Slaves Made* (New York: Vintage, 1974).

20. Dwight D. Eisenhower, Farewell Address, "Military-Industrial Complex Speech," 17 January 1961, http://www.ourdocuments.gov/doc.php?flash=true&doc=90&page =transcript.

21. See W. J. Cash, *The Mind of the South* (Garden City, N.Y.: Doubleday, 1941); C. Vann Woodward, *The Strange Career of Jim Crow* (New York: Oxford University Press, 1955); Woodward, *Tom Watson, Agrarian Rebel* (New York: Macmillan, 1938); Woodward, *American Counterpoint: Slavery and Racism in the North-South Dialogue* (Boston: Little, Brown, 1971); Woodward, *The Burden of Southern History* (Baton Rouge: Louisiana State University Press, 1960); Woodward, *Origins of the New South, 1877–1913* (Baton Rouge: Louisiana State University Press, 1971); John Hope Franklin, *A Southern Odyssey: Travelers in the Antebellum North* (Baton Rouge: Louisiana State University Press, 1976); Franklin, *Reconstruction: After the Civil War* (Chicago: University of Chicago Press, 1961); Franklin, *The Militant South, 1800–1861* (Cambridge, Mass.: Belknap Press of Harvard University Press, 1956); Fred Hobson, *Tell about the South: The Southern Rage to Explain* (Baton Rouge: Louisiana State University Press, 1983); and Clement Eaton, *Freedom of Thought in the Old South* (Durham, N.C.: Duke University Press, 1940).

1 African American Male Slaves' Honor

1. Stanley Elkins, *Slavery: A Problem in American Institutional and Intellectual Life* (Chicago: University of Chicago Press, 1959); Elkins, "Slavery and Ideology," in *The*

Debate over Slavery: Stanley Elkins and His Critics, ed. Ann J. Lane (Urbana: University of Illinois Press, 1971), 325–78; Elkins, "The Slavery Debate," *Commentary* 60 (December 1975): 40–54.

2. I acknowledge with gratitude the critical readings of Susan Marbury and Anne Marbury Wyatt-Brown. Also most helpful were Lawrence Friedman, David Hackett Fisher, Mark Smith, Vernon Burton, Ellen DuBois, David Brion Davis, and Wesley Joyner. Female honor is a matter of negatives, modesty not male-like bravado, chastity not male sexual license, submissiveness to male authority not male aggression or leadership, and so on. Therefore, the nature of female slave honor is not covered here. Some of the material in this chapter was borrowed from Bertram Wyatt-Brown, "The Mask of Obedience: Male Slave Psychology in the Old South," *American Historical Review* 93 (December 1988): 1228–52.

3. Unfortunately, we have almost no records of what the slaves thought because for many years few had sufficient command of English and the skill of writing needed for the task. Later interviews with old freedmen and memoirs, though, are helpful. Teaching the rudiments of writing and reading was prohibited in the slave states. Few anecdotes—or even legends—explain how newly arrived Africans reacted to this initial requirement in light of their African roots.

4. W. E. B. Du Bois, *Black Reconstruction in America, 1860–1880* (New York: Free Press, 1998), 52–53; Mark M. Smith, ed., *Stono: Documenting and Interpreting a Southern Slave Revolt* (Columbia: University of South Carolina Press, 2005); John K. Thornton, *Warfare in Atlantic Africa, 1500–1800* (London: UCL Press, 1999); Thornton, "African Dimensions of the Stono Rebellion," in *A Question of Manhood: A Reader in U.S. Black Men's History and Masculinity*, vol. 1, ed. Darlene Clark Hine and Earnestine Jenkins (Bloomington: Indiana University Press, 1999), 115–29. See also T. J. Desch Obi, *Fighting for Honor: The History of African Martial Art Traditions in the Atlantic World* (Columbia: University of South Carolina Press, 2008).

5. Sylviane A. Diouf, *Servants of Allah: African Muslims Enslaved in the Americas* (New York: New York University Press, 1998), 24. For Abdul Rahman Ibrahim Ibn Sori, see Terry Alford, *Prince among Slaves* (New York: Harcourt Brace Jovanovich, 1977), and T. H. Gallaudet, *A Statement with Regard to the Moorish Prince, Abduhl Rahhahman* (New York: Daniel Fanshaw, 1828). See also a series of articles that appeared in the periodical *African Repository and Colonial Journal:* "The Unfortunate Moor," *African Repository and Colonial Journal* 3 (February 1828): 364–67; "Abduhl Rahahman, The Unfortunate Moorish Prince," *African Repository and Colonial Journal* 4 (May 1828): 77–81; "Abduhl Rahahman, the Unfortunate Moor," *African Repository and Colonial Journal* 4 (October 1828): 243–50; "Error Corrected," *African Repository and Colonial Journal* 4 (February 1829): 379. See also "Prince among Slaves: The Cultural Legacy of Enslaved Africans," www.princeamongslaves.org.

6. Diouf, *Servants of Allah*, 10, 41; James Watt, *Journal of James Watt: Expedition to Timbo, Capital of the Fula Empire in 1794*, ed. Bruce L. Mouser (Madison: African Studies Program, University of Wisconsin–Madison, 1994), 44–46 (entries for 9–10 March

1794); Theophilus Conneau, *A Slaver's Log Book; or, 20 Years' Residence in Africa* (1855; reprint Englewood Cliffs, N.J.: Prentice-Hall, 1976), 66–70.

7. Conneau, *A Slaver's Log Book,* 141. Conneau remarks, of women wearing clothes only from the waist down, "No nation in the world can boast of better or equal forms" (140).

8. "The Unfortunate Moor," *African Repository and Colonial Journal* 3 (February 1828): 365.

9. Alford, *Prince among Slaves,* 21–24.

10. "Adbul Rahahman, The Unfortunate Moorish Prince," *African Repository and Colonial Journal* 4 (May 1828): 79; Alford, *Prince among Slaves,* 23, 29–30; Marcus Rediker, *The Slave Ship: A Human History* (New York: Penguin, 2008), 28.

11. "Abduhl Rahaman: The Unfortunate Moorish Prince," *African Repository and Colonial Journal* 4 (May 1828): 80.

12. See Alford, *Prince among Slaves,* especially 3–38, 42.

13. Alford, *Prince among Slaves,* 43–44; "The Unfortunate Moor," *African Repository and Colonial Journal* 3 (February 1828): 366.

14. Bertram Wyatt-Brown, *The Shaping of Southern Culture: Honor, Grace, and War, 1760s–1880s* (Chapel Hill: University of North Carolina Press, 2001), 4. See also Elizabeth Fox-Genovese, *Within the Plantation Household: Black and White Women of the Old South* (Chapel Hill: University of North Carolina Press, 1988), 189.

15. Alford, *Prince among Slaves,* 45–47; Stephen F. Power, comp., *The Memento: Old and New Natchez 1700 to 1897* (Natchez, Miss.: S. Power, 1897), 13.

16. Alford, *Prince among Slaves,* 47; Bernard Bailyn, *Voyagers to the West: A Passage in the Peopling of America on the Eve of the Revolution* (New York: Vintage, 1988), 491; Eron Rowland, ed., *Life, Letters and Papers of William Dunbar of Elgin, Morayshire, Scotland, and Natchez, Mississippi: Pioneer Scientist of the Southern United States* (Jackson: Mississippi Historical Society, 1930), 26–28 (entry for 12 July 1776).

17. Alford, *Prince among Slaves,* 47–48; Power, *The Memento,* 13–14.

18. Alford, *Prince among Slaves,* 79–82; Power, *The Memento,* 14; Christopher Morris, "The Strange Career of Gideon Gibson: An Early American Tragedy," in *Southern Character: Essays in Honor of Bertram Wyatt-Brown,* ed. Lisa Tendrich Frank and Daniel J. Kilbride (Gainesville: University of Florida Press, 2011), 38. See also "An African Prince," Washington *Daily National Intelligencer,* 8 May 1828, 2; T. H. Gallaudet, *A Statement with Regard to the Moorish Prince, Abduhl Rahhaman* (New York: Daniel Fanshaw, 1828), 3, 8; "The Unfortunate Moor," *African Repository and Colonial Journal* 3 (February 1828): 336–67; and "Abduhl Rahaman, the Unfortunate Moor," *African Repository and Colonial Journal* 4 (October 1828), 246. See also John W. Blassingame, ed., *Slave Testimony: Two Centuries of Letters, Speeches, Interviews, and Autobiographies* (Baton Rouge: Louisiana State University Press, 1977), 682–86.

In 1828, Ibrahim claimed to be a loyal Muslim but "anxious" to have a Bible in Arabic. See "Abduhl Rahaman, the Unfortunate Moorish Prince," *African Repository and Colonial Journal* 4 (May 1828): 78, and "An African Prince," Washington *Daily National Intelligencer,* 8 May 1828, 2. Gallaudet, *Statement,* 3, asserted that Ibrahim's "wife, and eldest son have been baptized, and are in connexion with the Baptist Church." She was apparently a Methodist. Omar Ibn Said, another formerly highly placed Fulani, enslaved in North Carolina, refused inquiries about returning to his homeland; he also submitted to Christian convictions after years of serving Allah in America. Blassingame, ed., *Slave Testimony*, 470–74.

19. Anthropologist Paul Riesman, as quoted by Patterson, notes that, like "chivalry," *pulaaku* signifies "at once certain moral qualities and a group of men possessing these qualities." Orlando Patterson, *Slavery and Social Death: A Comparative Study* (Cambridge, Mass.: Harvard University Press, 1982), 84; Alford, *Prince among Slaves*, 65.

20. Alford, *Prince among Slaves*, 58–61, 73–75, 90; Gallaudet, *Statement*, 4.

21. Philip D. Morgan, *Slave Counterpoint: Black Culture in the Eighteenth-Century Chesapeake and Lowcountry* (Chapel Hill: University of North Carolina Press, 1998), 276. Ibrahim Ibn Sori had five sons and four daughters by two marriages, many of whom had progeny that brings his lineage to the present. Two sons accompanied Ibrahim Ibn Sori and his second wife, Isabella, to Africa in his old age. Lewis Tappan and other New York philanthropists arranged for their passage to Monrovia after Foster released them from bondage. Unfortunately, the prince died of a fever before reaching Timbo and before he could pay for the freedom of the rest of his family. PBS produced a video on the life of Ibrahim; for more information visit http://www.pbs.org/programs/prince-among -slaves.

22. Shane White and Graham White, "Slave Clothing and African-American Culture in the Eighteenth and Nineteenth Centuries," *Past & Present* 148 (August 1995): 153.

23. Letter to John Bartram from Peter Collinson, 17 February 1737, in William Dar-lington, *Memorials of John Bartram and Humphrey Marshall, with Notices of Their Botani-cal Contemporaries* (Philadelphia: Lindsay and Blakiston, 1849), 89. See also Richard L. Bushman, *The Refinement of America: Persons, Houses, Cities* (New York: Knopf, 1992); White and White, "Slave Clothing and African-American Culture," 153; Jonathan Prude, "To Look upon the 'Lower Sort': Runaway Ads and the Appearance of Unfree Laborers in America, 1750–1800," *Journal of American History* 78 (June 1991): 145.

24. White and White, "Slave Clothing and African-American Culture," 152. For many newly imported Africans, European dress might have seemed commonplace because of Western incursions into the hinterlands. Owning foreign raiment was a sign in West Africa of special status and honor.

25. Jody R. Fernald, "In Slavery and in Freedom: Oliver C. Gilbert and Edwin War-field Sr.," *Maryland Historical Magazine* 106 (Summer 2011): 141–62.

26. Frederick Law Olmsted, *The Cotton Kingdom: A Traveller's Observations on Cotton and Slavery in the American Slave States, 1853–1861,* ed. Arthur M. Schlesinger (New York: Knopf, 1953), 28.

27. White and White, "Slave Clothing and African-American Culture," 149–86.

28. Ibid., 156.

29. Richard Hofstadter and Michael Wallace, eds., *American Violence: A Documentary History* (New York: Vintage, 1971), 196.

30. Mark M. Smith, *How Race Is Made: Slavery, Segregation, and the Senses* (Chapel Hill: University of North Carolina Press, 2006), 14, 24; Smith, "Producing Sense, Consuming Sense, Making Sense: Perils and Prospects for Sensory History," *Journal of Social History* 40, no. 4 (Summer 2007): 841–58.

31. Smith, *How Race Is Made,* 24.

32. Ibid., 34–36; Primo Levi, *Survival in Auschwitz: The Nazi Assault on Humanity,* trans. Stuart Woolf (New York: Collier, 1961), 23.

33. Olmsted, *The Cotton Kingdom,* 25–26, 28; Legrand H. Clegg II, "Ebonics: A Serious Analysis of African American Speech Patterns," *Maat News* 1, no. 2 (January 1997), http://www.melanet.com/clegg_series/ebonics.html.

34. Walt Wolfram, Erik R. Thomas, and Elaine W. Green, "The Regional Context of Earlier African-American Speech: Evidence for Reconstructing the Development of AAVE," *Language in Society* 29 (September 2000): 315–55; Michael Montgomery, Janet M. Fuller, and Sharon DeMarse, "'The Black Men Has Wives and Sweet Harts [and Third Person Plural-s] Jest Like the White Men': Evidence for Verbal -s from Written Documents on Nineteenth-Century African American Speech," *Language Variation and Change* 5 (1993): 335–57; Edgar W. Schneider, "The Origin of the Verbal -s in Black English," *American Speech* 58 (1983): 99–113.

35. "The Cultural Landscape of the Plantation: 'We'll Soon Be Free,'" http://www.gwu.edu/~folklife/bighouse/panel22.html.

36. Charles Reagan Wilson, *Southern Missions: The Religion of the American South in Global Perspective* (Waco, Texas: Baylor University Press, 2006), 6.

37. C. Eric Lincoln, "The Black Heritage in Religion in the South," in *Religion in the South: Essays,* ed. Charles Reagan Wilson (Jackson: University Press of Mississippi, 1985), 45.

38. Mechal Sobel, *The World They Made Together: Black and White Values in Eighteenth-Century Virginia* (Princeton, N.J.: Princeton University Press, 1987), 3.

39. "Cultural Landscape of the Plantation."

40. Diouf, *Servants of Allah,* 130.

41. Jon Butler, *Religion in Colonial America* (New York: Oxford University Press, 2000), 88, 93–94; Butler, *Awash in a Sea of Faith: Christianization of the American People* (Cambridge, Mass.: Harvard University Press, 1990), 154–56; Jeffrey K. Padgett, "The Christianization of Slaves in the West Indies," *Slave Resistance: A Caribbean Study: The Slave Trade,* scholar.library.miami.edu/slaves/slave_trade/individual_essays/jeffrey.html; Albert J. Raboteau, *Slave Religion: The Invisible Institution in the Antebellum South* (New York: Oxford University Press, 1978), 164; Richard Furman, "Rev. Dr. Richard Furman's Exposition of the Views of the Baptists, Relative to the Coloured Population in the United States in a Communication to the Governor of South-Carolina," 2nd ed., Charleston, 1838, http://eweb.furman.edu/~benson/docs/rcd-fmn1.htm; Barry Hankins, *The Second Great Awakening and the Transcendentalists* (Westport, Conn.: Greenwood Press, 2004), 65; "Religion in Colonial America: Trends, Regulations, and Beliefs," *Give Bigotry No Sanction,* http://nobigotry.facinghistory.org/content/religion-colonial

-america-trends-regulations-and-beliefs; Thomas P. Joswick, "'The Crown without the Conflict': Religious Values and Moral Reasoning in *Uncle Tom's Cabin*," *Nineteenth-Century Fiction* 39, no. 3 (December 1984): 253–74, especially 265–66.

42. See Halvor Moxnes, "Honor and Shame," in *The Social Sciences and New Testament Interpretation*, ed. Richard L. Rohrbaugh (Peabody, Mass.: Hendrickson, 2003), 22–23; David A. deSilva, *Honor, Patronage, Kinship and Purity: Unlocking New Testament Culture* (Downers Grove, Ill.: InterVarsity, 2000), 29–30; and J. Albert Harrill, "The Psychology of Slaves in the Gospel Parables: A Case Study in Social History," *Biblishe Zeitschrift* (January 2011): 66–68. Harrill analyses the Luke version of the parable about the good servant who serves his master honorably and efficiently while the master travels. On his return, he is rewarded for his integrity. But the story does not end there. Jesus asks, if the master were delayed, would the responsible slave continue as before or would he assume a degree of power? He becomes cruel and arbitrary, beating the women and children and over-drinking. The parable concludes that he will end up cut into pieces when his master returns.

43. See J. Albert Harrill, "The Use of the New Testament in the American Slave Controversy: A Case History in the Hermeneutical Tension between Biblical Criticism and Christian Moral Debate," *Religion and American Culture: A Journal of Interpretation* 10, no. 2 (2000): 149–86. For an example of proslavery theology, see Fred A. Ross, *Slavery Ordained of God* (Philadelphia: Lippincott, 1857).

44. Charles Reagan Wilson, "Mississippi Rebels: Elvis Presley, Fanny Lou Hamer, and the South's Culture of Religious Music," unpublished paper, presented at the St. George Tucker Society, Augusta, Georgia, 30 July 2011.

45. Jeffery E. Anderson, *Hoodoo, Voodoo, and Conjure: A Handbook* (Westport, Conn.: Greenwood Press, 2008), 25; Anderson, *Conjure in African American Society* (Baton Rouge: Louisiana State University Press, 2005), 106–7.

46. Halifax County (Va.) Commonwealth Cause, *Commonwealth vs. Jack [Slave]*, April 1802, Local Government Records Collection, Halifax County Court Records, The Library of Virginia, Richmond.

47. Anderson, *Conjure*, 1.

48. Ibid., 26–27, 92.

49. Ibid., 79, 17, 37, 14, 36.

50. Melville J. Herskovits, *The Myth of the Negro Past* (Boston: Beacon Press, 1990), 182.

51. Frederick Douglass, *My Bondage and My Freedom*, ed. William L. Andrews (1855; reprint Urbana: University of Illinois Press, 1987), 36.

52. Jennie Miller, "Harriet Jacobs and the 'Double Burden' of American Slavery," *International Social Science Review* 78 (2003): 33.

53. Marie Jenkins Schwartz, *Born in Bondage: Growing up Enslaved in the Antebellum South* (Cambridge, Mass.: Harvard University Press, 2000), 1.

54. Fox-Genovese, *Within the Plantation Household*, 24–26.

55. Solomon Northrup, *Twelve Years a Slave: Narrative of Solomon Northrup, a Citizen of New-York, Kidnapped in Washington City in 1841, and Rescued in 1853, from a Cotton*

Plantation near the Red River, in Louisiana (Auburn, N.Y.: Derby and Miller, 1853), especially 176, 202–3.

56. Louis D. Rubin Jr., *William Elliott Shoots a Bear: Essays on the Southern Literary Tradition* (Baton Rouge: Louisiana State University Press, 1975), 3–4.

57. A. B. Cooper to Charles Tait, 24 January 1835; Daniel McLeod (overseer) to Tait, 13 September 1834 (both concerning Tait's accomplished and literate manservant Harford); J. B. Grace (overseer) to Tait, 24 May 1835; Harford to Tait, 10 January 1827, 6 November 1826; and Grace to Tait, 1 May 1835, Charles Tait Papers, State of Alabama Department of Archives and History, Montgomery.

58. Paul Riesman, *Freedom in Fulani Social Life: An Introspective Ethnography,* trans. Martha Fuller (Chicago: University of Chicago Press, 1998), 76–79, 124, 197–200; Riesman, "The Art of Life in a West African Community: Formality and Spontaneity in Fulani Interpersonal Relationships," *Journal of African Studies* 2 (Spring 1975): 39–63; John Dollard, "The Dozens: The Dialect of Insult," in *Mother Wit from the Laughing Barrel: Readings in the Interpretation of Afro-American Folklore,* ed. Alan Dundes (Englewood Cliffs, N.J.: Prentice-Hall, 1973), 277–309, reprinted from *American Imago* 1 (November 1939): 3–25; Roger D. Abrahams, "Playing the Dozens," *Journal of American Folklore* 75 (July–September 1962): 209–20, especially 213, 215; Donald C. Simmons, "Possible West African Sources for the American Negro 'Dozens,'" *Journal of American Folklore* 76 (October–December 1963): 339–40; Millicent R. Ayoub and Stephen A. Barnett, "Ritualized Verbal Insult in White High School Culture," *Journal of American Folklore* 78 (October–December 1965): 337–44; William Labov, "Rules for Ritual Insults," in *Language in the Inner City: Studies in the Black English Vernacular* (Philadelphia: University of Pennsylvania Press, 1972), 297–353; Amuzie Chimezie, "The Dozens: An African-Heritage Theory," *Journal of Black Studies* 6 (June 1976): 401–20; Walter F. Edwards, "Speech Acts in Guyana: Communicating Ritual and Personal Insults," *Journal of Black Studies* 10 (September 1979): 20–39.

59. Lawrence J. Friedman, *The White Savage: Racial Fantasies in the Postbellum South* (Englewood Cliffs, N.J.: Prentice-Hall 1970), v.

60. B. A. Botkin, *Lay My Burden Down: A Folk History of Slavery* (Chicago: University of Chicago Press, 1945), 3.

61. Historians often refer to this episode as the Akin slave conspiracy, and many have written on the subject. The head of the conspiracy was supposedly an overseer named James Springer, who had left for a Northern colony long before the hearings and therefore could not be made a material witness. Philip D. Morgan and George D. Terry, "Slavery in Microcosm: A Conspiracy Scare in Colonial South Carolina," *Southern Studies* 21 (Summer 1982): 122, 126–27, 136; Council Journal 17, Part 1, 1 February 1749, pp. 98–99, South Carolina Department of Archives and History, Columbia.

62. Ibid., 122–24.

63. South Carolina Sessional Papers, Minutes of Council, December 1748–December 1749, Journal 17, Part 1, Public Record Office, British Manuscripts Project, Reel 34, I.C.O. 5/457, microfilm, 27 January 1749, 55–120, South Carolina Department of Archives and History, Columbia.

64. See Douglas R. Egerton, *Gabriel's Rebellion: Virginia Slave Conspiracies of 1800 and 1802* (Chapel Hill: University of North Carolina Press, 1993). On Denmark Vesey, see Michael Johnson, "Denmark Vesey and His Co-Conspirators," *William and Mary Quarterly*, 3d ser., 58 (October 2001): 915–76. On Nat Turner, see Kenneth S. Greenberg, *Nat Turner: A Slave Rebellion in History and Memory* (New York: Oxford University Press, 2003).

65. Junius Rodriguez, "Rebellion on the River Road: The Ideology and Influence of Louisiana's German Coast Slave Insurrection of 1811," in *Antislavery Violence: Sectional, Racial, and Cultural Conflict in Antebellum America,* ed. John R. McKivigan and Stanley Harrold (Knoxville: University of Tennessee Press, 1999), 65–88; "1811 Louisiana Slavery Rebellion," http://www.coax.net/people/lwf/1811-REBELLION.htm; Kris Broughton, "American Uprising Revisits Louisiana's 1811 Slave Revolt," *Big Think*, 7 January 2011, http://bigthink.com/ideas/26459. A recent interpretation of the Pointe Coupee insurrection of 1790 is Patrick Luck, "'The Blacks Have Been Taught an Important Lesson—Their Weakness': Insurrection and the Consolidation of Slavery in the Lower Mississippi Valley, 1790," in *Creating a Deep South: Making the Sugar and Cotton Revolutions in the Lower Mississippi Valley, 1790–1825,* Ph.D. dissertation, Johns Hopkins University (kindly lent by the author).

66. Nathalie de Fabrique et al., "Understanding Stockholm Syndrome," *FBI Law Enforcement Bulletin (Law Enforcement Communication Unit)* 76 (2007), http://www.fbi.gov/stats-services/publications/law-enforcement-bulletin/2007-pdfs/july07leb.pdf/at_download/file; M. Namnyak et al., "'Stockholm Syndrome': Psychiatric Diagnosis or Urban Myth?" *Acta Psychiatrica Scandinavica* 117 (January 2008): 4–11.

67. Laurence Rees, *Auschwitz: A New History* (New York: Public Affairs Books, 2005).

68. Kathleen Taylor, *Brainwashing: The Science of Thought Control* (New York: Oxford University Press, 2004). She notes that the psychoanalyst Robert J. Lifton recognized the same pattern in the Stalinist era over the minds of Russian citizens. That was particularly evident in the show trials of the 1930s, when Stalin purged the upper ranks of his leadership corps. See also Mikhail Heller, *Cogs in the Wheel: The Formation of Soviet Man,* trans. David Floyd (New York: Knopf, 1988), 4–5.

69. George Orwell, *Nineteen Eighty-Four* (London: Secker and Warburg, 1949); D. J. Taylor, *Orwell: The Life* (New York: Henry Holt, 2003); Maurice Merleau-Ponty, *Humanism and Terror: The Communist Problem,* trans John O'Neill (Boston: Beacon Press, 1969). "Every line of serious work that I have written since 1936 has been written, directly or indirectly, against totalitarianism and for democratic socialism, as I understand it." George Bott, ed., *Selected Writings of George Orwell* (London: Heinemann, 1958), 103.

70. John Iliffe, *Honour in African History* (Cambridge: Cambridge University Press, 2005), 123–26.

71. Bernd Baldus, "Responses to Dependence in a Servile Group: The Machube of Northern Benin," in *Slavery in Africa: Historical and Anthropological Perspectives,* ed. Suzanne Miers and Igor Kopytoff (Madison: University of Wisconsin Press, 1977), 446–56. The *machube* were Islamic in conviction as were their masters, a common identification of faith of masters and slaves.

72. John J. Grace, "Slavery and Emancipation among the Mende in Sierra Leone, 1896–1929," in *Slavery in Africa: Historical and Anthropological Perspectives*, ed. Suzanne Miers and Igor Kopytoff (Madison: University of Wisconsin Press, 1977), 419; Thomas L. Webber, *Deep Like the Rivers: Education in the Slave Quarter Community, 1831–1865* (New York: Norton, 1978), 33.

73. Evelin Lindner, *Making Enemies: Humiliation and International Conflict* (Westport, Conn.: Praeger Security International, 2006), 19.

74. Douglass, *My Bondage and My Freedom*, 177. For examples of black identity arising from skills and social status, see the account of John Drayton, lumberjack, in Botkin, ed., *Lay My Burden Down*, 11–12; and of May, harpoonist, in Rubin, *William Elliott Shoots a Bear*, 3–4.

75. Lorraine Hansbury to her mother, quoted in Patricia C. McKissack and Frederick L. McKissack, *Young, Black, and Determined: A Biography of Lorraine Hansberry* (New York: Holiday House, 1998), 77–78.

76. Frederick Douglass, *Narrative of the Life of Frederick Douglass* (New York: Dover, 1995), 7–8; Yuval Taylor, ed., *I Was Born a Slave: An Anthology of Classic Slave Narratives, 1770–1849*, vol. 1 (Chicago: Lawrence Hill Books, 1999), 542; Fran Smith, "Feels Americans Should Be 'Least Proud of Slavery,'" *New Milford Spectrum*, 9 February 2011, http://www.newmilfordspectrum.com/default/article/Feels-Americans-should-be-least-proud-of-slavery-1005990.php.

77. Lawrence J. Friedman, "Life 'in the Lion's Mouth': Another Look at Booker T. Washington," *Journal of Negro History* 59 (October 1974): 351; "A Conversation with Primo Levi by Philip Roth," in *Survival in Auschwitz: The Nazi Assault on Humanity* (New York: Touchstone, 1996), 179.

78. Douglass, *Narrative*, 69.

79. Josiah Henson, *Father Henson's Story of His Own Life* (Boston: Jewett and Company, 1858), 48, 51, 53.

80. Leon Litwack, *Been in the Storm So Long: The Aftermath of Slavery* (New York: Knopf, 1979), 253.

81. Richard A. Davis, "The Norm of Legitimacy in the Black Family," *Western Journal of Black Studies* 22 (1998): 145–52; Herbert G. Gutman, *The Black Family in Slavery and Freedom: 1750–1925* (New York: Vintage, 1977); Melville J. Herskovits, *The Human Factor in Changing Africa* (New York: Knopf, 1962), 78, 86–87, 91.

82. Herskovits, *Human Factor*, 98.

83. Henry Bibb, *Narrative of the Life and Adventures of Henry Bibb: An American Slave* (New York: Negro Universities Press, 1969).

84. Douglass, *Narrative*, 43.

85. John Matsui, *The First Republican Army: The Army of Virginia and the Radicalization of Union Citizen-Soldiers, 1862*, unpublished manuscript, kindly lent by the author.

86. Edward A. Miller, *Gullah Statesman: Robert Smalls from Slavery to Congress, 1839–1915* (Columbia: University of South Carolina Press, 1995); Orville Vernon Burton, *The Age of Lincoln* (New York: Hill and Wang, 2007), 151–52.

87. Russell Duncan, *Where Death and Glory Meet: Colonel Robert Gould Shaw and the 54th Massachusetts Infantry* (Athens: University of Georgia Press, 1999).

88. James M. McPherson, *Battle Cry of Freedom: The Civil War Era* (New York: Oxford University Press, 1988), 634.

89. Abraham Lincoln, *Abraham Lincoln: Complete Works, Comprising His Speeches, Letters, State Papers, and Miscellaneous Writings,* ed. John G. Nicolay and John Hay, 2 vols. (New York: Century, 1894), 2:562, 564; Burton, *Age of Lincoln,* 166.

2   White Male Honor, Shame, and Shamelessness in the Old South

1. See Bertram Wyatt-Brown, *Southern Honor: Ethics and Behavior in the Old South* (New York: Oxford University Press, 1982), and *The Shaping of Southern Culture: Honor, Grace, and War* (Chapel Hill: University of North Carolina Press 2001).

2. William Shakespeare, *The Merchant of Venice,* Act 2, scene 9, lines 1167–78.

3. Gabriella Slomp, *Thomas Hobbes and the Political Philosophy of Glory* (Houndmills, England: Macmillan, 2000), 34; Michal Jan Rozbicki, *Culture and Liberty in the Age of the American Revolution* (Charlottesville: University of Virginia Press, 2011).

4. Edmund Burke, *Stanford Encyclopedia of Philosophy,* http://plato.stanford.edu/entries/burke/#7; Edmund Burke, *Speech on Conciliation with America,* ed. Albert S. Cook (New York: Longmans, Green, 1898), 3–79.

5. Elliott J. Gorn, "'Gouge and Bite, Pull Hair and Scratch': The Social Significance of Fighting in the Southern Backcountry," *American Historical Review* 90 (February 1985): 18–43.

6. Curtis Brown Watson, *Shakespeare and the Renaissance Concept of Honor* (Princeton, N.J.: Princeton University Press, 1960), 79.

7. Bernard Mayo, *Myths and Men: Patrick Henry, George Washington, Thomas Jefferson* (Athens: University of Georgia Press, 1959), 17.

8. Michal Jan Rozbicki, "Conceptual Bridges and Antibodies: A Response," *Historically Speaking* 13 (April 2012): 18. This view runs counter to the current paradigm, to which Gordon S. Wood and others subscribe, that liberty is a static notion and is the same in every age.

9. Stephen W. Berry II, *All That Makes a Man: Love and Ambition in the Civil War South* (New York: Oxford University Press, 2003), 20.

10. Steven Shapin, *A Social History of Truth: Civility and Science in Seventeenth-Century England* (Chicago: University of Chicago Press, 1994), 69; James Cleland, *The Instruction of a Young Noble Man* (Oxford: Joseph Barnes, 1612), 199.

11. V. G. Kiernan, *The Duel in European History: Honour and the Reign of Aristocracy* (New York: Oxford University Press, 1989); John Lyde Wilson, *The Code of Honor; or, Rules for the Government of Principals and Seconds in Dueling* (Charleston, 1838), 88, 90, reprinted in Jack K. Williams, *Dueling in the Old South: Vignettes of Social History* (College Station: Texas A&M Press, 1980), 87–90; Dickson D. Bruce Jr., *Violence and Culture in the Antebellum South* (Austin: University of Texas Press, 1979), 21–43; Joanne B. Freeman, *Affairs of*

Honor: National Politics in the New Republic (New Haven, Conn.: Yale University Press, 2001).

12. George Washington, *Rules of Civility and Decent Behavior in Company and Conversation* (Washington, D.C.: W. H. Morrison, 1888).

13. David Hackett Fischer, *Washington's Crossing* (New York: Oxford University Press, 2004), 17, 13.

14. Ibid., 16, 17.

15. Ibid., 255.

16. Nathan Schachner, *Thomas Jefferson: A Biography* (New York: Thomas Yoseloff, 1957), 183–84.

17. Ron Chernow, *Alexander Hamilton* (New York: Penguin, 2004), 362–530; Michael Durey, *"With the Hammer of Truth": James Thomson Callender and America's Early National Heroes* (Charlottesville: University Press of Virginia, 1990), 102–6.

18. Schachner, *Thomas Jefferson*, 678; Fawn M. Brodie, *Thomas Jefferson: An Intimate History* (New York: Norton, 1974), 26; Dumas Malone, *Jefferson and His Time*, vol. 1 (Boston: Little, Brown, 1948), 396.

19. Schachner, *Thomas Jefferson*, 316–22, 352; Brodie, *Thomas Jefferson*, 230–32.

20. Annette Gordon-Reed, *Thomas Jefferson and Sally Hemings: An American Controversy* (Charlottesville: University of Virginia Press, 1997); Patricia Cohen, "Seeing Past the Slave to Study the Person," *New York Times*, 20 September 2008, B7; David Walton, review of Annette Gordon-Reed, *Thomas Jefferson and Sally Hemings: An American Controversy*, *New York Times*, 27 July 1997, http://www.nytimes.com/1997/07/27/books/books-in-brief-nonfiction-177199.html?ref=bookreviews.

21. Gordon-Reed, *Thomas Jefferson and Sally Hemings*; Brodie, *Thomas Jefferson*, 293; Merrill D. Peterson, *Thomas Jefferson and the New Nation: A Biography* (New York: Oxford University Press, 1970); Maura Singleton, "Anatomy of a Mystery: The Jefferson-Hemings Controversy in the Post-DNA Era," *University of Virginia Magazine* 96, no. 3 (Fall 2007): 30–34. Singleton comments, "1984 In one of his last interviews, Dumas Malone tells a *New York Times* reporter [that] Jefferson and Hemings may have had a sexual encounter 'once or twice.'" It was a concession from earlier denials. "The History of a Secret," *Frontline*, http://www.pbs.org/wgbh/pages/frontline/shows/jefferson/video/report4.html; Dumas Malone and Steven H. Hochman, "A Note on Evidence: The Personal History of Madison Hemings," *Journal of Southern History* 41, no. 4 (1975): 523–28.

22. B. J. Ramage, "Homicide in the Southern States," *Sewanee Review* 4 (1896): 215; Lawrence Stone, "Interpersonal Violence in English Society, 1300–1980," *Past & Present* 101 (November 1983): 22–33.

23. Freeman, *Affairs of Honor*; Randolph Roth, *American Homicide* (Cambridge, Mass.: Belknap Press of Harvard University Press, 2009), 219–20. See also Wyatt-Brown, "Andrew Jackson's Honor," in Wyatt-Brown, *Shaping of Southern Culture*, 56–80.

24. Richard L. Bushman, "The Genteel Republic," *Wilson Quarterly* 20, no. 4 (1996): 14. On dueling protocol, see John Lyde Wilson, *The Code of Honor; or, Rules for the*

Government of Principals and Seconds in Duelling (Charleston, S.C.: James Phinney, 1858), reprinted in Williams, *Dueling in the Old South*, 88–104.

25. Lawrence Stone, *The Causes of the English Revolution, 1529–1642* (New York: Routledge, 1996); Francis Bacon, *The Works of Lord Bacon* (London: William Ball, 1838), 680.

26. Clement Eaton, *Freedom of Thought in the Old South* (Durham, N.C.: Duke University Press, 1940), 52.

27. Roth, *American Homicide*, 160–61; J. A. Pitt-Rivers, *The People of the Sierra* (New York: Criterion, 1954), 140.

28. J. Russell Major, the early modern French scholar, is quoted in Kristen Brooke Neuschel, *Word of Honor: Interpreting Noble Culture in Sixteenth-Century France* (Ithaca, N.Y.: Cornell University Press, 1989), 7; Wyatt-Brown, *Shaping of Southern Culture*, 62–63.

29. James S. Jeffers, *The Greco-Roman World of the New Testament Era: Exploring the Background of Early Christianity* (Downers Grove, Ill.: Intervarsity Press, 1999), 192; John W. Schoenheit, "An Overview of Manners & Customs in the Bible," http://www.truthor tradition.com/modules.php?name=News&file=article&sid=701; Jerome H. Neyrey, ed., *Social World of Luke-Acts: Models for Interpretation* (Peabody, Mass.: Hendrickson, 1991); Joseph Plevnik, "Honor/Shame," in *Handbook of Biblical Social Values*, ed. John J. Pilch and Bruce J. Malina (Peabody, Mass.: Hendrickson, 1998), 106–14; Saul M. Olyan, "Honor, Shame, and Covenant Relations in Ancient Israel and Its Environment," *Journal of Biblical Literature* 115 (1996): 201–18.

30. Freeman, *Affairs of Honor*. See also Wyatt-Brown, "Andrew Jackson's Honor," 56–80; Roth, *American Homicide*, 160–61.

31. Charles M. Wiltse, *John C. Calhoun, Nationalist, 1782–1828* (Indianapolis: Bobbs-Merrill, 1944), 49–50, 213, 252, 254–55. See also Michael O'Brien, *A Character of Hugh Legaré* (Knoxville: University of Tennessee Press, 1985), 41–42, and William W. Freehling, *Prelude to Civil War: The Nullification Controversy in South Carolina, 1816–1836* (New York: Harper and Row, 1965), 145–46.

32. George Lewis Prentiss, ed., *A Memoir of S. S. Prentiss*, vol. 1 (New York: C. Scribner's Sons, 1855), 132–34; Joseph Dunbar Shields and Sargeant Prentiss Knut, *The Life and Times of Seargent Smith Prentiss* (Philadelphia: J. B. Lippincott, 1884), 69–73.

33. Christopher J. Olsen, "The Politics of Honor and Masculinity: Political Culture in the Deep South, 1820s-1861," in *Southern Character: Essays in Honor of Bertram Wyatt-Brown*, ed. Lisa Tendrich Frank and Daniel J. Kilbride (Gainesville: University of Florida Press, 2011), 52.

34. Daniel Justin Herman, *Hell on the Range: A Story of Honor, Conscience, and the American West* (New Haven, Conn.: Yale University Press, 2010).

35. Sheldon Hackney, "Southern Violence," *American Historical Review* 74 (February 1969): 906–25.

36. Roth, *American Homicide*, 387; Department of the Interior, Census Office, *Report on Vital and Social Statistics in the United States at the Eleventh Census: 1890, Part III—Statistics of Deaths*, "Table 18: Number of Deaths from Each Reported Cause, by State, State

Groups, and Registration Cities, During the Census Year Ended May 31, 1890," 971, 977, 1,000, 1,030.

37. See Wyatt-Brown, *Southern Honor*, 462–93.

38. Ted Ownby, *Subduing Satan: Religion, Recreation, and Manhood in the Rural South, 1865–1920* (Chapel Hill: University of North Carolina Press, 1990), is the most authoritative study of the Southern churches' response to public morals.

39. Wyatt-Brown, *Southern Honor*, 308.

40. David Hackett Fischer, *Albion's Seed: Four British Folkways in America* (Oxford: Oxford University Press, 1989), 342.

41. Wyatt-Brown, *Southern Honor*, 348.

42. Ibid., 341–48, 151; Robert Bailey, *The Life and Adventures of Robert Bailey, from His Infancy up to December, 1821: Interspersed with Anecdotes, and Religious and Moral Admonitions* (Richmond: J. & G. Cochran, 1822), 66–67.

43. Wyatt-Brown, *Southern Honor*, 349; *History of Gambling in the United States*, http://www.library.ca.gov/crb/97/03/Chapt2.html.

44. Wyatt-Brown, *Southern Honor*, 462–93.

45. Marjorie Pryse, "Miniaturizing Yoknapatawpha: *The Unvanquished* as Faulkner's Theory of Realism," *Mississippi Quarterly* 33 (Summer 1980): 343–54.

3   America's Antebellum Wars, 1776–1848

1. Gordon S. Wood, *The Creation of the American Republic, 1776–1787* (Chapel Hill: University of North Carolina Press, 1969), 146, 199, 209; Wood, *The Radicalism of the American Revolution* (New York: Vintage, 1993), 39–41, 207.

2. Wood, *Creation of the American Republic*, 4; Wood, "Rhetoric and Reality in the American Revolution," *William and Mary Quarterly*, 3d ser., 23 (January 1966): 4–32. The literature on republicanism and its origins includes Robert E. Shalhope, "Toward a Republican Synthesis: The Emergence of an Understanding of Republicanism in American Historiography," *William and Mary Quarterly*, 3d ser., 29 (January 1972): 49–80; Joyce Appleby, "Republicanism in Old and New Contexts," *William and Mary Quarterly*, 3d ser., 43 (January 1986): 20–34; Appleby, *Capitalism and a New Social Order: The Republican Vision of the 1790s* (New York: New York University Press, 1984); Appleby, *Inheriting the Revolution: The First Generation of Americans* (Cambridge, Mass.: Belknap Press of Harvard University Press, 2000); Bernard Bailyn, *The Ideological Origins of the American Revolution* (Cambridge, Mass.: Belknap Press of Harvard University Press, 1967); and Bailyn, "The Central Themes of the American Revolution: An Interpretation," in *Essays on the American Revolution*, ed. Stephen G. Kurtz and James H. Hutson (Chapel Hill: University of North Carolina Press, 1973), 3–31.

3. John E. Godfrey, "Captain Mowatt," March 1877, Collection 110, Maine Historical Society, Portland.

4. Thomas Bradford Chandler, *What Think Ye of Congress Now? or, An Enquiry How Far the Americans Are Bound to Abide By, and Execute, the Decisions of the Late Continental*

Congress? (New York: James Rivington, 1775), 61, 64–65; Janice Potter, *The Liberty We Seek: Loyalist Ideology in Colonial New York and Massachusetts* (Cambridge, Mass.: Harvard University Press, 1983), 137.

5. Potter, *The Liberty We Seek,* 137.

6. Keith Krawczynski, *William Henry Drayton: South Carolina Revolutionary Patriot* (Baton Rouge: Louisiana State University Press, 2001), 49.

7. Thomas Paine, "Common Sense," in *The Works of Thomas Paine* (London, 1796), 16.

8. See Jean G. Peristiany, ed., *Honour and Shame: The Values of Mediterranean Society* (Chicago: University of Chicago Press, 1966), and Michael Herzfeld, "Honour and Shame: Problems in the Comparative Analyses of Moral Systems," *Man,* 15 (June 1980): 339–51. On New England and secular honor, see Evarts B. Greene, "The Code of Honor in Colonial and Revolutionary Times with Special Reference to New England," *Publications of the Colonial Society of Massachusetts* 26 (1927): 367–88.

9. John Allen, "An Oration, on the Beauties of Liberty," 3 December 1772, quoted in *American Literature, 1764–1789: The Revolutionary Years,* ed. Everett Emerson (Madison: University of Wisconsin Press, 1977), 35.

10. Harry S. Stout, *The New England Soul: Preaching and Religious Culture in Colonial New England* (New York: Oxford University Press, 1986), 306.

11. Julian Pitt-Rivers, "Honor," in *International Encyclopedia of the Social Sciences,* ed. David Sills (New York: Macmillan, 1968), 504–5.

12. Marcel Mauss, *The Gift: Forms and Functions of Exchange in Archaic Societies,* trans. Ian Cunnison (Glencoe, Ill.: Free Press, 1954).

13. James Otis, *The Rights of the British Colonies Asserted and Proved,* 3rd ed. (Boston, 1766), 40.

14. Thomas Jefferson, "Virginia Resolutions on Lord North's Conciliatory Proposal [10 June 1775]," and "Resolutions of Congress on Lord North's Conciliatory Proposal: II. The Resolutions as Adopted by Congress," in *The Papers of Thomas Jefferson,* ed. Julian Parks Boyd (Princeton, N.J.: Princeton University Press, 1950), 1:171–73, 231. For an anthropological approach, see F. G. Bailey, *Gifts and Poison: The Politics of Reputation* (New York: Schocken Books, 1971).

15. Niccolò Machiavelli, "The Prince," in *The Prince and the Discourses* (New York: Modern Library, 1940), 62; see also 57–58.

16. Bailyn, *Ideological Origins,* 162. See also Conrad Russell, *Parliaments and English Politics, 1621–1629* (New York: Oxford University Press, 1979), 49–53, 56–57, 366–67 on subsidy issues. On Irish taxation, see "Four Letters on Interesting Subjects," in *Pamphlets of the American Revolution, 1750–1776, Vol. 1, 1750–1765,* ed. Bernard Bailyn (Cambridge, Mass.: Harvard University Press, 1965), 78.

17. Otis, *Rights of the British Colonies,* 65–66, 70.

18. William Gordon, *The Separation of the Jewish Tribes, after the Death of Solomon, Accounted for, and Applied to the Present Day, in a Sermon before the General Court, on Friday, July the 4th, 1777, Being the Anniversary of the Declaration of Independency* (Boston: J. Gill, 1777), 11.

19. John Adams, "Novanglus," in *The Political Writings of John Adams*, ed. George W. Carey (Washington, D.C.: Regnery, 2000), 40–41. Men of more temperate dispositions also spoke in passionate language.

20. J. G. A. Pocock, *The Ancient Constitution and the Feudal Law: A Study of English Historical Thought in the Seventeenth Century* (Cambridge: Cambridge University Press, 1987), 331–32. See also Lois G. Schwoerer, *"No Standing Armies!" The Antiarmy Ideology in Seventeenth-Century England* (Baltimore: Johns Hopkins University Press, 1974); J. G. A. Pocock, "Machiavelli, Harrington and English Political Ideologies in the Eighteenth Century," *William and Mary Quarterly*, 3d ser., 22 (October 1965): 549–83, esp. 558–64; Lewis D. Cress, *Citizens in Arms: The Army and the Militia in American Society to the War of 1812* (Chapel Hill: University of North Carolina Press, 1982), 15–33; and Jerrilyn Greene Marston, *King and Congress: The Transfer of Political Legitimacy from King to the Continental Congress, 1774–1776*, Ph.D. dissertation, Boston University, 1975, 144–46.

21. Caroline Robbins, *The Eighteenth-Century Commonwealthman: Studies in the Transmission, Development and Circumstances of English Liberal Thought from the Restoration of Charles II until the War with the Thirteen Colonies* (Cambridge, Mass.: Harvard University Press, 1961), 339. See also Bailyn, ed., *Pamphlets of the American Revolution*, 41–44, esp. 42n7, in which he points out that J. G. A. Pocock dates the issue only as far back as 1675, but there was a nostalgia in Commonwealthman writings for feudal times when "the 'nobility' secured 'the people against the insults of the prince and the prince against the popularity of the commons.'" See Robbins, *Commonwealthman*, 104.

22. Moses Coit Tyler, *Patrick Henry* (Boston: Houghton Mifflin, 1898), 145.

23. David Hackett Fischer, *Washington's Crossing* (Oxford: Oxford University Press, 2004), 28; Caroline Cox, *A Proper Sense of Honor: Service and Sacrifice in George Washington's Army* (Chapel Hill: University of North Carolina Press, 2004), vii.

24. Robert Howe to Henry Laurens, 9 June 9, quoted in Richard Walsh, ed., *The Writings of Christopher Gadsden, 1764–1805* (Columbia: University of South Carolina Press, 1966), xxiv.

25. Nathanael Greene to Joseph Reed, 9 March 1778, in Richard K. Showman, ed., *The Papers of Nathanael Greene, Vol. II, 1 January 1777–16 October 1778* (Chapel Hill: University of North Carolina Press, 1980), 307. See also Greene to Alexander McDougall, 28 March 1778, ibid., 326.

26. Charles Royster, *A Revolutionary People at War: The Continental Army and American Character, 1775–1783* (Chapel Hill: University of North Carolina Press, 1996), 199.

27. Alexander DeConde, *The Quasi-War: The Politics and Diplomacy of the Undeclared War with France, 1797–1801* (New York: Charles Scribner's Sons, 1966), 83; Frederick C. Leiner, *Millions for Defense: The Subscription Warships of 1798* (Annapolis, Md.: Naval Institute Press, 2000), 13–17.

28. John E. Ferling, *John Adams: A Life* (Knoxville: University of Tennessee Press, 1992), 364–68; Gregg Costa, "John Marshall, the Sedition Act, and Free Speech in the Early Republic," *Texas Law Review* 77 (1999): 1011–47; Andrew Roberts, "Talleyrand: The Old Fraud," *New Criterion* 25 (April 2007): 4–10.

29. DeConde, *Quasi-War,* 107.

30. Ibid., 159.

31. Ibid., 259.

32. Nathan Schachner, *Thomas Jefferson: A Biography* (New York: Thomas Yoseloff, 1957), 296.

33. Ray W. Irwin, *The Diplomatic Relations of the United States with the Barbary Powers, 1776–1816* (Chapel Hill: University of North Carolina Press, 1931); Alan Axelrod, *America's Wars* (New York: Wiley, 2002), 173; Barbara Fuchs, *Mimesis and Empire: The New World, Islam, and European Identities* (Cambridge: Cambridge University Press, 2001), 122; Peter Earle, *Corsairs of Malta and Barbary* (London: Sidgwick and Jackson, 1970), 44, 257, 261–62.

34. Glenn Tucker, *Dawn Like Thunder: The Barbary Wars and the Birth of the U.S. Navy* (Indianapolis: Bobbs-Merrill, 1963), 58, 66–70.

35. Joseph Wheelan, *Jefferson's War: America's First War on Terror 1801–1805* (New York: Carroll and Graf, 2003), 3; Jack Kenny, "Bane of the Barbary Pirates: During America's Early Years, Muslim Pirates from the Barbary Coast Demanded Tribute in Order to Let U.S. Ships Pass Unmolested. The Tribute Was a Source of Contention in America," *The New American,* 6 June 2011, 35–39; Robert F. Turner, "President Thomas Jefferson and the Barbary Pirates," in *Piracy and Maritime Crime: Historical and Modern Case Studies,* ed. Bruce A. Elleman, Andrew Forbes, and David Rosenberg (Newport, R.I.: Naval War College Press, 2010).

36. Wheelan, *Jefferson's War,* 43, 45–46, 54; Tucker, *Dawn Like Thunder,* 58.

37. Gerard W. Gawalt, "America and the Barbary Pirates: An International Battle against an Unconventional Foe," http://memory.loc.gov/ammem/collections/jefferson _papers/mtjprece.html; Tucker, *Dawn Like Thunder,* 70.

38. Michael B. Oren, *Power, Faith, and Fantasy: America in the Middle East, 1776 to the Present* (New York: Norton, 2007), 41, 18–23; Martha Elena Rojas, "'Insults Unpunished' Barbary Captives, American Slaves, and the Negotiation of Liberty," *Early American Studies* 1, no. 2 (2003): 159–86.

39. Alexander Slidell Mackenzie, *Life of Stephen Decatur: A Commodore in the Navy of the United States* (Boston: C. C. Little and J. Brown, 1846), 25, 64–82. See also Gardner Weld Allen, *Our Navy and the Barbary Corsairs* (Boston: Houghton, Mifflin, 1905).

40. Mackenzie, *Life of Stephen Decatur,* 81; Charles Lee Lewis, *The Romantic Decatur* (Philadelphia: University of Pennsylvania Press, 1937), 227.

41. Mackenzie, *Life of Stephen Decatur,* 139–64, 305–28; Lewis, *The Romantic Decatur,* 92–94.

42. John Clark Ridpath, *A Popular History of the United States of America: From Aboriginal Times to the Present Day* (New York: Nelson and Phillips, 1878), 389–90.

43. Norman K. Risjord, "1812: Conservatives, War Hawks, and the Nation's Honor," *William and Mary Quarterly,* 3rd ser., 18 (April 1961): 196–210.

44. Risjord, "1812: Conservatives," 204, 209.

45. Ibid., 209, 210.

46. Walter A. McDougall, *Freedom Just around the Corner: A New American History, 1585–1828* (New York: HarperCollins, 2004), 411–12; Samuel Eliot Morison, "Our Most Unpopular War," *Proceedings of the Massachusetts Historical Society,* 3rd ser., 80 (1968): 38–54, 166; Richard Chew, "The Origins of Mob Town: Social Divisions and Racial Conflict in the Baltimore Rioters of 1812," *Maryland Historical Magazine* 104 (Fall 2009): 272–301.

47. Nathaniel W. Stephenson, *Texas and the Mexican War: A Chronicle of the Winning of the Southwest* (New Haven, Conn.: Yale University Press, 1921), 71; Paul Foos, *A Short, Offhand, Killing Affair: Soldiers and Social Conflict during the Mexican-American War* (Chapel Hill: University of North Carolina Press, 2002), 25; Ted C. Hinckley, "American Anti-Catholicism during the Mexican War," *Pacific Historical Review* 31, no. 2 (May 1962): 121–37; Otis A. Singletary, *The Mexican War* (Chicago: University of Chicago Press, 1960), 15.

48. James Knox Polk, *Polk: The Diary of a President, 1845–1849, Covering the Mexican War, the Acquisition of Oregon, and the Conquest of California and the Southwest,* ed. Allan Nevins (New York: Longmans, Green, 1929), 87; Foos, *A Short, Offhand, Killing,* 84.

49. James Brewer Stewart, *Joshua R. Giddings and the Tactics of Radical Politics* (Cleveland: Case Western Reserve University Press, 1970), 114–15.

50. Foos, *A Short, Offhand Killing,* 22–25.

51. Ibid., 83; Polk, *Polk,* 87.

52. Foos, *A Short, Offhand Killing,* 84; Dwight G. Anderson, "Quest for Immortality: A Theory of Abraham Lincoln's Political Psychology," in *The Historian's Lincoln: Pseudohistory, Psychohistory, and History,* ed. Gabor S. Boritt (Urbana: University of Illinois Press, 1996), 261–62; Douglas Card, "We Forget That Lincoln Opposed a War, Too," *Register-Guard* (Eugene, Oregon), 7 January 2009, A7; David Donald, *Lincoln* (New York: Simon and Schuster, 1995), 122–25.

53. Orville Vernon Burton, *The Age of Lincoln* (New York: Hill and Wang, 2007), 30; Howard Zinn, *A People's History of the United States: 1492–Present,* 5th ed. (New York: HarperCollins, 2005), 154.

54. Richard Dillman, ed., *The Major Essays of Henry David Thoreau* (Albany, N.Y.: Whitston, 2001), 47–67; Burton, *Age of Lincoln,* 29.

55. J. Javier Rodríguez, "The U.S.–Mexican War in James Russell Lowell's *The Biglow Papers,"* *Arizona Quarterly* 63 (2007): 1–33.

56. Foos, *A Short, Offhand, Killing,* 113.

57. John W. Chambers II, ed., *The Oxford Companion to American Military History* (New York: Oxford University Press, 1999), 849.

58. "Bivouac of the Dead," Department of Veterans Affairs, http://www.cem.va.gov/hist/bivouac.asp; Bertram Wyatt-Brown, *Hearts of Darkness: Wellsprings of a Southern Literary Tradition* (Baton Rouge: Louisiana State University Press, 2003), 107–9.

4   Honor, Humiliation, and the American Civil War

1. Drew Gilpin Faust, *This Republic of Suffering: Death and the American Civil War* (New York: Random House, 2008).

2. John Nerone, *Violence against the Press: Policing the Public Sphere in U.S. History* (New York: Oxford University Press, 1994), 91.

3. Eugene D. Genovese and Elizabeth Fox-Genovese, *Fatal Self-Deception: Slaveholding Paternalism in the Old South* (New York: Cambridge University Press, 2011), 111.

4. Eric Foner, *The Fiery Trial: Abraham Lincoln and American Slavery* (New York: Norton, 2010), 118; Gregg D. Crane, *Race, Citizenship, and Law in American Literature* (Cambridge: Cambridge University Press, 2002), 48–49. See also Vernon Burton, *The Age of Lincoln* (New York: Hill and Wang, 2007).

5. Walter Edgar, *South Carolina: A History* (Columbia: University of South Carolina Press, 1998), 355; Michael Rosenfeld, ed., *Constitutionalism, Identity, Difference, and Legitimacy: Theoretical Perspectives* (Durham, N.C.: Duke University Press, 1994), 118; Burton, *Age of Lincoln*, 102.

6. Alexander Hamilton Stephens, *Recollections of Alexander H. Stephens: His Diary Kept When a Prisoner at Fort Warren, Boston Harbor, 1865, Giving Incidents and Reflections of His Prison Life and Some Letters and Reminiscences*, ed. Myrta Lockett Avary (Baton Rouge: Louisiana State University Press, 1998), 166, 198–201.

7. Bertram Wyatt-Brown, *The Shaping of Southern Culture: Honor, Grace, and War* (Chapel Hill: University of North Carolina Press, 2001), 178.

8. James M. McPherson, *For Cause and Comrades: Why Men Fought in the Civil War* (New York: Oxford University Press, 1997), 17.

9. Lacy K. Ford Jr., *Origins of Southern Radicalism: The South Carolina Upcountry, 1800–1860* (New York: Oxford University Press, 1988), 368. See also Margaret Burr DesChamps, "Union or Division? South Atlantic Presbyterians and Southern Nationalism, 1820–1861," *Journal of Southern History* 20 (November 1954): 493–94; James Henley Thornwell, *Fast Day Sermons; or, The Pulpit on the State of the Country* (New York: Rudd and Carleton, 1861).

10. James H. Otey to Edward Calohill Burks, 23 November 1860 and 12 March 1861, in James Elliott Walmsley, ed., "Documents: The Change of Secession Sentiment in Virginia in 1861," *American Historical Review* 31 (October 1925): 98–99.

11. Isaiah, 8:22; George Henry Clark, *The Union: A Sermon, Delivered in St. John's Church, Savannah, on Fast Day, Nov. 28, 1860* (Savannah: George N. Nichols, 1860).

12. Joseph D. Cushman, *A Goodly Heritage: The Episcopal Church in Florida, 1821–1892* (Gainesville: University of Florida Press, 1965), 42–44.

13. Cushman, *Goodly Heritage*, 42–44; entry for 4 January 1861, *The Diary of Edmund Ruffin, Vol. 1, Toward Independence, October 1856–April 1861*, ed. William Kauffman Scarborough (Baton Rouge: Louisiana State University Press, 1972), 524.

14. Cushman, *Goodly Heritage*, 45.

15. C. C. Goen, *Broken Churches, Broken Nation: Denominational Schisms and the Coming of the American Civil War* (Macon, Ga.: Mercer University Press, 1985), 173.

16. Edward R. Crowther, "Holy Honor: Sacred and Secular in the Old South," *Journal of Southern History* 58 (November 1992): 636.

17. Jabez Lamar Monroe Curry, "The Perils and Duty of the South, . . . Speech De-livered in Talladega, Alabama, November 26, 1860 (Washington, D.C.: Lemuel Towers, 1860)," in *Southern Pamphlets on Secession, November 1860–April 1861*, ed. Jon L. Wakelyn (Chapel Hill: University of North Carolina Press, 1996), 49.

18. "Speech of Hon. George S. Pugh, of Ohio, on the Condition of Affairs in Kansas Territory," Charleston *Courier*, 30 April 1860, 1 [quotation differs slightly from Murat Halstead, *Caucuses of 1860* (Columbus, Ohio: Follett, Foster, 1860), 48–50]; Stuart of Michigan, Charleston *Courier*, 2 May 1860, 4.

19. David Herbert Donald, *Charles Sumner and the Coming of the Civil War* (New York: Knopf, 1967), 233–60; Moorfield Storey, *Charles Sumner* (Boston: Houghton Mifflin, 1900), 147; T. Lloyd Benson, *The Caning of Senator Sumner* (Belmont, Calif.: Thomson/Wadsworth Learning, 2004), 99.

20. William E. Gienapp, "'The Crime against Sumner: The Caning of Charles Sum-ner and the Rise of the Republican Party," *Civil War History* 25 (1979): 218–45.

21. Storey, *Charles Sumner*, 152–53.

22. John Stauffer, *The Black Hearts of Men: Radical Abolitionists and the Transformation of Race* (Cambridge, Mass.: Harvard University Press, 2001), 108–9.

23. Adam Gopnik, *Angels and Ages: A Short Book about Darwin, Lincoln, and Modern Life* (New York: Vintage, 2009), 63.

24. Ibid.; David S. Reynolds, *John Brown, Abolitionist: The Man Who Killed Slavery, Sparked the Civil War, and Seeded Civil Rights* (New York: Vintage, 2005), 332.

25. Gopnik, *Angels and Ages*, 64.

26. Reynolds, *John Brown*, 333.

27. Yorkville *Enquirer*, 20 September 1860.

28. James Redpath, *The Public Life of Capt. John Brown* (Boston: Thayer and Eldridge, 1860), 42.

29. David Brion Davis and Steven Mintz, *The Boisterous Sea of Liberty: A Documentary History of America from Discovery through the Civil War* (New York: Oxford University Press, 1998), 23–24.

30. Daniel W. Crofts, *Reluctant Confederates: Upper South Unionists in the Secession Crisis* (Chapel Hill: University of North Carolina Press, 1989), 95.

31. Henry A. Wise, public letter dated 31 December 1860 in Richmond *Semi-Weekly Enquirer*, 8 January 1861, quoted in Daniel W. Crofts, *Reluctant Confederates: Upper South Unionists in the Secession Crisis* (Chapel Hill: University of North Carolina Press, 1989), 98.

32. Dickson D. Bruce Jr., *Violence and Culture in the Antebellum South* (Austin: Uni-versity of Texas Press, 1979), 192.

33. Genovese and Fox-Genovese, *Fatal Self-Deception*, 138.

34. Steven A. Channing, *Crisis of Fear: Secession in South Carolina* (New York: Norton, 1974), 287.

35. Drew Gilpin Faust, *Mothers of Invention: Women of the Slaveholding South in the American Civil War* (Chapel Hill: University of North Carolina Press, 1996), 21.

36. Donald E. Reynolds, *Editors Make War: Southern Newspapers in the Secession Crisis* (Nashville: Vanderbilt University Press, 1970), 43–44.

37. *Charlottesville Review,* 25 January 1861, cited in Dwight Lowell Dumond, *The Secession Movement, 1860–1861* (New York: Macmillan, 1931), 169.

38. Smith in 33rd Congress, 1st session, *Century of Lawmaking for a New Nation: U.S. Congressional Documents and Debates, 1774–1875* (Washington, D.C.: Government Printing Office, 1854), also available online through the Library of Congress, http://memory .loc.gov/ammem/amlaw/lawhome.html; Stauffer, *Black Hearts of Men,* 58, 195.

39. Gordon S. Barker, *Imperfect Revolution: Anthony Burns and the Landscape of Race in Antebellum America* (Kent, Ohio: Kent State University Press, 2011).

40. John Smith Dye, *History of the Plots and Crimes of the Great Conspiracy to Overthrow Liberty in America* (New York: n.p., 1866)

41. Burton, *Age of Lincoln,* 88.

42. David Brion Davis, *The Slave Power Conspiracy and the Paranoid Style* (Baton Rouge: Louisiana State University Press, 1969), 20; Eric Foner, *Free Soil, Free Labor, Free Men: The Ideology of the Republican Party before the Civil War* (New York: Oxford University Press, 1995), 64–65.

43. Elizabeth R. Varon, *Disunion! The Coming of the American Civil War, 1789–1859* (Chapel Hill: University of North Carolina Press, 2008), 43.

44. Lydia Maria Child, *An Appeal in Favor of That Class of Americans Called Africans,* ed. Carolyn L. Karcher (Amherst: University of Massachusetts Press, 1996), 69.

45. James M. McPherson, *Drawn with the Sword: Reflections on the American Civil War* (New York: Oxford University Press, 1996), 38.

46. Reynolds, *Editors Make War,* 232–33.

47. Kenneth M. Stampp, *America in 1857: A Nation on the Brink* (New York: Oxford University Press, 1990), 106.

48. Daniel W. Stowell, "Abraham Lincoln and Southern Honor," in *Southern Character: Essays in Honor of Bertram Wyatt-Brown,* ed. Lisa Tendrich Frank and Daniel Kilbride (Gainesville: University of Florida Press, 2011), 107, 109–10, 111–12.

49. Bertram Wyatt-Brown, "Church, Honor, and Secession," in *Religion and the American Civil War,* ed. Randall M. Miller, Harry S. Stout, and Charles Reagan Wilson (New York: Oxford University Press, 1998), 101.

50. James M. McPherson, *Abraham Lincoln and the Second American Revolution* (New York: Oxford University Press, 1990), 43–44.

51. Dora L. Costa and Matthew E. Kahn, *Heroes and Cowards: The Social Face of War* (Princeton, N.J.: Princeton University Press, 2008), 89–90; Catherine Clinton and Nina Silber, *Divided Houses: Gender and the Civil War* (New York: Oxford University Press, 1992), 51.

52. McPherson, *For Cause and Comrades;* Gary W. Gallagher, ed., *Lee and His Army in Confederate History* (Chapel Hill: University of North Carolina Press, 2001), 261; Edward L. Ayers, *In the Presence of Mine Enemies: The Civil War in the Heart of America, 1859–1863* (New York: Norton, 2003), 195.

53. Edward G. Longacre, *Joshua Chamberlain: The Soldier and the Man* (Conshohocken, Penn.: Combined Publication, 1999), 153.

54. Gallagher, ed., *Lee and His Army*, 95–96.

55. William A. Fletcher, *Rebel Private, Front and Rear: Memoirs of a Confederate Soldier* (Austin: University of Texas Press, 1954), 44.

56. McPherson, *For Cause and Comrades*, 80.

57. Christopher H. Hamner, *Enduring Battle: American Soldiers in Three Wars, 1776–1945* (Lawrence: University Press of Kansas, 2011), 64.

58. James M. McPherson, *Battle Cry of Freedom: The Civil War Era* (New York: Oxford University Press, 1988), 463.

59. James M. McPherson, "American Victory, American Defeat," in *Why the Confederacy Lost*, ed. Gabor S. Boritt (New York: Oxford University Press, 1992), 19–20.

60. McPherson, *Battle Cry of Freedom*, 662.

61. Jeff Davis to Cornelia Hancock, 23 August 1863, in *Letters of a Civil War Nurse: Cornelia Hancock, 1863–1865*, ed. Henrietta Stratton Jaquette (Lincoln: University of Nebraska Press, 1998), 22.

62. John David Smith, ed., *Black Soldiers in Blue: African American Troops in the Civil War Era* (Chapel Hill: University of North Carolina Press, 2002), 45–47; "Order of Retaliation," 30 July 1863, Abraham Lincoln, *The Collected Works of Abraham Lincoln*, ed. by Roy P. Basler (New Brunswick, N.J.: Rutgers University Press, 1953), 357. For more information on blacks and the Civil War, visit HarpWeek's Black American History Website, http://blackhistory.harpweek.com.

63. Michael Fellman, *Views from the Dark Side of American History* (Baton Rouge: Louisiana State University Press, 2011), 70.

64. Jack Hurst, *Born to Battle: Grant, Forrest, Shiloh, Vicksburg, and Chattanooga* (New York: Basic Books, 2012), 411.

65. Burton, *Age of Lincoln*, 183.

66. Costa and Kahn, *Heroes and Cowards*, 91, 115–16.

67. Gen. U. S. Grant to Brig. Gen. Richard Taylor, 22 June 1863; Taylor to Grant, 27 June 1863; Grant to Taylor, 4 July 1863; Gen. Henry W. Halleck to Grant, 12 August 1863; Grant to Halleck, 29 August 1863, all in *The War of the Rebellion: A Compilation of the Official Records of the Union and Confederate Armies*, ser. 1, vol. 24, part 3 (Washington, D.C.: Government Printing Office, 1889), 425–25, 443–44, 469, 589–90; "Order of Retaliation," 30 July 1863.

68. Richard Slotkin, *No Quarter: The Battle of the Crater, 1864* (New York: Random House, 2009), 246–47; John Y. Simon, ed., *The Papers of Ulysses S. Grant, Vol. XI: June 1–August 15, 1864* (Carbondale: Southern Illinois University Press, 1984), 361; John Y. Simon, ed., *The Papers of Ulysses S. Grant, Vol. XIII: November 16, 1864–February 20, 1865* (Carbondale: Southern Illinois University Press, 1985), 142; Wilmer L. Jones, *Generals in Blue and Gray: Volume 1, Lincoln's Generals* (Westport, Conn.: Praeger, 2004), 164; Emory M. Thomas, *Robert E. Lee* (New York: Norton, 1997), 342.

69. Faust, *This Republic of Suffering*, 73–75.

70. See Richard Orr Curry, *A House Divided: A Study of Statehood Politics and Copperhead Movement in West Virginia* (Pittsburgh: University of Pittsburgh Press, 1964), 75–76; Spencer C. Tucker, *Brigadier General John D. Imboden: Confederate Commander in the Shenandoah* (Lexington: University Press of Kentucky, 2003), 101–2; Hu Maxwell and Henry Clay Hyde, *History of Tucker County, West Virginia* (Kingwood, W.Va.: Preston, 1884), 344–45.

71. Michael Fellman, *In the Name of God and Country: Reconsidering Terrorism in American History* (New Haven, Conn.: Yale University Press, 2010), 90–92.

72. McPherson, *Battle Cry of Freedom*, 785–86.

73. Gary E. Gallagher, ed., *Fighting for the Confederacy: The Personal Recollections of General Edward Porter Alexander* (Chapel Hill: University of North Carolina Press, 1989), 530–33; Douglas Southall Freeman, *R. E. Lee: A Biography*, vol. 4 (New York: Charles Scribner's Sons, 1935), 122; Don Lowry, *Towards an Indefinite Shore: The Final Months of the Civil War, December 1864–May 1865* (New York: Hippocrene, 1995), 596–97; George M. Fredrickson, *Why the Confederacy Did Not Fight a Guerrilla War after the Fall of Richmond: A Comparative View* (Gettysburg, Penn.: Gettysburg College, 1996); Alice Rains Trulock, *In the Hands of Providence: Joshua L. Chamberlain and the American Civil War* (Chapel Hill: University of North Carolina Press, 1992), 500.

74. Ulysses S. Grant, *Personal Memoirs of U. S. Grant* (Lincoln: University of Nebraska Press, 1960), 263.

75. Joshua Lawrence Chamberlain, *"Bayonet! Forward": My Civil War Reminiscences* (Gettysburg, Penn.: Stan Clark Military Books, 1994), 235–36; Trulock, *In the Hands of Providence*, 302.

76. Chamberlain, *Bayonet! Forward*, 155.

77. Trulock, *In the Hands of Providence*, 303.

78. Glenn Lafantasie, "Joshua Chamberlain and the American Dream," in *The Gettysburg Nobody Knows*, ed. Gabor S. Boritt (New York: Oxford University Press, 1997), 34.

79. J. David Hacker, "Recounting the Dead," *New York Times*, 20 September 2011, http://opinionator.blogs.nytimes.com/2011/09/20/recounting-the-dead; J. David Hacker, "A Census-Based Count of the Civil War Dead," *Civil War History* 4 (December 2011): 307–48; Guy Gugliotta, "New Estimate Raises Civil War Death Toll," *New York Times*, 3 April 2012, D1.

80. These Georgians are cited in David Williams, *Rich Man's War: Class, Caste, and Confederate Defeat in the Lower Chattahoochee Valley* (Athens: University of Georgia Press, 1998), 173.

81. Dr. Samuel Preston Moore, quoted in entry for 17 April 1865, *Kate: The Journal of a Confederate Nurse*, ed. Richard Barksdale Harwell (Baton Rouge: Louisiana State University Press, 1987), 271; entries for 11, 14, and 20 April 1865, in the Samuel A. Agnew Diary, #923, Southern Historical Collection, The Wilson Library, University of North Carolina at Chapel Hill.

82. See entries for 11 and 17 April 1865 in "The Civil War Decade in Greensboro, N.C. as Recorded in the Diary of Rev. Mr. J. Henry Smith, Pastor of the Presbyterian Church of Greensboro," transcript, 118, 119, in the possession of O. Norris Smith, M.D.,

of Greensboro, N.C. I am indebted to Dr. Smith for the use of this valuable diary, written by his grandfather.

83. Georgia, Department of Public Health, Central State Hospital, Medical Case Histories, vol. 3 (9 October 1860–31 July 1873), 25 March 1866, 4 May 1869, 20 June 1873, ref. 732, drawer 350, box 19, Georgia Archives, Morrow; Dillon J. Carroll, *"The Living Souls, the Bodies Tragedies": Injured Veterans and Their Families in the American Civil War*, Ph.D. dissertation, University of Georgia, expected 2015.

84. Lesley J. Gordon, *General George E. Pickett in Life and Legend* (Chapel Hill: University of North Carolina Press, 1998), 164, 166.

85. Ellen House, quoted in Eugene D. Genovese, *The Consuming Fire: The Fall of the Confederacy in the Mind of the White Christian South* (Athens: University of Georgia Press, 1998), 66.

86. Josiah Gorgas, *The Journals of Josiah Gorgas, 1857–1878*, ed. Sarah Woolfolk Wiggins (Tuscaloosa: University of Alabama Press, 1995), 114.

5 Reconstruction

1. William Ian Miller, *Humiliation and Other Essays on Honor, Social Discomfort, and Violence* (Ithaca, N.Y.: Cornell University Press, 1993), 84; Leon Würmser, *The Mask of Shame* (Baltimore: Johns Hopkins University Press, 1981); Charles B. Dew, *Apostles of Disunion: Southern Secession Commissioners and the Causes of the Civil War* (Charlottesville: University of Virginia Press, 2001), 56.

2. John Wilkes Booth, "To the Editors of the *National Intelligencer,* Washington, D.C. 14 April 1865," in *"Right or Wrong, God Judge Me": The Writings of John Wilkes Booth,* ed. John Rhodehamel and Louise Taper (Urbana and Chicago: University of Illinois Press, 1997), 147.

3. Rhodehamel and Taper, eds., *"Right or Wrong, God Judge Me,"* 125.

4. Ibid., 150.

5. Warren Getler and Bob Brewer, *Shadow of the Sentinel: One Man's Quest to Find the Hidden Treasure of the Confederacy* (New York: Simon and Schuster, 2003), 67. See also Bertram Wyatt-Brown, "Honor and Theater: Booth, the Lincoln Conspirators, and the Maryland Connection," *Maryland Historical Magazine* 104 (Fall 2009): 302–25.

6. Michael W. Kauffman, *American Brutus* (New York: Random House, 2004), 134, 166; Doris Kearns Goodwin, *Team of Rivals: The Political Genius of Abraham Lincoln* (New York: Simon and Schuster, 2005), 728.

7. There are so many narratives of Booth's near escape apart from those already cited that only a few should be noted here: Jay Winik, *April 1865: The Month That Saved America* (New York: HarperCollins, 2001), 253; Elizabeth D. Leonard, *Lincoln's Avengers: Justice, Revenge, and Reunion after the Civil War* (New York: Norton, 2004), 4–5; and James L. Swanson, *Manhunt: The 12-Day Chase for Lincoln's Killer* (New York: HarperCollins, 2006), 45–49, 206, 389–90, 423n.

8. Entry for 21 April 1865, John Wilkes Booth diary, in Rhodehamel and Taper, eds., *"Right or Wrong, God Judge Me,"* 154–55.

9. Gene Smith, *American Gothic: The Story of America's Legendary Theatrical Family—Junius, Edwin, and John Wilkes Booth* (New York: Simon and Schuster, 1992), 209–13.

10. Hans L. Trefousse, *Andrew Johnson: A Biography* (New York: Norton, 1989), 85.

11. David G. Sansing, ed., *What Was Freedom's Price? Essays* (Jackson: University Press of Mississippi, 1978), ix.

12. Walter L. Fleming, *Documents Relating to Reconstruction* (Morgantown, W.Va., 1904), 3–4; Eric Foner, *Reconstruction: America's Unfinished Revolution, 1863–1877* (New York: Harper and Row, 1988), 69, 159–63. For the bureau's limitations, see Michael Perman, *Emancipation and Reconstruction* (Wheeling, W.Va.: Harlan Davidson, 2003), 53.

13. Willie Lee Rose, *Rehearsal for Reconstruction: The Port Royal Experiment* (Indianapolis: Bobbs-Merrill, 1964), 218, 234.

14. Bertram Wyatt-Brown, "Black Schooling during Reconstruction," in *The Web of Southern Social Relations: Women, Family, and Education,* ed. Walter J. Fraser Jr., R. Frank Saunders Jr., and Jon L. Wakelyn (Athens: University of Georgia Press, 1985), 146–65; Ronald E. Butchart, *Northern Schools, Southern Blacks, and Reconstruction: Freedmen's Education, 1862–1875* (Westport, Conn.: Greenwood Press, 1980), 170.

15. Butchart, *Northern Schools,* 188, 190.

16. James D. Anderson, *The Education of Blacks in the South, 1860–1935* (Chapel Hill: University of North Carolina Press, 1988), 27–28.

17. Benjamin T. Swartz, "'A Carnival of Crime' in America: Southern Honor, Morality, and the Reconstruction Ku Klux Klan in the Upcountry Carolinas, 1868–1872," M.A. thesis, Johns Hopkins University, 2012, 32–34; Steven Hahn, *A Nation under Our Feet: Black Political Struggles in the Rural South from Slavery to the Great Migration* (Cambridge, Mass.: Harvard University Press, 2003), 268–69, 181–84.

18. William S. McFeely, *Grant: A Biography* (New York: Norton, 1981), 278–79, 285, 369–73; Foner, *Reconstruction,* 452, 454–59.

19. Willie Lee Rose, "Jubilee & Beyond: What Was Freedom?" in Sansing, ed., *What Was Freedom's Price?,* 3.

20. Christopher Waldrep, ed., *Lynching in America: A History in Documents* (New York: New York University Press, 2006), 5, 19.

21. Claudine L. Ferrell, *Reconstruction* (Westport, Conn.: Greenwood Press, 2003), 28; James G. Hollandsworth, *An Absolute Massacre: The New Orleans Race Riot of July 30, 1866* (Baton Rouge: Louisiana State University Press, 2001); George Rable, *But There Was No Peace: The Role of Violence in the Politics of Reconstruction* (Athens: University of Georgia Press, 1984), 33–42, 43–58.

22. Edward Ayers, "In Black and White," in Waldrep, ed., *Lynching in America,* 18–19.

23. Ibid., 19.

24. Nina Silber, *The Romance of Reunion: Northerners and the South, 1865–1900* (Chapel Hill: University of North Carolina Press, 1993), 3–4.

25. Irving H. Bartlett, *Wendell Phillips, Brahmin Radical* (Boston: Beacon Press, 1961), 330.

26. Ibid.; Carla Wilson, "Black Women's Narratives of Slavery, the Civil War and Reconstruction," *Workers Vanguard,* no. 841, 4 February 2005, http://www.icl-fi.org/english/wv/

archives/oldsite/2005/Slavery-841.html; David W. Blight, *Race and Reunion: The Civil War in American Memory* (Cambridge, Mass.: Belknap Press of Harvard University Press, 2001), 312.

27. Lawrence J. Friedman, *The White Savage: Racial Fantasies in the Postbellum South* (Englewood Cliffs, N.J.: Prentice-Hall, 1970), 122.

28. Christopher Morris, "The Strange Career of Gideon Gibson: An Early American Tragedy," in *Southern Character: Essays in Honor of Bertram Wyatt-Brown*, ed. Lisa Tendrich Frank and Daniel J. Kilbride (Gainesville: University of Florida Press, 2011), 25–40.

29. Ibid.

30. See Friedman, *The White Savage*, 67–68, 80.

31. C. Vann Woodward, *Origins of the New South, 1877–1913* (Baton Rouge: Louisiana State University Press, 1951).

32. Richard Zuczek, *State of Rebellion: Reconstruction in South Carolina* (Columbia: University of South Carolina Press, 1996), 210; Stetson Kenney, *After Appomattox: How the South Won the War* (Gainesville: University Press of Florida, 1995), 56.

33. H. K. Beale, *The Critical Year: A Study of Andrew Johnson and Reconstruction* (New York: Ungar, 1958), 344–55; W. E. B. Du Bois, *Black Reconstruction in America, 1860–1880* (New York: Free Press, 1998), 465.

34. Andrew Slap, "The Spirit of '76: The Reconstruction of History in the Redemption of South Carolina," *The Historian* 63 (Summer 2001): 769.

35. C. Vann Woodward, *Reunion and Reaction: The Compromise of 1877 and the End of Reconstruction* (Boston: Little, Brown, 1951).

36. Robert W. Coakley, *The Role of Federal Military Forces in Domestic Disorders, 1789–1878* (Washington, D.C.: Center of Military History, U.S. Army, 1989), 344–45.

37. C. Vann Woodward, *The Burden of Southern History* (Baton Rouge: Louisiana State University Press, 1993), 107.

38. David Silkenat, *Moments of Despair: Suicide, Divorce, and Debt in Civil War Era North Carolina* (Chapel Hill: University of North Carolina Press, 2011), 14–21, 39–41; Randolph Roth, *American Homicide* (Cambridge, Mass.: Harvard University Press, 2009), 414.

39. See Silkenat, *Moments of Despair*.

40. Gaines M. Foster, *Ghosts of the Confederacy: Defeat, the Lost Cause, and the Emergence of the New South, 1865 to 1913* (New York: Oxford University Press, 1987), 5–6.

41. Ibid., 5; Gary W. Gallagher, *Jubal A. Early, the Lost Cause, and Civil War History: A Persistent Legacy* (Milwaukee: Marquette University Press, 1995), 14.

42. Blight, *Race and Reunion*, 272–74.

43. Foster, *Ghosts of the Confederacy*, 23–24.

44. Walter Lynwood Fleming, *The Sequel of Appomattox: A Chronicle of the Reunion of the States* (New Haven, Conn.: Yale University Press, 1919), 175–77, 181, 291.

45. Ibid., 21.

46. Ibid., 264.

47. See Michael W. Fitzgerald, *The Union League Movement in the Deep South: Politics and Agricultural Change during Reconstruction* (Baton Rouge: Louisiana State University Press, 1989).

48. Roth, *American Homicide*, 425; Jake Adam York, "The Burning Man," in *Murder Ballads* (Denver: Elixir Press, 2005), 3–20.

49. Michael Perman, *Struggle for Mastery: Disfranchisement in the South, 1888–1908* (Chapel Hill: University of North Carolina Press, 2001), 72.

50. Roth, *American Homicide*, 414–15.

51. Rayford Logan, *The Betrayal of the Negro from Rutherford B. Hayes to Woodrow Wilson* (New York: Da Capo Press, 1997), 88–90; Woodward, *Origins of the New South*, 350.

52. Rayford Logan, *The Betrayal of the Negro from Rutherford B. Hayes to Woodrow Wilson* (New York: Da Capo Press, 1997), 88–90; Woodward, *Origins of the New South*, 350; Glenda Elizabeth Gilmore, *Gender and Jim Crow: Women and the Politics of White Supremacy in North Carolina, 1896–1920* (Chapel Hill: University of North Carolina Press, 1996), 105–11.

53. James H. Cone, *The Cross and the Lynching Tree* (Maryknoll, N.Y.: Orbis Books, 2011), 6, 20–21; W. E. B. Du Bois, *The Negro* (New York: Cosimo Classics, 2007), 130.

54. Jennie Lightweis-Goff, *Blood at the Root: Lynching as American Cultural Nucleus* (Albany: State University of New York Press, 2011), 113–44.

55. For a full account, see Ralph Blumenthal, "Fresh Outrage in Waco at Grisly Lynching of 1916," *New York Times*, 1 May 2005, http://www.nytimes.com/2005/05/01/national/01lynch.html?_r=0; Sylvia Moreno, "In Waco, a Push to Atone for the Region's Lynch-Mob Past," *Washington Post*, 26 April 2006, http://www.washingtonpost.com/wp-dyn/content/article/2006/04/25/AR2006042502306.html; Patricia Bernstein, *The First Waco Horror: The Lynching of Jesse Washington and the Rise of the NAACP* (College Station: Texas A&M University Press, 2005); William G. Jordan, *Black Newspapers and America's War for Democracy, 1914–1920* (Chapel Hill: University of North Carolina Press, 2001), 43.

56. See "Lynchings in 1897," Cleveland *Gazette*, 8 January 1898, 2; U.S. Congress, "Antilynching Bill," Senate Report No. 837, 67th Congress, 2nd session, 1921–1922, vol. 2 (7951).

57. Mark Gado, "Carnival of Death: Lynching in America," *Crime Library*, http://www.trutv.com/library/crime/notorious_murders/mass/lynching/index_1.html.

58. "Lynchings: By State and Race, 1882–1968," http://law2.umkc.edu/faculty/projects/ftrials/shipp/lynchingsstate.html. The statistics were supplied by the archives at the Tuskegee Institute.

6   America as World Power, 1898–1918

1. Michael Perman, *Struggle for Mastery: Disfranchisement in the South, 1888–1908* (Chapel Hill: University of North Carolina Press, 2001), 119–20; Joseph A. Fry, *Dixie Looks Abroad: The South and U.S. Relations, 1789–1973* (Baton Rouge: Louisiana State University Press, 2002), 124–25.

2. C. Vann Woodward, *Tom Watson, Agrarian Rebel* (New York: Macmillan, 1938), 334–35.

3. See Fry, *Dixie Looks Abroad*, 110–11; "Hannis Taylor," *Lewiston Daily Sun*, 20 April 1899, 5. See also Tennant S. McWilliams, *Hannis Taylor: The New Southerner as an American* (Tuscaloosa: University of Alabama Press, 1978).

4. See Fry, *Dixie Looks Abroad*, 112–13; Hugh B. Hammett, *Hilary Abner Herbert: A Southerner Returns to the Union* (Philadelphia: American Philosophical Society, 1976); Joseph A. Fry, *John Tyler Morgan and the Search for Southern Autonomy* (Knoxville: University of Tennessee Press, 1992).

5. H. Wayne Morgan, *William McKinley and His America* (Kent: Kent State University Press, 2003), 272–77; Louis Fisher, "Destruction of the *Maine* (1898)," Law Library of Congress, 4 August 2009, http://loc.gov/law/help/usconlaw/pdf/Maine.1898.pdf.

6. Phillip J. Morledge, *"I Do Solemnly Swear": Presidential Inauguration Speeches from George Washington to George W. Bush* (Sheffield, England: PJM Publishing, 2008), 143.

7. Louis A. Pérez Jr., *The War of 1898: The United States and Cuba in History and Historiography* (Chapel Hill: University of North Carolina Press, 1998), 18–21.

8. Fry, *Dixie Looks Abroad*, 120–21.

9. Ibid., 121–22; Kristin L. Hoganson, *Fighting for American Manhood: How Gender Politics Provoked the Spanish-American and Philippine-American Wars* (New Haven, Conn.: Yale University Press, 1998), 47, 62; George Coleman Osborn, *John Sharp Williams: Planter-Statesman of the Deep South* (Baton Rouge: Louisiana State University Press, 1943), 83–87.

10. Fry, *Dixie Looks Abroad*, 123.

11. Hoganson, *Fighting for American Manhood*, 72; Fry, *Dixie Looks Abroad*, 123.

12. Edmund Morris, *Theodore Rex* (New York: Modern Library, 2002), 453–63, 465–68, 471–75.

13. Ibid.; Gerald Horne, *Black and Brown: African Americans and the Mexican Revolution, 1910–1920* (New York: New York University Press, 2005), 98; Mike Cox, *Time of the Rangers: Texas Rangers from 1900 to the Present* (New York: Tom Doherty Associates, 2009), 388n37.

14. John Hope Franklin and Evelyn Brooks Higginbotham, *From Slavery to Freedom: A History of African Americans*, 9th ed. (New York: McGraw-Hill, 2010), 279; Frank N. Schubert, *Black Valor: Buffalo Soldiers and the Medal of Honor, 1870–1898* (Lanham, Md.: Rowman and Littlefield, 1997), 153; Anthony L. Powell, "An Overview: Black Participation in the Spanish-American War," *Centennial Spanish-American War Website*, http://www.spanamwar.com/AfroAmericans.htm.

15. Woodward, *Tom Watson*, 334.

16. Fry, *Dixie Looks Abroad*, 127.

17. Willard B. Gatewood Jr., *Smoked Yankees and the Struggle for Empire: Letters from Negro Soldiers, 1898–1902* (Urbana: University of Illinois Press, 1971), ix.

18. Ibid., 8.

19. Ibid., 8, 45.

20. Ibid., 39.

21. Ibid., 87.

22. See Theophilus G. Steward, *Colored Regulars in the United States Army* (Philadelphia: A.M.E. Book Concern, 1904).

23. Fry, *Dixie Looks Abroad*, 128–29; Stephen Kantrowitz, *Ben Tillman and the Reconstruction of White Supremacy* (Chapel Hill: University of North Carolina Press, 2000), 263.

24. Hoganson, *Fighting for American Manhood*, 135; Gregg Jones, *Honor in the Dust: Theodore Roosevelt, War in the Philippines, and the Rise and Fall of America's Imperial Dream* (New York: New American Library, 2012), 115.

25. Gatewood, *Smoked Yankees*, 184, 241; David J. Silbey, *A War of Frontier and Empire: The Philippine-American War, 1899–1902* (New York: Hill and Wang, 2007), 107, 109.

26. Gatewood, *Smoked Yankees*, 245.

27. Ibid., 281.

28. Harvey Rosenfeld, *Diary of a Dirty Little War: The Spanish-American War of 1898* (Westport, Conn.: Praeger, 2000), 181; H. W. Brands, *Bound to Empire: The United States and the Philippines* (New York: Oxford University Press, 1992), 46.

29. Rosenfeld, *Diary of a Dirty Little War*, 181; Donald H. Dyal, Brian B. Carpenter, and Mark A. Thomas, eds., *Historical Dictionary of the Spanish American War* (Westport, Conn.: Greenwood Press, 1996), 7.

30. Robert F. Rogers, *Destiny's Landfall: A History of Guam* (Honolulu: University of Hawai'i Press, 1995), 113. For the full text of the Treaty of Paris, see "Treaty of Paris between the United States and Spain; December 10, 1898," Yale Law School Avalon Project, http://avalon.law.yale.edu/19th_century/sp1898.asp.

31. Brands, *Bound to Empire*, 123. See also Hazel M. McFerson, ed., *Mixed Blessing: The Impact of the American Colonial Experience on Politics and Society in the Philippines* (Westport, Conn.: Greenwood Press, 2002).

32. Brian McAllister Linn, *The U.S. Army and Counterinsurgency in the Philippine War, 1899–1902* (Chapel Hill: University of North Carolina Press, 1989), 23, 155.

33. Silbey, *A War of Frontier and Empire*, 164. In the Second World War, the United States hanged Japanese soldiers who had used water boarding. It was also employed in the 2000s by the CIA on some Al-Qaeda suspects. The Bush-Cheney-Rumsfeld administration justified water boarding as not constituting actual torture. See Scott Shane, David Johnston, and James Risen, "Secret U.S. Endorsement of Severe Interrogations," *New York Times*, 4 October 2007, A1; "McCain: Japanese Hanged for Waterboarding," *CBS News*, 29 November 2007; Caitlin Price, "CIA Chief Confirms Use of Waterboarding on 3 Terror Detainees," *JURIST*, 5 February 2008.

34. Daniel B. Schirmer and Stephen Rosskamm Shalom, eds., *The Philippines Reader: A History of Colonialism, Neocolonialism, Dictatorship, and Resistance* (Boston: South End Press, 1987), 13.

35. Spencer C. Tucker, ed., *The Encyclopedia of the Spanish-American and Philippine-American Wars: A Political, Social, and Military History* (Santa Barbara, Calif.: ABC-CLIO, 2009), 354, 958, 964; McAllister, *U.S. Army and Counterinsurgency in the Philippine War*, 145–46.

36. Morris, *Theodore Rex*, 101–2.

37. Schirmer and Shalom, eds., *Philippines Reader*, 189, 319.

38. Fry, *Dixie Looks Abroad*, 129, 128.

39. Richard E. Welch Jr., *Response to Imperialism: The United States and the Philippine-American War, 1899–1902* (Chapel Hill: University of North Carolina Press, 1979), 46, 123, 124, 158.

40. Senator Edward Carmack, 25 April 1902, *Congressional Record* 35, part 5, 4669.

41. Tucker, *Encyclopedia of the Spanish-American and Philippine-American War*, 22, 625; William B. Hixson, *Moorfield Storey and the Abolitionist Tradition* (New York: Oxford University Press, 1972); John Carlos Rowe, *Literary Culture and U.S. Imperialism: From the Revolution to World War II* (New York: Oxford University Press, 2000), 122, 124.

42. James Joll, *The Second International, 1889–1914* (New York: Praeger, 1956), 107.

43. Ernest R. May, *The World War and American Isolation, 1914–1917* (Cambridge, Mass.: Harvard University Press, 1959); Luigi Albertini, *The Origins of the War of 1914*, 3 vols. (Oxford: Oxford University Press, 1952–1957); Martin Gilbert, *The First World War: A Complete History* (New York: Henry Holt, 1994); Paul M. Kennedy, *The Rise of the Anglo-German Antagonism, 1860–1914* (Boston: Allen and Unwin, 1980).

44. Avner Offer, "Going to War in 1914: A Matter of Honor?" *Politics and Society* 23, no. 2 (June 1995): 213–41; Lamar Cecil, *Wilhelm II: Prince and Emperor, 1859–1900* (Chapel Hill: University of North Carolina Press, 1989), 335.

45. Emil Ludwig, *Wilhelm Hohenzollern, The Last of the Kaisers*, trans. Ethel Colburn Mayne (New York: G. P. Putnam's Sons, 1927), 10.

46. Miranda Carter, *George, Nicholas, and Wilhelm: Three Royal Cousins and the Road to World War I* (New York: Vintage, 2011), 97.

47. John C. G. Röhl, *The Kaiser and His Court: Wilhelm II and the Government of Germany*, trans. Terence F. Cole (New York: Cambridge University Press, 1994), 20, 28–69.

48. John C. G. Röhl and Nicolaus Sombart, eds., *Kaiser Wilhelm II: New Interpretations: The Corfu Papers* (New York: Cambridge University Press, 1982), 304.

49. Kevin McAleer, *Dueling: The Cult of Honor in Fin-de-Siecle Germany* (Princeton, N.J.: Princeton University Press, 1994), 140, 82.

50. Offer, "Going to War in 1914," 216–17.

51. John C. G. Röhl, *1914: Delusion or Design?* (London: Elek, 1973), 59–60; Ludwig, *Wilhelm Hohenzollern*, 292.

52. Offer, "Going to War in 1914," 221, 227; David Stevenson, *The First World War and International Politics* (Oxford: Oxford University Press, 1988), 1–40.

53. Fry, *Dixie Looks Abroad*, 140.

54. John Milton Cooper Jr., *The Warrior and the Priest: Woodrow Wilson and Theodore Roosevelt* (Cambridge, Mass.: Harvard University Press, 1983), 182–86.

55. Arthur S. Link, *Wilson: The Struggle for Neutrality,* vol. 3 (Princeton, N.J.: Princeton University Press, 1960), 105; Charles Seymour, *Woodrow Wilson and the World War: A Chronicle of Our Own Times* (New Haven, Conn.: Yale University Press, 1921), 49.

56. Gilbert, *First World War,* 318.

57. Ibid., 333–34, 299, 256; Geoffrey Wheatcroft, "Hello to All That!" *New York Review of Books,* 23 June 2011, 30–32.

58. Gilbert, *First World War,* 260, 299–300, 391, 540–41; Wheatcroft, "Hello to All That!"; Martin Gilbert, *The Somme: Heroism and Horror in the First World War* (New York: Henry Holt, 2006), 243; John Keegan, *The First World War* (London: Pimlico, 1999), 319–21. The death toll of the Great War was huge: Germany, 1,800,000; Russia, 1,700,000; France 1,300,000; Britain 743,000; United States, 48,000. Gilbert, *First World War,* 256, 299, 333–34, 391, 540–41.

59. Seymour, *Woodrow Wilson,* 49–57; Anthony Gaughan, "Woodrow Wilson and the Rise of Militant Interventionism in the South," *Journal of Southern History* 65 (November 1999): 771–808. William Jennings Bryan resigned because of the president's intractability about German submarine warfare: William N. Tilchin and Charles E. Neu, eds., *Artists of Power: Theodore Roosevelt, Woodrow Wilson, and Their Enduring Impact on U.S. Foreign Policy* (Westport, Conn.: Praeger Security International, 2006), 80.

60. Fry, *Dixie Looks Abroad,* 157.

61. Zachary Smith, "Tom Watson and Resistance to Federal War Policies in Georgia during World War I," *Journal of Southern History* 78 (May 2012): 293–326.

62. "Wilson's Fifth Annual Message to Congress (Delivered before Congress in Joint Session, December 4, 1917)," in Albert Shaw, *The Messages and Papers of Woodrow Wilson,* vol. 1 (New York: Review of Reviews, 1924), 445, 453–54.

63. Lewis Sorley, *Honor Bright: History and Origins of the West Point Honor Code and System* (New York: McGraw-Hill, 2009).

64. David M. Kennedy, *Over Here: The First World War and American Society* (Oxford: Oxford University Press, 1982), 158–59.

65. William G. Jordan, *Black Newspapers and America's War for Democracy, 1914–1920* (Chapel Hill: University of North Carolina Press, 2001), 10–11.

66. Kennedy, *Over Here,* 156; Jami Bryan, "Fighting for Respect: African-American Soldiers in WWI," *Military History Online* (2003), http://www.militaryhistoryonline.com/wwi/articles/fightingforrespect.aspx.

67. Kennedy, *Over Here,* 159–60.

68. Ibid., 162; Bryan, "Fighting for Respect."

69. Bryan, "Fighting for Respect."

70. William Alexander Percy, *Lanterns on the Levee: Recollections of a Planter's Son* (New York: Knopf, 1941), 198. See also Bertram Wyatt-Brown, *The House of Percy: Honor, Melancholy and Imagination in a Southern Family* (New York: Oxford University Press, 1994), 210–12.

71. See Edward M. Coffman, *The War to End All Wars: The American Military Experience in World War I* (New York: Oxford University Press, 1968), 314–20; Jennifer D. Keene, *World War I* (Westport, Conn.: Greenwood Press, 2006), 101–3.

72. "Remarks at a Ceremony for the Posthumous Presentation of the Medal of Honor to Corporal Freddie Stowers," *Arlington National Cemetery,* 24 April 1991, http://www.arlingtoncemetery.net/fstowers.htm; "Black Hero of World War I Is Posthumously Awarded Medal of Honor 72 Yrs. Late," *Jet,* 13 May 1991, 9; 369th Infantry Regiment

"Harlem Hellfighters," *BlackPast.org,* http://www.blackpast.org/?q=aah/369th-infantry
-regiment-harlem-hellfighters.

73. Jordan, *Black Newspapers,* 36–39, 41–45, 75–78.

74. Ibid., 33; Katherine A. Bitner, "The Role of the *Chicago Defender* in the Great
Migration of 1916–1918," *Negro History Bulletin* 48, no. 2 (1985): 20–26.

75. W. E. B. Du Bois's "Returning Soldiers" originally appeared in the May 1919 issue
of *The Crisis,* quoted in David Levering Lewis, *W. E. B. Du Bois: A Biography, 1868–1963*
(New York: Henry Holt, 2009), 380.

76. Entry for Sergeant Alvin C. York in Ron Owens, ed., *Medal of Honor: Historical
Facts and Figures* (Paducah, Ky.: Turner, 2004), 98; "Alvin C. York" in *Tennessee Through
Time: The Later Years,* ed. Valerie Thursby Hatch (Layton, Utah: Gibbs Smith, 2008),
167; Laurence Stallings, *The Story of the Doughboys: The AEF in World War I* (New York:
Harper and Row, 1966), 153–61.

77. William J. Bennett, *The Book of Man: Readings on the Path to Manhood* (Nashville:
Thomas Nelson, 2011), 52.

78. Robert Niemi, *History in the Media: Film and Television* (Santa Barbara, Calif.:
ABC-CLIO, 2006), 50–51; David Thomson, *Gary Cooper* (New York: Faber and Faber,
2010), 78; David Welky, *The Moguls and the Dictators: Hollywood and the Coming of World
War II* (Baltimore: Johns Hopkins University Press, 2008), 294–95; David D. Lee, *Sergeant York: An American Hero* (Lexington: University Press of Kentucky, 1985), 103.

79. Edward M. Coffman, *The Regulars: The American Army, 1898–1941* (Cambridge,
Mass.: Harvard University Press, 2004), 213.

80. Carlo D'Este, *Patton: A Genius for War* (New York: HarperCollins, 1995), 248–65;
W. E. B. Du Bois, "The Souls of White Folk," in *Darkwater: Voices from within the Veil*
(New York: Harcourt, Brace, and Howe, 1920), 29–52.

81. Paul Fussell, *Thank God for the Atomic Bomb and Other Essays* (New York: Summit
Books, 1988), 226–27.

7   Honor, Race, and Humiliation in World War II and Korea

1. George H. Stein, *The Waffen SS: Hitler's Elite Guard at War, 1939–1945* (Ithaca, N.Y.:
Cornell University Press, 1966), 121–22, 242. See also David Art, *The Politics of the Nazi
Past in Germany and Austria* (New York: Cambridge University Press, 2006).

2. Adolf Hitler, *Mein Kampf* (New York: Reynal and Hitchcock, 1939), 102, 228–29.

3. Norman Rich, *Hitler's War Aims: Ideology, the Nazi State, and the Course of Expansion,* vol. 1 (New York: Norton, 1973), 154.

4. Freeman Dyson, "The Bitter End," *New York Review of Books,* 28 April 2005, 4–6;
Max Hastings, "The Most Terrible of Hitler's Creatures," *New York Review of Books,*
9 February 2012, 38–39, review of Peter Longerich, *Himmler: Hitler's Hangman.*

5. Rich, *Hitler's War Aims,* 47–51, 57–58, 62.

6. Ibid., 234–35; Ernst L. Presseisen, *Germany and Japan: A Study in Totalitarian Diplomacy 1933–1941* (The Hague: Martinus Nijhoff, 1958), 314–16.

7. Paul Herbig, *Innovation Japanese Style: A Cultural and Historical Perspective* (Westport, Conn.: Quorum Books, 1995), 193; William Scott Wilson, *Ideals of the Samurai: Writings of Japanese Warriors* (Burbank, Calif.: Ohara, 1982), 122.

8. Tsunetomo Yamamoto, *The Way of the Samurai,* trans. Minoru Tanaka, ed. Justin F. Stone (Garden City, N.Y.: Square One, 2002); Robin L. Rielly, *Kamikaze Attacks of World War II: A Complete History of Japanese Suicide Strikes on American Ships, by Aircraft and Other Means* (Jefferson, N.C.: McFarland, 2010).

9. Evelin Lindner, *Making Enemies: Humiliation and International Conflict* (Westport, Conn.: Praeger, 2006), 109; H. Paul Varley, *Japanese Culture,* 4th ed. (Honolulu: University of Hawai'i Press, 2000), 143.

10. Charles S. Nichols Jr. and Henry I. Shaw Jr., *Okinawa: Victory in the Pacific* (Washington, D.C.: Branch, G-3 Division, Headquarters, U.S. Marine Corps, 1955), 143; John Toland, *The Rising Sun: The Decline and Fall of the Japanese Empire, 1936–1945* (New York: Random House, 1970), 698–701, 704–13, 718–26.

11. Paul Fussell, *Thank God for the Atomic Bomb and Other Essays* (New York: Summit Books, 1988), 15–18, 20–21.

12. "Battle of Okinawa: The Bloodiest Battle of the Pacific War," *HistoryNet,* 12 June 2006, http://www.historynet.com/battle-of-okinawa-the-bloodiest-battle-of-the-pacific -war.htm; William Manchester, "The Bloodiest Battle of All," *New York Times Magazine,* 14 June 1987, 42.

13. David D. Roberts, *The Syndicalist Tradition and Italian Fascism* (Chapel Hill: University of North Carolina Press, 1979), 4, 5.

14. Geoffrey Wheatcroft, "Hello to All That!" *New York Review of Books,* 23 June 2011, 30–32; Joseph A. Fry, *Dixie Looks Abroad: The South and U.S. Foreign Relations, 1789–1973* (Baton Rouge: Louisiana State University Press, 2002), 169–74, 188–200, 203–4, 207–10.

15. Fry, *Dixie Looks Abroad,* 203.

16. Neil R. McMillen, ed., *Remaking Dixie: The Impact of World War II on the American South* (Jackson: University Press of Mississippi, 1997); Justus D. Doenecke, "American Isolationism, 1939–1941," *Journal of Libertarian Studies* 6 (Summer–Fall 1982): 201–16.

17. Wayne S. Cole, *Charles A. Lindbergh and the Battle against American Intervention in World War II* (New York: Harcourt Brace Jovanovich, 1974), 11, 115–24; Philip Jenkins, *Hoods and Shirts: The Extreme Right in Pennsylvania, 1925–1950* (Chapel Hill: University of North Carolina Press, 1997), 11, 134, 137, 141–65; Lynne Olson, *Those Angry Days: Roosevelt, Lindbergh, and America's Fight over World War II, 1939–1941* (New York: Random House, 2013), 123. See also Sander Diamond, *The Nazi Movement in the United States, 1924–1941* (Ithaca, N.Y.: Cornell University Press, 1974).

18. Mattie E. Treadwell, *The Women's Army Corps: United States Army in World War II* (1954; Washington, D.C.: Office of the Chief of Military History, Department of the Army, 1991), 25–28, 460; *American Army Women Serving on All Fronts,* Universal Newsreel, 1944, http://www.youtube.com/watch?v=7Paw_MZEMlo; Kenneth Paul O'Brien and Lynn Hudson Parsons, eds., *The Home-Front War: World War II and American Society* (Westport, Conn.: Greenwood Press, 1995), 120; William O'Neill, *A Democracy at War:*

America's Fight at Home and Abroad in World War II (Cambridge, Mass.: Harvard University Press, 1993), 331–32.

19. Dan Shiffman, "Richard Wright's '12 Million Black Voices' and World War II–Era Civic Nationalism," *African American Review* 41, no. 3 (2007): 447.

20. *NAACP 1940–55. General Office File: Lynching. Fort Benning, Ga., 1941* (Frederick, Md.: University Publications of America, 1982); Bernard C. Nalty, *Strength for the Fight: A History of Black Americans in the Military* (New York: Free Press, 1987), especially 164, 204–6.

21. Fry, *Dixie Looks Abroad*, 215.

22. William E. Alt and Betty L. Alt, *Black Soldiers, White Wars: Black Warriors from Antiquity to the Present* (Westport, Conn.: Praeger, 2002), 91; Allene G. Carter and Robert L. Allen, *Honoring Sergeant Carter: A Family's Journey to Uncover the Truth about an American Hero* (New York: HarperCollins, 2003), 4, 98–99.

23. Gerald A. White Jr., "Tuskegee (Weather) Airmen: Black Meteorologists in World War II," *Air Power History* 53, no. 2 (2006): 20–31.

24. "General Patton's Forgotten Troops: African American Soldiers in World War II in Their Own Words," http://www.history.com/images/media/interactives/African AmericansWWII.pdf.

25. Nurith C. Aizenman, "Black Soldiers Battled Fascism and Racism: Veterans Remember Bitterness of Bias-Tainted Homecomings," *Washington Post,* 26 May 2004, B1; Robert Hodges Jr., "African American 92nd Infantry Division Fought in Italy during World War II," *World War II Magazine,* 12 June 2006, http://www.historynet.com/african -american-92nd-infantry-division-fought-in-italy-during-world-war-ii.htm.

26. Aizenman, "Black Soldiers Battled Fascism"; Donald L. Miller and Henry Steele Commager, *The Story of World War II* (New York: Simon and Schuster, 2001), 504–5; William L. Shirer, *The Rise and Fall of the Third Reich: A History of Nazi Germany* (New York: Simon and Schuster, 1960), 1090. See also Charles B. MacDonald, *A Time For Trumpets: The Untold Story of the Battle of the Bulge* (New York: Bantam Books, 1984).

27. Aizenman, "Black Soldiers Battled Fascism."

28. Gary Y. Okihiro, *Whispered Silences: Japanese Americans and World War II* (Seattle: University of Washington Press, 1996), 94.

29. Ibid., 159.

30. Franklin Odo, *No Sword to Bury: Japanese Americans in Hawai'i during World War II* (Philadelphia: Temple University Press, 2004), 104.

31. Ibid., 136–40.

32. Ibid., 132, 230–39.

33. Rudi Williams, "Army Secretary Lionizes 22 World War II Heroes," http://www .defense.gov/specials/medalofhonor/; "442nd Veterans Club," http://www.442.us.com/ decorations/medalofhonor.html.

34. Christopher Hamner, *Enduring Battle: American Soldiers in Three Wars, 1776–1865* (Lawrence: University Press of Kansas, 2011), 44–46.

35. Ibid., 185–90.

36. Ibid., 190–91.

37. Robert B. Edgerton, *Hidden Heroism: Black Soldiers in America's Wars* (Boulder, Col.: Westview Press, 2001), 127–28, 130.

38. William R. Levesque, "An Uneasy Question for the Tuskegee Airmen: The Heroism of the Tuskegee Airmen Is Legendary, but Some Wonder If They Really Never Lost a Bomber. And That Doesn't Sit Well," St. Petersburg *Times,* 26 January 2008, http://www .sptimes.com/2008/01/26/Worldandnation/An_uneasy_question_fo.shtml. In January 2009, the surviving Tuskegee Airmen, some 180, attended the inauguration of Barack Obama. See Jill S. Schiefelbein, "Tuskegee Airmen," in *Icons of Black America: Breaking Barriers and Crossing Boundaries,* ed. by Matthew C. Whitaker (Santa Barbara, Calif.: ABC-CLIO, 2011), 894.

39. Jeremy Black, *World War Two: A Military History* (London: Routledge, 2003), 250.

40. Edgerton, *Hidden Heroism,* 130.

41. Stephen R. Taaffe, *Marshall and His Generals: U.S. Army Commanders in World War II* (Lawrence: University Press of Kansas, 2011), 3, 5.

42. "Lucian Adams," *Congressional Medal of Honor: Heroes of the Battles through France,* http://www.worldwariihistory.info/Medal-of-Honor/France.html; "Bernard P. Bell," ibid.

43. Carlo D'Este, *Patton: A Genius for War* (New York: HarperCollins, 1995), 516–20.

44. Ibid., 508–10.

45. Rick Atkinson, *The Day of Battle: The War in Sicily and Italy, 1943–1944* (New York: Henry Holt, 2007), 147–48; Stanley P. Hirshson, *General Patton: A Soldier's Life* (New York: HarperCollins, 2002), 393.

46. D'Este, *Patton,* 534–38.

47. Brian M. Sobel, ed., *The Fighting Pattons* (Westport, Conn.: Praeger, 1997), 9.

48. "Along the N.A.A.C.P. Battlefront: Southern Schrecklichkeit," *The Crisis* 53 (September 1946): 276–77; Carol Anderson, *Eyes off the Prize: The United Nations and the African American Struggle for Human Rights, 1944–1955* (Cambridge: Cambridge University Press, 2003), 58.

49. Laura Wexler, *Fire in a Canebrake: The Last Mass Lynching in America* (New York: Scribner, 2003).

50. "NAACP: 100 Years of History," http://www.naacp.org/pages/naacp-history; Steven Greenhouse, "Herbert Hill, a Voice against Discrimination, Dies at 80," *New York Times,* 21 August 2004, http://www.nytimes.com/2004/08/21/us/herbert-hill-a-voice-against -discrimination-dies-at-80.html.

51. Steve Estes, "A Question of Honor: Masculinity and Massive Resistance to Integration," in *White Masculinity in the Recent South,* ed. Trent Watts (Baton Rouge: Louisiana University Press, 2008), 102; Charles M. Payne, *I've Got the Light of Freedom: The Organizing Tradition and the Mississippi Freedom Struggle* (Berkeley: University of California Press, 2007), 34–35. See also Neil R. McMillen, *The Citizens' Council: Organized Resistance to the Second Reconstruction* (Urbana: University of Illinois Press, 1994).

52. Estes, "Question of Honor," 104–5. See also Trent Watts, "The Boycotting of Coach Rutter: Manhood, Race, and Authority in Post-1970 Mississippi," in Watts, ed., *White Masculinity,* 124–25.

53. Estes, "Question of Honor," 107.

54. Ibid., 108.

55. Ibid., 105–6; Stephen J. Whitfield, *A Death in the Delta: The Story of Emmett Till* (Baltimore: Johns Hopkins University Press, 1988).

56. Dennis D. Wainstock, *Truman, MacArthur and the Korean War* (Westport, Conn.: Greenwood Press, 1999), 24.

57. Chen Jian, *China's Road to the Korean War: The Making of the Sino-American Confrontation* (New York: Columbia University Press, 1994), 13–14, 59, 140.

58. Wainstock, *Truman, MacArthur and the Korean War*, 121; William Manchester, *American Caesar: Douglas MacArthur, 1880–1964* (New York: Little, Brown, 1978), 3; Michael David Pearlman, *Truman & MacArthur: Policy, Politics, and the Hunger for Honor and Renown* (Bloomington: Indiana University Press, 2008), 176.

59. "Donn F. Porter, Sergeant, United States Army," Arlington National Cemetery Website, http://www.arlingtoncemetery.net/dfporter.htm.

60. George C. Mitchell, *Matthew B. Ridgway: Soldier, Statesman, Scholar, Citizen* (Mechanicsburg, Penn.: Stackpole Books, 2002), 63, 35, 55, 31; Bill McWilliams, *On Hallowed Ground: The Last Battle for Pork Chop Hill* (Annapolis, Md.: Naval Institute Press, 2004), 21–22; Billy A. Arthur, "Obituary: General Matthew Ridgway," *The Independent*, 10 August 1993, http://www.independent.co.uk/news/people/obituary-general-matthew-ridgway-1460281.html.

61. "The Beginnings of a New Era for African-Americans in the Armed Forces," http://jackiewhiting.net/USHistory/ColdWar/AfAmKorea.htm; Charles B. Rangel, *And I Haven't Had a Bad Day Since: From the Streets of Harlem to the Halls of Congress* (New York: Thomas Dunne Books, 2007).

62. Lt. Col. Charles M. Bussey, *Firefight at Yechon: Courage and Racism in the Korean War* (Lincoln: University of Nebraska Press, 2002), 99, 108.

8   Honor and Shame in Vietnam and Iraq

1. Wilfred Owen, "Dulce et Decorum Est," in *War Poems and Manuscripts of Wilfred Owen,* http://www.oucs.ox.ac.uk/ww1lit/collections/item/3303?CISOBOX=1&REC=1; Gary Jacobson, "It Don't Mean Nuthin'," 2003, http://gloryriders.com/nuthin.html.

2. "Safety," in *The Poetical Works of Rupert Brooke*, ed. Geoffrey Keynes (London: Faber and Faber, 1946), 20.

3. Blema S. Steinberg, *Shame and Humiliation: Presidential Decision Making on Viet Nam* (Pittsburgh: University of Pittsburgh Press, 1996), 33–34.

4. Doris Kearns Goodwin, *Lyndon Johnson and the American Dream* (New York: Harpers, 1976), 336; Steinberg, *Shame and Humiliation*, 307–9.

5. Frank Newport, "Almost All Americans Consider World War II a 'Just' War," *Gallup*, 3 June 2004, http://www.gallup.com/poll/11881/almost-all-americans-consider-world-war-just-war.aspx.

6. Donald Kagan, "Honor, Interest, and the Nation-State," in *Honor among Nations: Intangible Interests and Foreign Policy*, ed. Elliott Abrams (Washington, D.C.: Ethics and

Public Policy Center, 1998), 5; Dean Rusk, "Memorandum by the Assistant Secretary of State for Far Eastern Affairs (Rusk) to the Deputy Under Secretary of State (Matthews)" (Freeman Matthews), 31 January 1951, in *Foreign Relations of the United States, 1951,* vol. 6, *Asia and the Pacific,* part 1 (Washington, D.C.: Government Printing Office, 1977), 20; General Lyman Lemnitzer, "Memorandum for the Secretary of Defense," 13 January 1962, attached to Robert S. McNamara, "Memorandum for the President," 27 January 1962, *United States-Vietnam Relations, 1945–1967: Study Prepared by the Department of Defense,* book 12, *U.S. Involvement in the War, Internal Documents: The Kennedy Administration: January 1961–1963,* book 2 (Washington, D.C.: Government Printing Office, 1971), 449–50.

7. Arthur Radford, "Memorandum by the Joint Chiefs of Staff to the Secretary of Defense (Wilson)," 20 May 1954, in *Foreign Relations of the United States, 1952–1954,* vol. 13, *Indochina,* part 2 (Washington, D.C.: Government Printing Office, 1982), 1592.

8. Joseph A. Fry, *Dixie Looks Abroad: The South and U.S. Relations, 1789–1973* (Baton Rouge: Louisiana State University Press, 2002), 261; Stanley Karnow, *Vietnam: A History* (New York: Viking Press, 1983), 375. See also Edwin E. Moise, *Tonkin Gulf and the Escalation of the Vietnam War* (Chapel Hill: University of North Carolina Press, 1996).

9. Fry, *Dixie Looks Abroad,* 261, 268, 275; Karnow, *Vietnam,* 326, 375, 507; David Halberstam, *The Best and the Brightest* (New York: Random House, 1972), 507.

10. Goodwin, *Lyndon Johnson,* 261–65.

11. Randy Roberts and James S. Olson, *A Line in the Sand: The Alamo in Blood and Memory* (New York: Free Press, 2001), 281; Robert Dallek, *Lone Star Rising: Lyndon Johnson and His Times, 1908–1960* (New York: Oxford University Press, 1991), 241, 476.

12. Ronnie Dugger, *The Politician: The Life and Times of Lyndon Johnson: The Drive for Power, from the Frontier to Master of the Senate* (New York: Norton, 1982), 146, 147. "Sacrificing lives to protect the flag or to maintain the honor or safety of the nation is an old and accepted value in this country." Hyman L. Muslin and Thomas H. Jobe, *Lyndon Johnson, The Tragic Self: A Psychohistorical Portrait* (New York: Insight Books, 1991), 205.

13. Hugh Sidey, *A Very Personal Presidency: Lyndon Johnson in the White House* (New York: Atheneum, 1968), 224.

14. Gregory Ross, *Cold War America, 1946 to 1990* (New York: Infobase Publishing, 2003), 600.

15. Robert D. Schulzinger, *A Time for War: The United States and Vietnam, 1941–1975* (New York: Oxford University Press, 1997), 264.

16. Goodwin, *Lyndon Johnson,* 253; Steinberg, *Shame and Humiliation,* 98.

17. "Former Secretary of Defense Clark M. Clifford Recalls His Post-Tet Questions (1968) 1969," in *Major Problems in American Foreign Relations: Documents and Essays, Volume II: Since 1914,* ed. Dennis Merrill and Thomas G. Paterson (Boston: Houghton Mifflin, 2000), 457.

18. George C. Herring, "Why the United States Failed in Vietnam," in Merrill and Paterson, eds., *Major Problems,* 467.

19. Robert Dallek, *Flawed Giant: Lyndon Johnson and His Times, 1961–1973* (New York: Oxford University Press, 1998), 569.

20. John M. Coski, *The Confederate Battle Flag: America's Most Embattled Emblem* (Cambridge, Mass.: Harvard University Press, 2005), 156.

21. Halberstam, *The Best and the Brightest,* 179, 180; Douglas Kinnard, *The War Managers* (Hanover, N.H.: University Press of New England, 1977), 109.

22. Halberstam, *The Best and the Brightest,* 178, 505–6; Steinberg, *Shame and Humiliation,* 120–21.

23. See Gerard J. De Groot, *A Noble Cause? America and the Vietnam War* (Harlow, England: Longman, 2000), 348; Eric T. Dean Jr., *Shook over Hell: Post-Traumatic Stress, Vietnam, and the Civil War* (Cambridge, Mass.: Harvard University Press, 1997), 180–81.

24. "The Bloods of 'Nam," *Frontline,* 20 May 1986, http://www.pbs.org/wgbh/pages/frontline/programs/info/414.html; Catherine Reef, *African Americans in the Military* (New York: Infobase, 2010), 149–50; "Winston-Salem Entertainment-Sports Complex," http://www.ljvm.com/lawrencejoel.html; "Medal of Honor Recipients—Vietnam (A–L)," http://www.history.army.mil/html/moh/vietnam-a-l.html.

25. "Background on Naturalization Ceremony for Active Duty Service Members," *Sigourney News Review,* http://sigourneynewsreview.com/background-on-naturalization-ceremony-for-active-duty-service-members-p3140.htm; "Peter C. Lemon: Biography," http://peterlemon.com/BIOGRAPHY.html; "Medal of Honor Recipients—Vietnam (A–L)."

26. Walter Goodman, Movie Review, "Black Soldiers in Vietnam," *New York Times,* 20 May 1986, C18.

27. Niall Ferguson, "Cowboys and Indians," *New York Times,* 24 May 2005, A25.

28. David E. Sanger, "Powell Says C.I.A. Was Misled about Weapons," *New York Times,* 17 May 2004, A8.

29. Edward N. Luttwak, "Iraq: The Logic of Disengagement," *Foreign Affairs* 84 (January–February 2005): 28–30. See also Bernard Lewis, "Freedom and Justice in the Modern Middle East," *Foreign Affairs* 84 (May–June 2005): 36–51, esp. 50–51.

30. Bob Woodward, *State of Denial* (New York: Simon and Schuster, 2006), 194–95; Larry Diamond, *Squandered Victory: The American Occupation and the Bungled Effort to Bring Democracy to Iraq* (New York: Henry Holt, 2005), 39–40.

31. Michael R. Gordon and Bernard E. Trainor, *Cobra II: The Inside Story of the Invasion and Occupation of Iraq* (New York: Pantheon Books, 2006), 476–79.

32. Dexter Filkins, "Desert Sturm," *New York Times,* 26 February 2006, sec. 7, 8; "The Mess," *New York Review of Books,* 9 March 2006, 27–30.

33. David Pryce-Jones, "Death of a Fantasy: Everything Saddam Hussein Built Up, in Utter Collapse," *National Review,* 31 December 2003, 18.

34. Victoria Firmo-Fontan, "The Dialectics of Humiliation: Polarization between Occupier and Occupied in Post-Saddam Iraq," August 2001, 3, 11; "Polarization between Occupier and Occupied in Post-Saddam Iraq: Humiliation and the Formation of Political Violence," January 2004, unpublished papers; "Expressions of Humiliation in 'New Iraq': Torture, Simulacra and Polarization," May 2004, unpublished paper; all three kindly lent by the author. Thomas Friedman observed the same issue. Friedman, "The Humiliation Factor," *New York Times,* 9 November 2003, sec. 4, 11. For employment

numbers, see "Reconstructing Iraq," *International Crisis Group Report,* 2 September 2004, 16n157, http://www.crisisgroup.org/~/media/Files/Middle%20East%20North%20 Africa/Iraq%20Syria%20Lebanon/Iraq/Reconstructing%20Iraq.pdf.

35. Firmo-Fontan, "Polarization," 11–14; Firmo-Fontan, "Dialectics of Humiliation," 1–16; Raphael Patai, *The Arab Mind* (1976; reprint New York: Hatherleigh Press, 2002), 91; Jan Goodwin, *The Price of Honor: Muslim Women Lift the Veil of Silence in the Islamic World* (Boston: Little, Brown, 1995), 51, 65, 87, 179, 248, 339–40; Sandra Mackey, *The Saudis: Inside the Desert Kingdom* (New York: Norton, 2002), 147–49, 166–68; Sana al-Khayyat, *Honour and Shame: Women in Modern Iraq* (London: Saqi Books, 1990); N. C. Aizenman, "A Killing Commanded by Tradition: Afghan Adultery Case Reflects Challenge of Extending Modern Law to Tribal Lands: Woman Accused of Adultery in Rural Afghanistan Killed under Tribal Law," *Washington Post,* 6 May 2005, A1; Saïd K. Aburish, *Saddam Hussein: The Politics of Revenge* (London: Bloomsbury, 2001), 81–82, 126–27.

36. Andrew J. Bacevich, *Washington Rules: America's Path to Permanent War* (New York: Henry Holt, 2010), 113; Jack Shulimson, "The Marine War: III MAF [Marine Amphibious Force] in Vietnam, 1965–1971," paper presented at "After the Cold War: Reassessing Vietnam," Vietnam Symposium, U.S. Marine Corps Historical Center, 18–20 April 1996. At a meeting of the City Club, Cleveland, Ohio, I heard General Walt explain the policy in the most optimistic terms.

37. George Packer, "The Lesson of Tal Afar: Is It Too Late for the Administration to Correct Its Course in Iraq?" *New Yorker,* 10 April 2006, 48–65.

38. David Leverenz, *Honor Bound: Race and Shame in America* (New Brunswick, N.J.: Rutgers University Press, 2012), 138; "President Discusses War on Terror and Operation Iraqi Freedom," White House Press Release, 20 March 2006, http://georgewbush -whitehouse.archives.gov/news/releases/2006/03/20060320-7.html.

39. A. Kevin Reinhart and Gilbert S. Merritt, "Reconstruction and Constitution Building in Iraq," addresses by Professor A. Kevin Reinhart and the Honorable Gilbert S. Merrit at Vanderbilt University Law School, 23 January 2004, published in *Vanderbilt Journal of Transitional Law* 37 no. 3 (May 2004): 765–90.

40. Michel Nolan, "SB High Grad Earns Silver Star for Bravery in Iraq," 29 January 2006, http://www.sbsun.com/news/ci_3448472#ixzz208WzSTtE; "The Wars in Iraq and Afghanistan: A Roll Call of the Fallen," *Chicago Tribune,* 9 September 2007, http:// articles.chicagotribune.com/2007-09-09/news/0709080478_1_baghdad-anbar-taji.

41. Eric Schmitt, "Officer Criticizes Detainee Abuse Inquiry," *New York Times,* 28 September 2005, A10. Tom Malinowski, the director for Human Rights Watch in Washington, declared that "Even officers [like Fishback] who wanted to behave honorably found it difficult to do so because there was no clarity about what the rules are." Josh White, "New Reports Surface about Detainee Abuse," *Washington Post,* 24 September 2005, A1.

42. Packer, "The Lesson of Tal Afar"; Fred Kaplan, "Challenging the Generals," *New York Times,* 26 August 2007, http://www.google.com/url?sa=t&rct=j&q=&esrc=s&source =web&cd=1&cad=rja&ved=0CDMQFjAA&url=http%3A%2F%2Fwww.nytimes.com%2F

2007%2F08%2F26%2Fmagazine%2F26military-t.html%3Fpagewanted%3Dall&ei=kw
FWUdSlEoXOyAGJroDoDA&usg=AFQjCNET3GpfAGhVhsUI92udtB7fH7kKcg&sig2=
mxwXG9O5KJdczKA4PRtDjA; "McMaster to Take Reins at Maneuver Center," *Army Times*, 11 June 2012, http://www.armytimes.com/news/2012/06/army-mcmaster
-maneuver-center-excellence-command-061112/; H. R. McMaster, *Dereliction of Duty: Lyndon Johnson, Robert McNamara, the Joint Chiefs of Staff, and the Lies That Led to Vietnam* (New York: HarperCollins, 1997).

43. Packer, "The Lesson of Tal Afar."

44. John McChesney, "The Death of an Iraqi Prisoner," NPR, 27 October 2005.

45. Mark Mazzetti, "C.I.A. Document Details Destruction of Tapes," *New York Times*, 16 April 2010, A17; Ralph Blumenthal and Timothy Williams, "Judge Declares Mistrial in Abu Ghraib Prison Abuse Case," *New York Times*, 4 May 2005, http://www.nytimes.com/2005/05/04/national/04cnd-abuse.html?_r=0; "Rumsfeld Tried to Resign during Prison Scandal," MSNBC, 3 February 2005, http://www.nbcnews.com/id/6909202/#.UVYHYlcaCrg; Sheryl Gay Stolberg and Jim Rutenberg, "Rumsfeld Resigns as Defense Secretary after Big Election Gains for Democrats," *New York Times*, 8 November 2006, http://www.nytimes.com/2006/11/08/us/politics/09BUSHCND.html?pagewanted=all; "Statement by CIA Director of Public Affairs Jennifer Millerwise," 18 March 2005, https://www.cia.gov/news-information/press-releases-statements/press-release-archive-2005/pr03182005.html.

46. Bertram Wyatt-Brown and Victoria C. Fontan, "The Honor Factor," *Baltimore Sun*, 23 January 2005, 5; Steven Strasser, ed., *The Abu Ghraib Investigations: The Official Reports of the Independent Panel and Pentagon on the Shocking Prisoner Abuse in Iraq* (New York: Public Affairs, 2004).

47. Mark Danner, "Iraq: The Real Election," *New York Review of Books*, 28 April 2005, 41–44.

48. "Graner Sentenced to 10 Years in Military Prison," *USA Today*, 14 January 2005, http://usatoday30.usatoday.com/news/nation/2005-01-14-graner_x.htm; David S. Cloud, "Private Gets 3 Years for Iraq Prison Abuse," *New York Times*, 28 September 2005, A20; Eric Schmitt, "Four Top Officers Cleared by Army in Prison Abuses," *New York Times*, 23 April 2005, http://www.nytimes.com/2005/04/23/politics/23abuse.html?ref=janiskarpinski.

49. "Full Text of Bin Laden's 'Letter to America,'" *The Observer*, 24 November 2002, http://observer.guardian.co.uk/worldview/story/0,11581,845725,00.html.

50. "Terror in America (30) Retrospective: A Bin Laden Special on Al-Jazeera Two Months before September 11," *Memri (Middle East Media Research Institute)*, 24 December 2001, no. 319, a transcription of an interview held on 10 July 2001 on the Al-Jazeera talk show "Opposite Direction"; Karen J. Greenberg, ed., *Al Qaeda Now: Understanding Today's Terrorists* (New York: Cambridge University Press, 2005), 194.

Conclusion

1. See Robert S. McKelvey, *Gift of Barbed Wire: America's Allies Abandoned in South Vietnam* (Seattle: University of Washington Press, 2002); McKelvey, *The Dust of Life:*

America's Children Abandoned in Vietnam (Seattle: University of Washington Press, 1999).

2. For Gallup poll figures on the Iraq invasion, see www.gallup.com/poll/1633/iraq .aspx.

3. Barry O'Neill, *Honor, Symbols, and War* (Ann Arbor: University of Michigan Press, 1999), 92–99.

4. James Bowman, "Lost Sense of Honor," *National Affairs* 149 (Fall 2002): 35. For an example of a failure to appreciate Middle Eastern notions of honor, consider Jimmy Carter's mishandling of the hostage situation in Iran. William J. Daugherty, "A Look Back: Jimmy Carter and the 1979 Decision to Admit the Shah into the United States," *American Diplomacy,* 2003, http://www.unc.edu/depts/diplomat/archives_roll/2003_01 -03/dauherty_shah/dauherty_shah.html; James A. Bill, *The Eagle and the Lion: The Tragedy of American-Iranian Relations* (New Haven, Conn.: Yale University Press, 1988).

5. Walter Kirn, "Tumultuous Lowell," *New York Times Book Review,* 26 June 2005, 10.

INDEX